AMERICAN LABOR

FROM CONSPIRACY
TO
COLLECTIVE BARGAINING

ADVISORY EDITORS

Leon Stein   *Philip Taft*

ADJUSTING IMMIGRANT AND INDUSTRY

William M. Leiserson

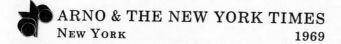
ARNO & THE NEW YORK TIMES

NEW YORK   1969

Reprint edition 1969 by Arno Press, Inc.

Library of Congress Catalog Card No. 73–89747

Reprinted from a copy in
The State Historical Society of Wisconsin Library

Manufactured in the United States of America

ADJUSTING IMMIGRANT
AND INDUSTRY

AMERICANIZATION STUDIES
ALLEN T. BURNS, DIRECTOR

ADJUSTING
IMMIGRANT AND INDUSTRY

BY

WILLIAM M. LEISERSON, PH.D.

*Professor in the University of the City of Toledo,
Chairman, Arbitration Boards, Clothing Industry,
New York and Baltimore*

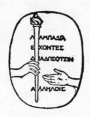

HARPER & BROTHERS PUBLISHERS
NEW YORK AND LONDON
1924

ADJUSTING IMMIGRANT AND INDUSTRY

First Edition
M-Y

PUBLISHER'S NOTE

THE material in this volume was gathered by the Division of Legal Protection and Correction of Studies in Methods of Americanization.

Americanization in this study has been considered as the union of native and foreign born in all the most fundamental relationships and activities of our national life. For Americanization is the uniting of new with native-born Americans in fuller common understanding and appreciation to secure by means of self-government the highest welfare of all. Such Americanization should perpetuate no unchangeable political, domestic, and economic régime delivered once for all to the fathers, but a growing and broadening national life, inclusive of the best wherever found. With all our rich heritages, Americanism will develop best through a mutual giving and taking of contributions from both newer and older Americans in the interest of the commonweal. This study has followed such an understanding of Americanization.

FOREWORD

THIS volume is the result of studies in methods of Americanization prepared through funds furnished by the Carnegie Corporation of New York. It arose out of the fact that constant applications were being made to the Corporation for contributions to the work of numerous agencies engaged in various forms of social activity intended to extend among the people of the United States the knowledge of their government and their obligations to it. The trustees felt that a study which should set forth, not theories of social betterment, but a description of the methods of the various agencies engaged in such work, would be of distinct value to the cause itself and to the public.

The outcome of the study is contained in eleven volumes on the following subjects: Schooling of the Immigrant; The Press; Adjustment of Homes and Family Life; Legal Protection and Correction; Health Standards and Care; Naturalization and Political Life; Industrial and Economic Amalgamation; Treatment of Immigrant Heritages; Neighborhood Agencies and Organization; Rural Developments; and Summary. The entire study has been carried out under the general direction of Mr. Allen T. Burns. Each volume appears in the

FOREWORD

name of the author who had immediate charge of
the particular field it is intended to cover.

Upon the invitation of the Carnegie Corporation a committee consisting of the late Theodore
Roosevelt, Prof. John Graham Brooks, Dr. John
M. Glenn, and Mr. John A. Voll has acted in an
advisory capacity to the director. An editorial
committee consisting of Dr. Talcott Williams, Dr.
Raymond B. Fosdick, and Dr. Edwin F. Gay has
read and criticized the manuscripts. To both of
these committees the trustees of the Carnegie Corporation are much indebted.

The purpose of the report is to give as clear a
notion as possible of the methods of the agencies
actually at work in this field and not to propose
theories for dealing with the complicated questions
involved.

TABLE OF CONTENTS

CONTENTS

x

CONTENTS

CONTENTS

LIST OF TABLES

AUTHOR'S NOTE

Acknowledgment is due to Miss Bertha M. Stevens, who directed the gathering of facts relating to immigrant workingwomen, and to Miss Henrietta Walter, who assisted her; to David J. Saposs, who gathered the material relating to immigrants and trade-unions; to John J. Meily and to Willis W. Wisler, who assisted in the investigation of employers' methods of managing immigrant employees. For any shortcomings of the work, however, I alone am responsible.

W. M. L.

ADJUSTING
IMMIGRANT AND INDUSTRY

ADJUSTING IMMIGRANT AND INDUSTRY

CHAPTER I

INDUSTRY AND AMERICANIZATION

IF Americanization means that the immigrant must be made over into an Anglo-Saxon, with the temperament, traditions, and characteristics of that race, then deliberate and organized efforts in that direction would be impractical, and a study of methods of Americanization futile. Only mixing of blood with Anglo-Saxon influences predominating could bring this result; and centuries must be allowed for the process. A uniting of minds, however, that enables immigrants of the most diverse races to coöperate with one another and with the native-born population to further national ends, may be created in the first generation; and this can be promoted by deliberate organization and education.

WHAT IS AMERICANIZATION?

Was it more than the development of such a unity of mind that made Americans of immigrants like Carl Schurz, Jacob Riis, Joseph Pulitzer, Oscar Straus, Franklin Lane, Edward Bok, Samuel Gompers, and many others that will readily come to mind? In beliefs, culture, and tradition these men differed as the nations from which they came differ; it was not necessary for them to renounce their family ties, their religions, or the traditions of the races from which they sprang in order to be recognized as great Americans.

3

Only political allegiance did they have to give up, and manners and habits unsuited to the American environment.

There are unhopeful prophets who see in the gathering together of men into one community the possibility of violent race conflicts,—conflicts for ascendency, but that is to suppose that civilization is incapable of adjustments by which men of different qualities and temperaments and appearances will live side by side, following different rôles and contributing diverse gifts. The weaving of mankind into one community does not imply the creation of a homogeneous community, but rather the reverse: the welcome and the adequate utilization of distinctive quality in an atmosphere of understanding. It is the almost universal bad manners of the present age which make race intolerable of race. The community to which we may be moving will be more mixed—which does not necessarily mean more interbred—more serious and more interesting than any existing community. Communities all to one pattern, like boxes of toy soldiers, are things of the past rather than the future.[1]

It was a common observation during the recent war that the united thought and action demanded by the great enterprise stimulated tremendously the weaving of all our diverse peoples into one nation. The recent immigrants from southern and eastern Europe were drawn together with the older immigrants from northern Europe and with the native-born population in rapid and dramatic fashion by the common tasks that the conflict imposed on all our people, just as the Civil War united the Irish and German immigrants of the forties and fifties with the rest of the population. A similar, and perhaps more permanent, union of the minds of immigrants with the native born is constantly being developed by the common experiences of every-day life in America, as the careers of well-known Americans of foreign birth serve to show. Through their experiences in neighborhood activities, in public

---

[1] H. G. Wells, *The Outline of History*, Vol. II, pp. 592–593.

schools, in politics, on farms and in their places of employment, immigrants learn to know America, learn to understand their neighbors, to work with them, and to develop that unity of mind with their fellow citizens which creates the common nationality.

How the immigrant is brought into the web of American life through the formal processes of education, through naturalization and political activity, through his press, his home, his neighborhood, etc., has been treated in other volumes of this series. In the present volume we are concerned only with his industrial experiences in America. How do the common experiences of gaining a livelihood in American industry develop unity of mind between native born and immigrant employees? How do the mutual adjustments that have to be made between the immigrant and his fellow-workers and employers bring all into a united American citizenship?

INDUSTRY AND THE IMMIGRANT

If the task of fusing immigrant and native-born population into a united nation is any more urgent or more difficult to-day than it was fifty or sixty years ago, it is because greater need and greater difficulty have developed among the wage-earners in our industries. In total numbers the ratio of foreign born to native population has been practically the same since 1860—about 1 to 7.[1] But while only about one seventh of the total population is foreign born, immigrants constitute a very much larger proportion of our industrial popula-

---

[1] Per cent Foreign Born of Total Population 1860 to 1920

1860,	*Per cent Foreign Born,*		13.2	1900,	*Per cent Foreign Born,*		13.6
1870,	"	" "	14.4	1910,	" "	"	14.7
1880,	"	" "	13.3	1920,	" "	"	13.0
1890,	"	" "	14.7				

5

tion. Such factory towns as Lowell, Fall River, Lawrence, Woonsocket, and Perth Amboy, as well as New York City, had more than 40 per cent foreign born in 1910; and in at least twenty other cities, including Chicago, Detroit, Cleveland, and Boston, more than a third were of foreign birth.

The Fourteenth Census, 1920, has not greatly changed these figures. The percentage of foreign born for leading industrial cities are: New York, 35.4; Boston, 31.9; Cleveland, 30.1; Chicago, 29.8; Detroit, 29.1; Duluth, 30.4; Bridgeport, 32.3; Lawrence, 41.4; Fall River, 35.1; New Bedford, 40.2; Passaic, 41.3; Paterson, 33.2; Perth Amboy, 35.8; Woonsocket, 36.8. In all the large industrial centers, the foreign born, together with their children, make up a majority of the population.

Something of the concentration of immigrants in industrial employment may be seen in the following table giving the proportions of foreign born in the general divisions of occupations as classified by the United States Census:

It will be noted that in agriculture less than 10 per cent of the persons engaged are immigrants, a smaller proportion than the number of foreign born to the population as a whole. On the other hand, immigrants constitute 36 per cent of the men engaged in manufacturing industries and more than 45 per cent of those in mining. In the extraction of minerals the total number of women employed is negligible, but in manufacturing women are an important factor and more than a fourth of these are foreign born. The building and hand trades, in which skilled mechanics predominate, have a somewhat smaller proportion of immigrants than mining and manufacturing, namely 27 per cent, and in the transportation industries just one fourth of the men engaged were born abroad.

TABLE I

Number and Per Cent Foreign Born in General Divisions of Occupations, 1910[1]

Occupational Division	Total			Foreign Born		Per Cent Foreign Born	
	Both Sexes	Male	Female	Male	Female	Male	Female
All Occupations	38,167,336	30,091,564	8,175,772	6,588,711	1,222,791	21.9	15.1
Agricultural Pursuits	12,665,693	10,857,488	1,808,205	1,038,913	57,995	9.6	3.2
Extraction of Minerals	1,059,961	1,057,408	2,553	480,251	435	45.4	17.0
Manufacturing Industries	7,464,404	6,094,423	1,369,981	2,193,019	351,000	36.0	25.6
Building and Hand Trades	3,410,819	2,797,249	614,570	763,310	87,563	27.3	14.2
Transportation	3,199,070	3,039,764	159,306	758,349	8,187	25.0	5.1
Trade	4,327,014	3,555,477	771,537	746,645	93,502	21.0	12.1
Public Service	532,753	509,176	23,577	107,973	1,272	21.2	5.4
Professional Service	1,712,489	933,165	779,324	138,273	60,355	14.8	7.7
Domestic and Personal Service	3,795,183	1,248,414	2,546,719	361,978	562,482	29.0	22.1

[1] U. S. Census, 1910, Table VI, Vol. IV Occupation Statistics, p. 302.

7

ADJUSTING IMMIGRANT AND INDUSTRY

These percentages represent averages of all the industries in each group, some of which have quite a small proportion of foreign born, while others have a much higher percentage than the average. When we look to the individual industries in each group, the concentration of immigrants in industrial employment stands out more clearly. In Table II we have tabulated all those industries in each general group which have a greater percentage of foreign born than is shown for the group as a whole.

TABLE II

PER CENT FOREIGN BORN BY INDUSTRIES, SHOWING GREATER PERCENTAGE THAN AVERAGE OF GENERAL DIVISION OF OCCUPATIONS, 1910 [1]

INDUSTRY	PER CENT FOREIGN BORN
Agricultural Pursuits	9.6 [2]
Forestry	24.4
Animal Husbandry	19.5
Extraction of Minerals	45.4
Coal Mines	48.3
Copper Mines	65.4
Iron Mines	66.8
Salt Mines, Wells, etc	46.3
Transportation	25.0
Water Transportation	38.7
Construction of Roads, etc	46.0
Street and Electric Railways	27.7
Steam Railroads	26.7
Manufacturing Industries	36.0
Soap Factories	38.2
Miscellaneous Chemical Factories	39.2
Lime Factories	40.0
Marble Factories	44.2
Clothing Factories (M.)	75.3

[1] Compiled from U. S. Census, Vol. IV, Table VI, p. 302.
[2] Percentages are for males only, except where F. indicates female.

8

INDUSTRY AND AMERICANIZATION

INDUSTRY	PER CENT FOREIGN BORN
Manufacturing Industries (Continued)	
Clothing Factories (F.)	45.2
Hat Factories	42.4
Bakeries	50.5
Slaughter and Packing Houses	45.8
Sugar Refineries	54.0
Agricultural Implements	37.5
Blast Furnaces	51.0
Car Factories	45.6
Iron	39.9
Leather Belt	50.9
Tanneries	52.9
Breweries	49.2
Furniture Factories	37.7
Piano Factories	43.2
Brass Factories	45.8
Copper Factories	64.0
Lead Factories	44.2
Tin Plate Mills	47.6
Miscellaneous Metal Factories	41.6
Paper and Pulp Mills	36.2
Carpet Factories	48.3
Cotton Mills (M.)	36.4
Cotton Mills (F.)	36.0
Hemp Mills (M.)	50.8
Hemp Mills (F.)	75.7
Lace Mills (M.)	57.2
Lace Mills (F.)	32.8
Rope Mills (M.)	44.0
Rope Mills (F.)	34.6
Silk Mills (M.)	46.5
Silk Mills (F.)	21.8
Woolen Mills (M.)	48.7
Woolen Mills (F.)	50.0
Dyeing	48.7
Other Textiles (M.)	40.2
Other Textiles (F.)	24.7
Charcoal	57.3
Oil Refineries	36.2
Rubber Factories	40.3

This table reveals that almost one fourth of those in forestry occupations and practically one fifth of those in animal husbandry are immigrants. These occupations are included in agriculture as a whole, for which less than 10 per cent is the proportion of foreign born. They are industrialized occupations and immigrants are found in them in much greater proportions than in straight farm work.

In the mining industries, while the percentage of foreign born for the whole group is 45, a higher percentage is shown by each of the three most important industries in the group—coal, copper, and iron mines. Almost half the men connected with coal mining and two thirds of those in copper and iron mining are immigrants. Similarly in the transportation industries, road construction shows 46 per cent foreign born as compared with 25 per cent for the whole group of industries.

While but slightly over a third of the men engaged in manufacturing are immigrants, all the more important industries in this group show a larger proportion—iron and steel, clothing and textiles, slaughter and packing houses, bakeries, rubber factories, tanneries and sugar refineries, all show more than 40 per cent foreign born, and in a good many manufacturing industries more than half the people engaged are immigrants.

But even these figures in Table II do not show the full extent of the concentration of immigrants in industrial employments. They include all persons engaged in the industries, proprietors, firm owners, salaried officials, and clerical help as well as wage earners. Among these "office workers," the proportion of immigrants is comparatively small. It is as a wage worker in the manual occupations that the immigrant stands out most plainly.

This is clearly shown in Table III, which lists the

10

principal occupations in which half or more of the
workers are foreign born.

TABLE III

PRINCIPAL OCCUPATIONS IN WHICH HALF OR MORE OF THE WAGE-
EARNERS WERE FOREIGN BORN IN 1910 [1]

OCCUPATION	PER CENT FOREIGN BORN
Extraction of Minerals	
Coal Miners	53.1 [2]
Coal Mine Laborers	51.1
Copper Miners	69.4
Copper Mine Laborers	68.1
Iron Miners	72.2
Iron Mine Laborers	69.3
Quarry Men	49.7
Quarry Laborers	51.1
Transportation	
Electric and Steam Railway Laborers	55.9
Longshoremen	56.3
Sewer and Road Laborers	51.5
Steam Railways Track Laborers	50.5
Manufacturing Industries	
Chemical Industries Laborers	56.0
Lime, Cement and Gypsum Laborers	51.1
Stone Cutters	49.8
Clothing Workers	79.2
Bakers	56.7
Butchers and Dressers	47.5
Laborers in Slaughter and Packing Houses	64.2
Sugar Refineries	71.4
Blast Furnaces and Rolling-Mill Laborers	70.0
Car and Railroad Shops Laborers	60.8
Foundry Laborers	62.6
Tanners	66.5

[1] U. S. Census, Vol. IV, Table VI, p. 302.
[2] Percentages are for males only, except where F. indicates female.

11

Occupation	Per Cent Foreign Born
Manufacturing Industries (Continued)	
Tannery Laborers..................................	60.6
Cabinet Makers..................................	56.6
Carpenters in Mills..............................	57.5
Brass Mill Laborers..............................	74.3
Copper Factories Laborers.......................	79.8
Lead and Zinc Laborers..........................	58.4
Tin Plate Mill Laborers..........................	69.0
Carpet Weavers..................................	51.1
Cotton Weavers (M.).............................	46.1
Cotton Weavers (F.).............................	48.0
Silk Weavers....................................	56.8
Textile and Dyeing and Finishing..................	57.1
Woolen Mills Laborers...........................	61.4
Woolen Weavers (M.).............................	53.2
Woolen Weavers (F.).............................	48.0
Woolen Spinners (M.)............................	44.5
Woolen Spinners (F.)............................	55.1
Coke Drawers...................................	73.1
Coke Laborers..................................	58.1
Electric Supply.................................	51.7
Gas Works Laborers.............................	56.1
Oil Refineries Laborers..........................	55.1
Rubber Factory Laborers.........................	57.1

It will be noted that the occupations which in point of numbers are most important have the largest proportions of immigrants. In most of the great industries of the country at least half of the wage workers are foreign born, while many occupations show two thirds and some as high as 70 per cent foreign born. In general, it is plain also from this table that the less skilled the labor, the greater the percentage of foreign born employed.

The United States Immigration Commission in 1909 made a study of the wage earners in twenty principal

INDUSTRY AND AMERICANIZATION

mining and manufacturing industries and found that of 500,000 workers employed, 60 per cent of the men and 47 per cent of the women were foreign born. In sixteen minor industries similarly studied the percentage of immigrants was found to be only slightly less.[1]

TABLE IV

Per Cent of Foreign-born Employees in Twenty Principal Mining and Manufacturing Industries and Sixteen Minor Industries

Principal Industries	Per Cent of Employees Foreign Born
Agricultural implement and vehicle manufacturing....	59.6
Boot and shoe manufacturing......................	27.3
Cigar and tobacco manufacturing..................	32.6
Clothing manufacturing...........................	72.2
Coal mining, bituminous..........................	61.9
Collar, cuff, and shirt manufacturing...............	13.4
Construction work................................	76.6
Copper mining and smelting.......................	65.3
Cotton goods manufacturing in the North Atlantic States..	68.7
Furniture manufacturing..........................	59.1
Glass manufacturing..............................	39.3
Glove manufacturing..............................	33.5
Iron and steel manufacturing......................	57.7
Iron ore mining..................................	52.6
Leather manufacturing............................	67.0
Oil refining......................................	66.7
Silk goods manufacturing and dyeing...............	37.7
Slaughtering and meat packing....................	60.7
Sugar refining...................................	85.3
Woolen and worsted goods manufacturing...........	61.9
Total—20 principal industries....................	57.9

[1] U. S. Immigration Commission *Abstract of Reports,* Vol. I, p. 501.

13

MINOR INDUSTRIES	PER CENT OF EMPLOYEES FOREIGN BORN
Carpet manufacturing	58.0
Car building and repairing	54.9
Cutlery and tool manufacturing	63.1
Electric railway transportation	33.9
Electric supplies manufacturing	44.9
Firearms manufacturing	40.1
Foundry and machine shop products manufacturing	54.5
Hosiery and knit goods manufacturing	29.0
Locomotive building and repairing	48.6
Paper and wood pulp manufacturing	38.8
Paper products manufacturing	31.3
Rope, twine, and hemp manufacturing	77.8
Sewing machine manufacturing	55.9
Steam railway transportation	39.0
Typewriter manufacturing	19.7
Zinc smelting and manufacturing	61.1
Total—16 minor industries	46.9

If all immigrants, representing as they do now less than one seventh of the population of the United States, were distributed evenly among the native population, the chances would be excellent that the common contacts of American life might in a reasonable time teach them to think and act in unison with Americans. Actually, however, this even distribution has not taken place. And when we find immigrants spending their lives in industrial occupations where they form more than a third and often half and two thirds of all the employees, and living in communities where a majority of the population is of foreign stock, then the problem of uniting native with foreign born takes on quite a different character. Picture a community where every seventh person is an immigrant and then contrast it with the following description of

14

INDUSTRY AND AMERICANIZATION

"Community E" as given by the United States Immigration Commission.[1]

This town in western Pennsylvania, although located in a bituminous coal-mining district, supports a number of important glass factories, which constitute its chief industry. In 1908 the estimated population was 9,000, composed of the following races:

Americans	3,000
Belgians (including French)	1,200
Croatians	100
Germans	500
Hebrews	100
Italians	1,200
Magyars	100
Poles	500
Russians	300
Slovaks	1,700
All other races	300
Totals	9,000

To develop a unity of mind in a community of this kind is obviously a much more serious and difficult task. And the untraveled reader may find scores of replicas of this community in the reports of the Immigration Commission.[2]

Not only the larger proportion of immigrants in industry but also the greater number of races in a particular industry makes the development of a unity of mind more difficult.

The immigrants in agriculture . . . are usually grouped in more or less homogeneous colonies or settlements; frequently a community is composed entirely of one foreign race and perhaps some American farmers. . . . The number of immigrants (in any agricultural occupation) is so small compared with the total number engaged in the occupation that it is insignificant.[3]

[1] *Ibid.*, Vol. I, p.525.

[2] U. S. Immigration Commission, *Abstract of Reports*, vol. I, pp. 502, 530, and vols. VI–XX, "Immigrants in Industries."

[3] *Ibid.*, p. 555.

Contrast this with the situation in manufacturing industries—cotton mills for example: [1]

The Americans, who formerly composed the bulk of the cotton mill operatives in the North Atlantic States, at the present time form only about one tenth of the total number of the employees in the cotton mills, and are divided in about equal proportions between males and females. . . . Of the total foreign born operatives, about one half are representatives of races of southern and eastern Europe and the Orient, the remainder being composed mainly of English, Irish, and French Canadians, with a relatively small number of Scotch, Germans, Swedes, Dutch, and French. The French Canadians among the foreign born are employed at present in greater proportions than any other races, the proportion of French Canadian cotton-mill operatives exceeding that of the Americans. The English furnish about one tenth and the Irish about one twentieth of the total number of employees in the industry. Of the operatives from southern and eastern Europe, the Poles, Portuguese, and Greeks, in the order named, furnish the largest proportions, the total number of these races constituting more than one fourth of the total number employed. More than thirty other races from southern and eastern Europe are working in the cotton mills of the North Atlantic States; the North and South Italians, Lithuanians, and Russians are numerically the most important. Several Oriental races, including Turks, Persians, and Syrians, are also found. The larger part of the female employees at the present time is made up of English, Irish, and French Canadian operatives, of both the first and second generations together with large proportions of Portuguese and Polish women. The American females, as already stated, form only about one tenth of the total number of female operatives.

In the twenty leading branches of mining and manufacturing the Immigration Commission found more than sixty different races. [2]

---

[1] *Ibid.*, pp. 511–512.
[2] *Abstract of Reports*, vol. I, pp. 321–322.

INDUSTRY AND AMERICANIZATION

*Races found by the Immigration Commission in Twenty
Leading Branches of Mining and Manufacturing*

Abyssinian
Albanian
Arabian
Armenian
Bohemian and Moravian
Bosnian
Bulgarian
Canadian, French
Canadian, Other
Croatian
Cuban
Dalmatian
Dutch
Danish
Egyptian
English
Filipino
Finnish
Flemish
French
German
Greek
Hebrew, Russian
Hebrew, Other
Herzegovinian
Hindu
Irish
Italian, North
Italian, South
Italian (not specified)
Japanese

Korean
Lithuanian
Macedonian
Magyar
Montenegrin
Mexican
Negro
Norwegian
Persian
Polish
Portuguese
Roumanian
Ruthenian
Russian
Scotch
Scotch-Irish
Servian
Slovak
Slovenian
Spanish
Swedish
Syrian
Turkish
Welsh
West Indian (other than Cuban)
Alsatian (race not specified)
Australian (race not specified)
Austrian (race not specified)
Belgian (race not specified)
South American (race not specified)
Swiss

This immigrant industrial population, it must also
be remembered, is composed mainly of adults who are
rarely reached by the public schools, and whose constant association with fellow workers of foreign birth
limits greatly their opportunities for contacts with
American influences. Only 10 per cent of the immi-

grants in the industries are between fourteen and nineteen years of age, whereas more than 25 per cent of the native born are in these younger age groups. Fifty per cent of the immigrant workers are under thirty years of age, but more than 60 per cent of the native-born workers were under this age. A larger percentage of the total foreign-born employees appears in every age group above twenty-five years, and a smaller proportion of the total under twenty-five.[1]

TABLE V

Per Cent of Employees within Each Age Group by Sex and General Nativity

	Number	Per Cent within Each Age Group							
		Under 14	14–19	20–24	25–29	30–34	35–44	45–54	55 and over
Male									
Native born.....	161,589	.2	18.7	20.0	16.4	12.7	17.7	10.1	4.2
Foreign born.....	246,702	—	7.1	19.8	20.1	15.4	21.9	10.9	4.8
Female									
Native born.....	51,533	.3	45.1	24.5	11.4	6.4	8.1	3.1	.9
Foreign born.....	45,460	—	27.4	29.7	14.6	9.0	12.8	5.0	1.3
Total									
Native born.....	213,122	.2	25.1	21.1	15.2	11.2	15.4	8.4	3.4
Foreign born.....	292,162	—	10.3	21.3	19.2	14.4	20.5	10.0	4.3

The adult enters the shop, the child goes to school. What the difference means is thus described by an immigrant girl.[2]

Although almost five years now had passed since I had started for America it was only now that I caught a glimpse of it. For though I was in America I had lived in practically the same environ-

---

[1] U. S. Immigration Commission, *Abstract of Reports*, vol. I, pp. 463–467.

[2] Rose Cohen, *Out of the Shadow*, George H. Doran Co., 1918, p. 246.

INDUSTRY AND AMERICANIZATION

ment which we brought from home. Of course there was a difference in our joys, our sorrows, in our hardships, for after all this was a different country; but on the whole we were still in our village in Russia. A child that came to this country and began to go to school had taken the first step into the New World. But the child that was put into the shop remained in the old environment with the old people, held back by the old traditions, held back by illiteracy. Often it was years before he could stir away from it, sometimes it would take a life time. Sometimes, too, it happened, as in fairy tales, that a hand was held out to you and you were helped out.

POINTS OF VIEW

Because the immigrant industrial population is necessarily so largely an adult population, because it is made up of so many races, and because of the great concentration of immigrants in certain industrial occupations and communities, industry presents at once the greatest need and the greatest difficulty for organized effort to bring about a merging of the native with the foreign born.

In industry, however, the conflict of interests between economic groups, such as employers and employees, skilled mechanics and common laborers, is so bitter that an impersonal conception of Americanism is difficult to maintain.

A native American woman drove over to the house of a Polish neighbor to inquire if the daughter of the Polish family would accept work as a servant for the American household. The American woman was displeased with the attitude of the Polish girl, but she thought the old Polish woman was "nice." The girl did not seem at all pleased about the opportunity to work as a servant. The mother, however, was quite evidently anxious that the daughter should get the work. The girl asked in good English about the wages offered and the privileges as to days off and evenings out, and she stipulated the kind of work she would do

19

in the household and what she would not do. The mother, in broken English, apologized for her daughter's attitude, apparently fearing that her questions might lose her the job. But the daughter explained that her teacher in the public school told her to be independent like an American and to ask questions like that.

To the American woman seeking a maid this effect of Americanization was quite displeasing, and she preferred the attitude of the un-Americanized Polish mother. It is possible, of course, that the Polish-speaking mother will prove to be a better American than the English-speaking daughter, but apparently it was the Americanization of the daughter that was most displeasing to her prospective native-born employer.

Similarly the employers in most of the great industries of the country which employ immigrants in such large numbers, object to unionism among their employees on the ground that a union shop itself is un-American; and they have named their policy of maintaining non-union shops, the "American Plan."

On the other hand, the American trade unions and a large section of the public generally condemn the immigrant for not joining labor unions and for being content with conditions which the native born will not accept, and thus lowering the standards of American workers.

. . . The extensive employment of southern and eastern European immigrants in manufacturing and mining has in many places resulted in the weakening of labor organizations or in their complete disruption. . . . The tendency of recent immigrants to thrift and their desire for immediate gains have made them reluctant to enter labor disputes involving loss of time or to join labor organizations to which it was necessary to pay regular dues. As a consequence, the recent immigrant has not, as a rule, affiliated himself with labor unions unless compelled to do so as a preliminary step toward

INDUSTRY AND AMERICANIZATION

acquiring work, and after becoming a member of a labor union, he has manifested but little interest in the tenets or policy of the organization.[1]

If Americans differ thus completely in their conception of Americanism, what confusion there must be in the mind of the immigrant. When he follows the example of his native fellow wage earners and wishes to join a labor union to improve his conditions and is prevented from doing it, what is he to think? When he is permitted to join a union or organize one, and is condemned as an alien or Bolshevik for this action, what must be his bewilderment? Is he not justified in thinking that we really do not want him to do what a free American may do, that we prefer him to keep his place as an inferior servant? Is not the public exhortation to become Americanized likely to strike him as hypocritical, when he finds the people who urge his Americanization also condemn him when he strives to achieve American standards of living by the methods that American workers use?

A group of industrial relations managers, representing some of the very largest industrial enterprises in the country, were questioning a national organizer of a labor union numbering 175,000 members, most of whom are immigrants. The organizer was an Italian by birth, an American citizen.

"What is the attitude of your organization toward Americanization?" asked a director of industrial relations for a corporation operating plants in many states.

"What do you mean by Americanization?" countered the labor man.

"You know what I mean. I can't just define it, but we all know what the word Americanization means as ordinarily used."

"I know what some employers mean by Americanization," continued the labor organizer, "and our people resent that kind of Americanization. I have my own ideas of Americanization which

---

[1] *Abstracts of Reports*, vol. I, pp. 530–531.

are quite different from those employers' ideas, and you will have to explain what you mean by Americanization."

Another member of the group then suggested that "We take Americanization to mean a knowledge of the English language, a knowledge of the American government and its methods, a desire to assume the responsibilities of citizenship, and a sympathetic attitude toward American traditions and ideals."

The Americanized Italian then answered: "Our organization is constantly striving to raise the standards of our people, most of whom are foreign born. We try to make them independent, self-respecting men and women. We want them to earn enough to live as Americans live. We have raised wages during the last four years by means of our organization, so that now they can maintain an American standard of living. We want them to have leisure enough for education, recreation, and enjoyment of life in American fashion, and we have brought the hours of labor in our industry down to forty-four per week to permit them to do this.

"Our organization conducts English and Naturalization classes. We do not force our people to join these classes, but we get the Board of Education to provide the teachers and then we organize classes in the shops, that meet at 4:30, immediately after working hours. We are not getting all the people, but we get enough to run the classes and we feel that these classes have been made possible by our forty-four-hour week. When we quit at 4:30 we have time to attend such classes. We also have evening classes at our headquarters in each city and the eight-hour day enables our people to go home for supper after work and be on time at the classes. In the steel industry where many still work seventy-two hours a week it is impossible for the worker to attend classes after a twelve-hour day.

"In our industry the workers are not afraid. They have freedom to assert their rights. They are not overworked. They walk with their heads erect. I can see myself the change in the workers of this city, who have been organized for only about a year and a half. They are a different people. They walk straighter. They are independent, they live better, they aren't afraid of losing their jobs, they are free men and women and not servile employees.

"If this is Americanization, then we are strongly for it and we are Americanizing all the time. But because we do this some employers call us foreigners and Bolshevists. As long as we were satisfied with low wages and long hours, as long as we were afraid of losing our jobs, stood for black lists and did not strike, we were all right. We were preferred to American employees. But when we strike, as we did recently because a girl was fired for no other reason than that she exercised her American right to join a union, when we ask for higher wages and a shorter work day to raise our standards, then the employer says we are not Americans.

"Can you blame us if we resent this? We (Italians) are sensitive people. We object to the word "Americanization" because it is used by employers as a camouflage to hide their desire to keep foreigners down to low standards. Our people have been overworked and exploited by employers, so that many of them in ten years have had to go back to the old country like squeezed-out lemons. This is what some employers want to perpetuate under the name Americanization. When we object to it they call us foreigners and they want to 'Americanize' us so we will accept what they want to give us.

"We are raising standards for our people constantly providing leisure, education, and wages enough to maintain good living conditions. This is Americanization. We don't want the camouflage which these employers call 'Americanization.'"

If immigrant industrial workers are to live and act in unison with Americans, they cannot be treated as members of an inferior economic class, who are to be content with lower standards and live among us to do the hard and disagreeable labor that Americans will not do. Under such conditions they cannot maintain the respect and consideration we must have for them if they are to be "of us" and we are to live and work with them as equal citizens. In the army all were treated alike and all could work together without regard to economic status. In industry, if immigrant wage-earners are not to be solidified into an inferior caste, there must be a similar mutual adjustment of relations between them and the native-born population.

Most immigrants are willing enough. They come here as to the Promised Land. If some show antagonism, may it not be that treatment and conditions in America have developed it? If the foreign-born population is to be fused with the native-born, the same freedom of opinion and action that is allowed to Americans will have to be granted to the immigrants. Equal opportunity, equal protection, equal treatment, and equal right of self-assertion are as necessary for them in the process of becoming Americans, as it is to maintain the ideal of American citizenship.

IMMIGRANT INDUSTRIAL EXPERIENCES AND THEIR EFFECT

From the day the immigrant lands in America he begins to have experiences that affect his mind and character vitally. Whatever we may mean by Americanism, these everyday experiences develop or retard his capacity to acquire it. Favorable economic experiences, steady work, rising standards, equality of rights and opportunity, property, prosperity, incline the immigrant favorably toward things American. Unfavorable experiences, unemployment, exploitation by labor agents, abuse by foremen and employers, poverty and low standards will make him antagonistic to things American and cause him to idealize his old home. For he sees in the injustices which he often suffers at the hands of employers, trade-unions, government officials, labor agents, and boarding house keepers, not the criminality of irresponsible individuals, but the acts of the American nation. He thinks these are the ways of American life which he must learn. It is the "American Game," a phrase commonly used by immigrants.

Industrial managers have recently discovered that human nature in working people, be they native or immigrant, men or women, skilled or unskilled, is very much the same. It responds normally to the treatment it gets in a perfectly reasonable way. The employer who pays a skilled mechanic $27\frac{1}{2}$ cents an hour, as many did before the war, gets a man who says he "would give $27\frac{1}{2}$ cents worth of work and no more." The manager who imposes his will upon his workers and enforces his policies without consulting the wishes of his employees must expect the same reaction from immigrants as from native born. The industry that herds its immigrant workers like cattle, makes no distinction among personalities, but treats its unskilled labor as a class of commodity to be paid for at a market price, finds such employees as balky, as actuated by class or herd spirit, as little interested or concerned in the enterprise of which they are a part as American workers are under the same treatment.

To a certain extent America has the kind of immigrant population it creates. To a certain extent clannishness, low standards of living, indifference to things American, and apparent loyalty to foreign lands, of which so many people complain, are the fruits of American policy or lack of policy in dealing with the immigrant industrial population? If industrial management has found that the native laborer responds to humane, considerate, and democratic treatment with an aroused interest in the business, with increased output and ambition, and with a spirit of coöperation and loyalty to the industrial establishment; then may it not be equally true that under similar treatment at the hands of immigration officials, courts, police, employment agencies, employers, trade-unions, social agencies, and other institutions of American community life, the immigrant will develop a similar spirit of coöperation and loyalty to the nation?

It behooves the nation, therefore, to study the experience of the immigrants whom we have permitted to land, in much the same way that enlightened employers are now studying the experiences in the shops of the people whom they employ. Under various names such employers have established what has been aptly described as a "Square Deal Department." Sometimes it is called an employment department, sometimes a welfare department or service department, and often an industrial relations department. But whatever the name, its purpose is to follow the careers of the workers in the plant and see to it that in hiring, in promotion, in wage payment, in treatment at the hands of subordinate officials, and in all the other experiences of a worker in the shop, he shall be protected against injustice. And since abuses are bound to creep in, provision is made for hearing complaints and giving redress where wrongs are proved.

Employers have found all this necessary, in order to build up a spirit of loyalty and coöperation among their employees. And it is hard to see how the nation can win the active and loyal coöperation of its immigrants without something of the same kind.

Whether we decide upon a policy of exclusion or not, fourteen million foreign born are in our midst, and many of them are having experiences every day with labor agencies, employers, unions, public authorities, and immigrant agencies which are described in later chapters. These experiences may assimilate them into American industrial life, or may set them apart as outsiders. So far as we have given any attention to the problem of immigration, we have centered it almost entirely on selection and exclusion, trusting that somehow, automatically, those who are admitted will be assimilated. Social science, however, has long ago taught us to reject the assumption of a benevolent providence that works automatically for the public weal through so-called natural laws. Deliberate organization has been found necessary to make the laws work to human ends and social well-being. If we wish to weave the immigrants into our American communities, we must provide the administrative organization that is capable of accomplishing such a purpose.

If ever there was a time when this could be done most effectively, the present is that time. The war aroused the public to a realization of the futility of depending upon undirected assimilation. It appears that the automatic melting pot has failed to melt. The draft and the various agencies created to further the war have made the facts of immigrant life in America common knowledge. For a good many years it is probable that immigration into the country will remain at a minimum, because of restrictive laws, and many immigrants will return to their native land.[1]

The problem is becoming limited to reasonable proportions. We can see around it and we can work out the program, and the administrative machinery necessary to carry it into effect, with complete knowledge of the number, kind, and nature of the immigrants we have to deal with. We may go at the task of conscious and deliberate assimilation without fear that our efforts will be upset by a deluge of new immigrants.

---

[1] The number leaving the country during the past fiscal year was 198,712. The total number of immigrant aliens admitted during the same period was 309,556, leaving a permanent addition to the population through immigration and emigration of only 110,844.

A casual inspection of the statistics relative to the distribution of immigrants by states for the past fiscal year indicates that a considerably larger proportion have gone to the western and agricultural states than was the case for many years prior to the war. This is due, of course, to the increased proportion of the older type of immigration in the movement, for it is a well-known fact that while the more recent immigrants have largely congregated in the cities and industrial districts, the northern and western Europeans have always become widely scattered throughout the country and that a far larger proportion of them have found their way into agricultural activities. If this trend continues, as it promises to do, immigration will in a corresponding degree become less of a problem.

Commissioner of Immigration, W. W. Husband, Sept. 12, 1922.

CHAPTER II

FINDING A PLACE IN AMERICAN INDUSTRY

WHATEVER the motives may be that lead immigrants to pull up stakes and come to the Promised Land, practically all of them are confronted from the first with the necessity of earning a living. Few of those who come over have sufficient funds to support themselves without work for more than a few weeks. According to the Commissioner General of Immigration,[1]

Immigrants applying for admission to the U. S. are not required to state how much money they bring with them unless the amount is under $50 but as a rule those having larger sums report the amounts they possess to the examining officials. In 1920, 141,799 immigrant aliens out of a total of 276,049 showing money, exhibited less than $50 each. This was 51.4 per cent of the total number showing money compared with 44.6 per cent in 1919 and 82.7 per cent in 1910–14.

The average amount possessed by all who showed money in 1921 was $45.50, in 1920 $119, in 1919 $112. During the period from 1910–1914 the average amount was $44.

Here we have a common level where all may touch each other, a common experience on the basis of which a community of mind may be built up. The first task of the immigrant is to root himself in the economic life of the country, that he may derive life and nourishment in the new land.

The officials of the government who admit the immigrant looking for work, however, must see to it that he has secured no job in this country in advance of his coming. This is their sworn duty. The alien contract

---

[1]Report of Commissioner General of Immigration, 1920, p. 43.

labor law prohibits the entry of any immigrant who has a definite promise of employment after he lands.

The absurd contradiction between the immigrant's need for work and the government's insistence that he shall have no job before he lands is the direct result of the lack of any domestic immigration policy. Having no means of protecting the American workman, or indeed the immigrant himself, from unfair labor contracts by which employers might exploit cheap foreign labor and use it to displace American workers, the government has been compelled by American labor to declare illegal any contracts made with aliens abroad for work in this country.

BLIND SEARCH FOR WORK

The immigrant lands, therefore, with no assurance of work; and ignorant as he is of our language and economic opportunities, he must find his place in American industry as best he can.

In the absence of a systematic national organization for distribution and placement of labor, he resorts to all sorts of devices. The saloon used to be one of the most important places to get information about jobs. Political district leaders make finding work for immigrants a part of their duties. Pool rooms, cafés, grocery stores, lodging houses, even street corners and public parks, become improvised labor markets. In these places many and strange abuses are met with. Groundless rumors send people scurrying over the city and country on wild goose chases. One job seeker sells information to another, and quite often it is false or misleading. Foremen sell real and bogus jobs in the factories where they work and "man catchers" pick up laborers, for whom they receive so much per head from their employers.

ADJUSTING IMMIGRANT AND INDUSTRY

Walking through Seward Park on New York's East Side one summer day, we were accosted by an elderly man, who asked: "Need a hand?" He wanted work in a clothing shop. And looking around we saw many such workmen standing around in groups and sitting on park benches—carpenters, glaziers, tinsmiths, and workers of many other hand trades. Window washers and other unskilled workers also congregated in this outdoor employment exchange, on the chance of getting something to do; and washwomen and scrubwomen were to be found here in the early morning hours.

The institution arose with the first Russian Jewish immigration and came to be known as the "Pig Market." In Baltimore, we were told of a similar market by clothing workers, who had used it before the union established itself in the city and provided an employment bureau for its members. In those days it was common for workers to furnish their own sewing machines, and when a man was hired he lifted his machine on his back and carried it to his place of employment. One of the first demands made by the unions organized among these clothing workers was the abolition of the "Pig Market," and the hiring of all help through the union offices.

Wherever there are immigrants looking for work, the same opportunities for service or abuse appear. From St. Louis an Assistant Commissioner of Labor of the State of Missouri reports: [1]

An interpreter came from a distant city and opened up head-quarters in a foreign settlement, using a saloon conducted by a foreigner as a base of his operations. He used the saloon keeper as a confederate to obtain money from unsuspecting foreigners, whom the saloon keeper informed there was plenty of work to be

---

[1] Annual Report of the Missouri Commissioner of Labor, 1917, p. 68.

had if they paid a fee of $5 to $10 to the assistant foreman. The interpreter, posing as the assistant foreman, lured over 150 men, collected the money, paid a commission to the saloon keeper, and left town without putting a man to work, thereby defrauding these foreigners out of hundreds of dollars. . . .

We have picked up twenty-five unlicensed labor agents who were operating in and around the union station. . . . A practice was in vogue here of the saloons and boarding houses advertising for laborers and securing help for railroads and quarries. In every case it was found that the men employed were compelled to board with the people who advertised for help.

FRIENDS AND RELATIVES HELP

"I would like to be in another trade but I never had any friend to take me to any other trade," said Sofia Caruso, a little Sicilian buttonhole maker in New York City.[1] Of 874 Italian girls who told how they secured their first positions, 685, over 75 per cent, said they secured it by the friend or relative method. The feeling of being "ashamed to go alone" has been found especially among Italian and Syrian girls. The "friend" is so important that quite often, if she happens to quit her place, the immigrant girl whom she brought to the shop will leave with her, for no other reason than that her friend is leaving.

Groups of Italian girls, six or seven perhaps, will go from place to place seeking work, strong in each other's protection; but not meeting with much success because the employer has not enough positions to observe their rule of "take one, take all."[2] Sometimes it is the effect of shyness that causes girls to depend so much on friends in seeking work; or it may be a desire for the comradeship in work of those whom they already know. More often it grows out of helplessness in getting about the city, ignorance of other

[1] L. Odencranz, *Italian Women in Industry*, p. 283.
[2] *Ibid.*, p. 275.

means of finding employment, and inability to make terms with an English-speaking employer.

Sofia Caruso was a buttonhole maker neither by choice nor interest. It was to buttonhole making her friend had taken her. A man, especially one with university education and training, will be more self-reliant; but in the end he may not fare much better.

After dinner I went up and down Broadway looking for something to do. All that day I had walked the streets looking for work, guided in my wanderings by the want ads in the New York *Staats Zeitung*. Bartenders headed the list of those wanted, barbers came next, bakers too were in demand, and butchers and clothing cutters. Although my eyes wandered over and over again to the letter U, there seemed to be no need for university men. That day I had nothing to eat.

With morning came the still unsolved question, what to do for a living. My friends suggested that I go from one hotel to another in the hope that my languages would be of value. Altogether I visited some twenty of the leading hotels. I walked from Twenty-third Street to Eightieth Street and arrived home tired and discouraged.

Fortunately the next day was Sunday; not only could I rest, but it was an opportunity to find a job. Sunday is the day when acquaintances meet in the coffee houses and the greenhorn becomes a subject of conversation and consideration. This particular coffee house was frequented by cloak shop workers, many of them acquaintances of my relatives. To them the greenhorn was introduced and by them his problem was discussed. . . . At last my fate was decided: I was to report on Monday at a certain number on Canal Street, bring an apron and try my luck at pressing cloaks.[1]

"WANT ADS"

A Turkish immigrant who arrived in 1913 told us how he secured employment through an advertisement calling for men less than six months in the country. On applying he was employed as a packer in a cotton house at $5 per week. He worked at this wage for

---

[1] Ed. Steiner, *From Alien to Citizen*, pp. 49–52.

five months, and then, when he asked for more he was promptly discharged. The employer, presumably, would be able to get other newcomers at $5 a week as he had secured this one.

Another, who had served an apprenticeship as a 'spinning master" in his native country, thought he would himself advertise in a newspaper of his own language for an opportunity to work at his trade. In reply a man called at his home and promised to get him the work he was looking for if he would pay an initiation fee and join the union. The end of it all was that the man got away with $8 belonging to the immigrant. After that he gave up the idea of finding work at his own trade and got a job as a painter, later as a paper hanger. He worked as a laborer, a clothing cutter, and a moving picture operator. And now he is a dentist!

A self-reliant Russian who arrived in 1914 did not care to avail himself of help offered by his friends. He preferred to shift for himself and got most of his numerous jobs through advertisements. First he was a painter at $4 a week. Then he became a machinist's helper at $6 per week. The employer promised to teach him the machinist's trade but did not do so. Finding the helper's work too hard, he quit and got work as a metal polisher. After changing around in many places at this work he learned the trade well and at the time we interviewed him, he was earning $25.00 a week.

Let an immigrant tell his own experiences with want advertisements: [1]

The two days allotted to a guest being over, I was given to understand that I must enter the race for American dollars. During the remainder of that week and throughout the entire week follow-

---

[1] M. E. Ravage, *An American in the Making*, pp. 91 ff.

ing I went about "trying." Early in the morning I would go downstairs to buy a *World*, and after breakfast I would get one of the
children to translate the want advertisements for me. When I
glanced at the length and the number of those columns, I saw that
I would not be long in getting rich. There were hundreds of shops
and factories and offices, it seemed, that wanted my help. They
literally implored me to come. They promised me high wages, and
regular pay, and fine working conditions. And then I would go and
blunder around for hours, trying to find where they were, stand in
line with a hundred other applicants, approach timidly when my
turn came, and be passed up with a significant glance at my appearance. . . . I could not bridge the gulf between the advertised appeals for help and this arrogant indifference of the employing
superintendent.

Half the time I had not the remotest idea of what was wanted.
I had been told what a butcher was and what was meant by a grocery
store. But what were shipping clerks, and stock clerks, and bill
clerks, and all the other scores of varieties of clerks that were so
eagerly sought? However, I did not let trifles discourage me. There
was only one way to succeed in America, my friends continually
told me, and that was by constant, tireless; undiscriminating trying.
If you failed in one place, or in ten places, or in a hundred places,
you must not give up. Keep on trying, and you are bound to be
taken somewhere. Moreover, American occupations were so flimsy,
they required so little skill or experience, that a fellow with a little
intelligence and the normal amount of daring could bluff his way
into almost any job. The main thing was to say "yes" whenever
you were asked whether you could do this or that. That was the
way everybody got work. The employer never knew the difference.
So I followed the counsel of the wise, insofar as my limited spunk
permitted, and knocked at every door in sight. Time and time
again I applied, at department stores in need of floor-walkers (that,
I thought, could certainly require no special gifts), at offices where
stenographers were wanted, at factories demanding foremen. . . .

Then there was the problem of distances. I could not dream of
paying car fares everywhere I went. Even if I had had the nickel,
the mere thought of spending twenty-five bani at every turn would
have seemed an appalling extravagance. And, somehow, the jobs
that I supposed I had a fair chance of getting were always at the
ends of creation. An errand boy was wanted in Long Island City,
and a grocer was looking for an assistant in Hoboken. By the time
I had reached one place and had had my services refused, I was too
late in getting to the others. And always I was refused. Why?
At last one morning, a butcher in the upper Eighties gave me the

answer with pungent frankness. I had got to the spot before anyone else, and when I saw it in his eye that he was about to pass me up, I gathered all the pluck that was in me and demanded the reason. He looked me over from head to foot, and then, with a contemptuous glance at my shabby foreign shoes (the alien's shoes are his Judas), he asked me whether I supposed he wanted a greenhorn in his store. I pondered that query for a long time. Here, I thought, was indeed new light on America. Her road to success was a vicious circle, and no mistake. In order to have a job one must have American clothes and the only way to get American clothes was to find a job and earn the price. Altogether a desperate situation.

EMPLOYMENT AGENTS

Failing to get the good job he is looking for, through his friends or through his own efforts, the immigrant turns to the private labor agent for help. How these agencies serve the immigrant may be illustrated by the experiences recounted to investigators of this study. A German who came over in 1912 wrote out his experiences as follows:

I was a few weeks in this country, one man advertised in a German paper, his place was on Sixth Ave., he charged a dollar. At that time I did not know enough to look for the license in the room. I now think there was none. That man was a downright faker. He soon moved from the place. (Without getting the immigrant a job.)

An ad in the German paper brought me to a German agency in Yorkville. He offered me a job on a dairy farm. He should not have offered me the job and I should not have taken it. I went to the place and was sent home the same day. It caused me about $10 expenses. I didn't know enough to press my case in the agency. I was offered a poor job (as a substitute) and was too discouraged to go back to the agency again.

I paid $2 to an agency in Yorkville, worked one day, quit, went to the agency, and got my money back.

A downtown high class employment agency advertised for a German stenographer. It was *bona fide*, but it cost me a week's salary.

In Chicago I paid $5 to an agency for a clerical position, which I didn't take. The law, as printed on the blank, wasn't clear to me, so I thought I had to submit to try another job. This other job was a cleancut frameup. I went back for my money and the agent made difficulties. A (compulsory) rubber stamp on back of my receipt gave the name and address of the Commissioner of private agencies. I went to see him. He had his feet on the desk, his hat on, a cigar in his mouth, talking privately to somebody. With an air of benevolence he listened to me, and put my report with pencil on a slip of paper. He seemed to be familiar with the sort of story I told him and with the whole situation. He spoke to the agent over the phone and settled the matter for me. I went back and got the money.

A Bulgarian farm worker paid a Chicago labor agent $10 for work as a track laborer in West Virginia at $1 a day. Subsequently he used labor agencies several times and had to pay only $2, although the wages he received were higher. This seems to be the universal experience. The first job secured through an employment agent is paid for with a high fee. Later, when the immigrant knows the ropes better, fees become more reasonable.

A superintendent of Alien Poor in New York State writes to the New York Bureau of Industries and Immigration: [1]

A number of cases of what seem to be imposition upon immigrant laborers have been brought to the attention of this department. It is stated that immigrants arriving at the port of New York apply to an employment bureau known as . . . of New York City. These aliens, according to their story, upon the payment of a fee of $3 are given to understand that a position awaits them at a certain point on the Erie Railroad at so much per day. Upon arriving at the designated point they are assigned to an agent, kept for a few days, after which they are told they are no longer wanted. As they have paid the agency almost the last cent they have, these aliens are obliged to suffer hardship, going without food for several days and compelled to walk a long distance to Buffalo or some other city. Very frequently these shipments are made along the line of the Erie Railroad. . . . At my request Mr. Elson has forwarded

---

[1] First Annual Report, 1911, p. 37.

four sample labor contracts obtained from the aliens at the Municipal Lodging House. All of these seem to have paid the agency a fee of $3. On November 23d, another contract of the same kind was picked up from a poor person at our Buffalo office. I trust it will be possible for your new Bureau of Industrial Immigration to prevent impositions of this character. I enclose the contracts to you.

It is not within our province to follow the immigrant in his experiences outside of industry. But one example may serve to show what inducement there is for him to follow the advice so often given him to leave the city and go out on the land. The Executive Officer of the California Commission of Immigration and Housing said in a public address:

Several years ago a large tract of land was opened for colonization in the Sacramento Valley. The sales agents made a particular point of inducing immigrants to purchase this land in lots of from twenty to thirty acres. Agents were employed who spoke many languages and the value of the land was represented in advertising and orally, in the most glowing terms. There was much exaggeration and even misrepresentation, and some 150 families, mostly immigrants, were induced to pay from $100 to $150 an acre for this land. Some eighty settlers have left the colony after three years of fruitless labor, and their life savings are gone. The land is honeycombed with hardpan and the university's soil experts have said that no one could possibly make a living on these twenty or thirty acre lots. The families that remain are practically destitute, but the commission is coöperating with them in bringing action against the owners and agents for fraud, and there is some hope for recovery.

This is only one of some 500 land fraud cases that have been handled by the State Immigration Commission. It shows that we exploit immigrants even in their attempt to get back to the land. . . the place where many wise students of the problem say they must be before our immigrant problem will be settled.

Many similar experiences are given in *A Stake in the Land*, by Peter A. Speek, the Americanization Studies' report on efforts of immigrants to settle on the land.

In contrast with all this antagonizing experience there is "Mother Makowski." Mother Makowski is proprietress of an employment agency in the Polish section of a western city. She is herself Polish and a worker. Her employment agency is her staple source of income, but she leaves it without ceremony any day when her services as high grade cook receive a desirable call. When immigration was active, Polish girls came to this inland city, straight from the steamer, arriving bundle in hand, guided thither by "Mother Makowski's" card brought with them from overseas. A bath in her own bathtub was often a first ceremony, followed soon after by a trip to the store, where she helped them buy a few American clothes for an American "job," and a *hat*. If these girls were not being looked after by their own people, the "lady next door" lodged them for fifty cents a night; or if her house was not full, Mrs. Makowski kept them herself.

No Polish woman, who is ignorant of the English language or the streets of the city, need be troubled about finding the position of which she learns at the agency; for Mrs. Makowski, herself, will go with her to the new employer—not only once perhaps, but two or three times in some cases, until the woman has learned the way and lost her fear. Mrs. Makowski finds a Polish girl at the place of employment, if she can, who lives in the new woman's neighborhood, and she asks this girl to see that the woman gets safely home when the day's work is done. If this new worker is new in the country and there is no Polish-speaking person in charge, Mrs. Makowski may actually instruct her, after they reach the place, in the dish washing, cleaning, or other work that she is to do. "I roll my sleeves up and show her just how she should do it. I'm not ashamed," she said.

But the job is not all. Mrs. Makowski sends immigrant Polish women to the dentist if necessary, and

she recommends doctors. She is the best friend some
arriving girls know. They come to her about illness
and other troubles, and sometimes she arranges for
hospital care, and visits them while there. In short,
she does just what a practical kindly woman would do
who mentally puts herself in the other woman's place;
and since she is herself Polish, in a strange country,
and must earn her own living, she has not a very far
journey to travel.

What Mrs. Makowski does, as an employment agent,
for her countrywomen, is done by many another foreign-born agent like her. The custom is general to
escort non-English-speaking women all the way to the
work given them, even if it necessitates some expenditure of carfare; and it is not unusual for necessary instruction to be given on the spot, in the restaurant
kitchen or wherever the work may be, as Mrs. Makowski gives it. In addition to the special friendly
services already noted, some agents combine, with their
employment business, such work as selling steamship
tickets in times of immigration, or interpreting and
translating; and the combination of the employment
business with the midwife profession is also common.
But these friendly services have come from one whom
the immigrant thinks of as a fellow foreigner, not an
American.

PHILANTHROPIC PLACEMENT AGENCIES

There are, in all the larger cities, philanthropic organizations of various kinds which attempt to find work
for immigrants. Almost every nationality has an Immigrant Aid Society, one of whose functions is to assist those who need help in finding employment. The
most prominent examples of these are the Society for
Italian Immigrants and the Hebrew Sheltering and

Immigrant Aid Society.[1] Then there are organizations
which, like the Immigrants' Protective League of Chicago, do not devote themselves to any one nationality.
The Y. M. C. A., Y. W. C. A., and similar organizations among other religious bodies, also assist to some
extent in securing employment for immigrants.

The total amount of placing of immigrants done by
all these organizations, however, is negligible. Their
employment work is usually incidental to other functions of the organizations which occupy their main attention. The immigrant aid societies maintained by
the various nationalities are content if they get the
immigrants safely into the hands of relatives or friends,
and their employment bureaus are designed primarily
to help those whom they have to shelter. The other
organizations are mainly concerned with protecting the
immigrant against fraud and exploitation, or with educational work, and while they are often helpful to individuals seeking employment, they are not equipped
to handle the industrial problem of placement.

TRADE-UNION HELP

In 1920, when immigration assumed something like
pre-war proportions, a number of labor organizations
became interested in the proper placement of new arrivals. In New York City a joint committee, representing unions of all trades employing immigrants, was
organized for the purpose of preventing the use of the
incoming immigrants by employers to break down the
wages and standards of employment gained by the
unions; and also for distributing the immigrants properly among the trades. The committee asked for permission to station representatives at Ellis Island, but
apparently this could not be done under existing laws.

---

[1] See Chapter XIV for detailed descriptions of their work.

FINDING A PLACE IN AMERICAN INDUSTRY

A subcommittee was appointed to work out a method of pro-rating immigrants among the various unions, as there were some charges that the organizations were trying to pass them on to each other. Arrangements were also made with labor organizations abroad, by which they would be informed when times are dull, so that prospective immigrants could be advised against coming here.

The efforts of this trade-union committee called public attention to the meager results that may be expected of labor organizations as placement agencies for the immigrant. Where the trade is completely organized, it is customary for the union to furnish all the help the employer needs, and before the immigrant can get work he must apply and be admitted to membership in the union. Most unions, however, are opposed to immigration into this country, and their opposition is sometimes extended to excluding from membership by various indirect means immigrants who have already landed. All unions fear the overcrowding of their trades, and even those whose membership consists mainly of immigrants, and who are not in favor of restricting immigration into the country, adopt policies which are designed to keep new workers out of the industry as much as possible.

The masses of foreign born who come to us can expect little help from trade-unions in finding places in American industry. The unskilled occupations, where the immigrant finds most of his opportunities, are as a rule unorganized, and the skilled trades, which are well organized, usually have restrictions on apprenticeship and the employment of learners which make it very difficult for an immigrant to acquire the skill necessary to work at the trade.

ADJUSTING IMMIGRANT AND INDUSTRY

EMPLOYERS' EFFORTS

Some employers, on the other hand, are over-anxious to give employment to immigrants. During 1919 the complaint was general among them that it was the "foreigners" who were causing all the strikes, and they attributed most of the industrial unrest of the time to the radical ideas prevalent among their foreign-born laborers. Many of them advertised for "American labor" in their efforts to break the strikes. Later (October, 1920), however, we find several writing to the Commissioner of Immigration at Ellis Island anxiously soliciting immigrant laborers.[1]

The Carbide and Carbon Corporation, at Niagara Falls, wrote it will place newly arrived laborers according to its needs. The Oliver Coal Company, at Yoleskie, Ohio, a mining town on the Baltimore and Ohio Railroad, can place several hundred experienced coal miners at $7 and $8 a day. The M. Rice Company, 1220 Spring Garden Street, Philadelphia, wants basket makers. D. R. Talbott, a tobacco grower of Dunkirk, Md., says there are fine chances in that section for persons willing to do farm work. The George M. Jones Company, bituminous coal operators, Toledo, Ohio, wants experienced miners. The Alpha Portland Cement Corporation, with plants at Alpha, New Jersey; Martin's Creek, Pennsylvania; Manheim, West Virginia; Cementon and Jamesville, New York, has been forced to take on negro helpers and would like to get immigrants. The Cleveland Stone Company, with quarries at Berea, Ohio; will pay immigrants 47 to 55 cents an hour. These few give the trend of the letters.

The tendency of these efforts is to draw over-supplies of immigrants into these industries and to increase the number of floating laborers.

A number of employers' associations maintain free employment offices for distributing workers among their members. These, however, do not ordinarily concern themselves with unskilled labor, and their

---

[1] New York *Globe*, October 19, 1920.

main object is to prevent their shops from being organized by trade unions. The National Metal Trades Association, the National Erectors' Association, the Lake Carriers' Association and the Employers' Associations of Detroit, Indianapolis, Los Angeles, and other cities, which conduct these offices, are all opposed to dealing with trade-unions, and the employment bureaus are conducted as one of the means of maintaining their "open shop" policies. They do not place many immigrants, but in so far as they do, the aliens are brought into an atmosphere antagonistic to the American organized workers, thus increasing the difficulties of merging the native with the foreign born along the lines suggested by the U. S. Immigration Commission.

RESULTS

What it has meant to the immigrant and to the country to leave to his own ignorant efforts the finding of a place in American industry is well illustrated in the results of an investigation by the statistical division of the Americanization Study. Between 1900 and 1910 the number of foreign-born laborers working on farms in this country increased from 259,000 to 336,000 or about 30 per cent. During these same ten years, however, over 1,600,000 agricultural laborers from foreign countries landed in the United States. Many of these returned to their native lands, no doubt, but even though we assume that 50 per cent went back, it still remains true that over 800,000 immigrant farm laborers were available and less than 100,000 of them found their way to farms in this country. And this during a time when we were suffering from a serious shortage of agricultural labor.

Where did these immigrant farm laborers who remained in the country go? The answer can well be imagined. They found places in mines and factories to which they were unaccustomed, and many of which had ample supplies of labor without them. Sixty-four per cent of the immigrant wage earners in our iron and steel industries, 58 per cent of our foreign-born bituminous coal miners, almost 61 per cent of the immigrants working in oil and sugar refineries, about half of the foreign furniture workers and 58 per cent of those in the leather and tanning industry were farmers or farm laborers before they came to this country.[1]

Of 17,000 households studied by the United States Immigration Commission the heads of which were working as wage earners in mines or manufacturing establishments, 62 per cent of the men were farmers or farm laborers before they came to the United States.[2] Another investigation made by the same Commission covering over 180,000 employees in factories and mines showed that 54 per cent were farmers or farm laborers in their native lands.[3]

The country lacked agricultural labor; hundreds of thousands of immigrant farm workers came to us, but they found their way into mines and factories, not on to farms. The conditions of agricultural labor and living and the attractions of the cities, have, of course, a good deal to do with the drift of immigrant farm workers, as well as of the native rural population, into industrial occupations. And no doubt many immigrants come to America to get away from farm work, but much of the failure of immigrant farmers to settle on the land also is to be ascribed to the fact that finding work in America is a matter of drifting for most immigrants, and the nation has had no organized machinery for guiding and

---

[1] United States Immigration Commission, *Abstract of Reports*, vol. I, pp. 297–313.

[2] *Ibid.*, pp. 356–361.

[3] *Ibid.*, pp. 297–313.

directing them into ocupations where they will most readily be able to earn a living as well as be of most benefit to their adopted country. Again and again we have been told by immigrant factory employees that they wished they knew how to earn a living on a farm.

Quite aside from the economic loss resulting from the maladjustment between the labor demands of the country and its labor supplies, there is a tremendous waste of agricultural and industrial skill involved in the scrapping of the years of experience that our immigrants have had in the countries from which they come.

This loss of industrial capacity becomes much more plain when we follow the experiences of immigrant skilled workers in finding work in America. The statistical study referred to above found that "about 84 per cent of the males and about 67 per cent of the females (in manufacturing and mining operations) were not utilizing such skill and experience as they may have acquired in the occupations they had been engaged in before coming to the United States." [1]

While the census figures for individual occupations on which this estimate is based must be considered only as approximately correct, still they show unmistakably the tremendous scrapping of skill and experience that goes on as the immigrant gives up his native calling and takes up work in America. Of sixteen typical skilled occupations only the barbers, plasterers, and lumberers seem to have absorbed the immigrants of these occupations who came to this country between 1900 and 1910. Only a fourth of the foreign-born cabinetmakers, however, and less than half of the painters and carpenters who came to the United States during the same decade, followed their occupations in this country, while two thirds of the masons, 90 per

[1] Reports of the Immigration Commission, vol. XIX, pp. 95–98

45

cent of the blacksmiths, and practically all of the bookbinders, tanners, printers, shoemakers and saddlers had apparently changed their occupations when they went to work in this country.

The same striking fact is confirmed in another way by the U. S. Immigration Commission, which found that less than one per cent of the immigrants in our oil and sugar refineries, $5\frac{1}{2}$ per cent of those engaged in slaughtering and meat packing, 6 per cent of the foreign-born workers in our tanneries, $8\frac{1}{2}$ per cent of the immigrants in iron and steel mills, and 20 per cent of those in coal mines were working in the same industries before they came to this country. Only in the clothing and textile industries did the Commission find that half or more of these immigrants had been in the same occupations abroad.[1]

More significant, perhaps, than the loss of industrial skill and experience involved in this changing of occupations is the tremendous readjustment that must take place in the immigrant's life and habits when he does find a place in American industry. For, obviously, it can not be assumed to be desirable either for the immigrant or the country that he should always follow the same calling in America that he had in his native land. There may be no demand here for the skill that he had and quite often he leaves his home because of a desire to change his occupation as well as his country. But the difficulties of adjustment are greatly multiplied when, in addition to everything else that is new, the immigrant must adjust himself to new methods of earning a living.

The place the immigrant does find in American industry is often a most temporary one. And the nature of the life to which he may be led by seasonal or casual

---

[1] *Abstract of Reports*, vol. I, pp. 297-313.

FINDING A PLACE IN AMERICAN INDUSTRY

labor is illustrated by two "life stories" secured by an investigator in California:[1]

The first a Mexican, I was passing on the road to Hume, and as this type of casual worker is becoming of very great importance in California, I determined to find out what I could from him. He could speak but little English, but by using a combination of English and Spanish we got along capitally.

Twenty-eight years old, he was of typical Mexican build, medium in stature, but supple and strong. He had been in California four years. His wife and a ten-year-old boy at school were in Mexico, and he sent money to them regularly. By trade he was a carpenter, but not being able to speak English he was unable to work at this here. He was at present doing construction work on a railroad line near Reedly, working in a gang containing fifty Mexicans and no others. He had been working at this for two months, earning $1.25 a day above his board. By questioning him in regard to the work he did each month, I was able to find out approximately what his yearly labor schedule was. In January and February he said he dug ditches and did similar work. There is, probably, considerable work at this period on the numerous irrigation ditches throughout this region. In March and April he hoed and planted, while in May he picked oranges or worked on the railroads. In June, July, and August he picked other fruit or did construction work, going north sometimes in July or August to work on hops. During the months of September and October I judge that work must be slack, for he says that then he wanders over the state, doing nothing in particular. During these trips, alone or with small groups, he has covered the whole state, having gone across the Oregon border. In November and December he usually picks oranges. This schedule is, of course, not all-embracing, but it does represent what a typical Mexican does throughout the year. He worked practically all the time, with the exception of a month or so in each year, staying with each job until it was over. In this last regard is found the great difference between these men and most American casuals. This man said that most Mexicans spent their money as they earned it, saving none, but as to the exact truth of this, I cannot say.

Antonio Frau, or "Tony" as he told me to call him, was a fellow worker in the grading crew at Hume. Twenty-three years old, he was born on the Island of Sardinia. Short but stockily built, brown faced, black-haired, black-mustached, with sparkling black eyes,

---

[1] F. C. Mills, "Scenes and Incidents on the Road," an unpublished report.

47

he was a typical son of sunny Italy. One of a family of four children, he was raised on a small farm. One can make there about 60 cents a day according to Tony, but there is no chance to save money So five years ago, when he was eighteen years old, Tony came to New York. For one year, he worked around New York State, returning home at the end of that time. He had made $250, but his trip having cost him $160, his net earnings were $90. He stayed in Sardinia for three years, and then took a trip to Panama, where he worked for a considerable period with a construction crew and returned home again. Fourteen months ago, Tony, this time with a brother, came again to New York, leaving a married and an unmarried sister at home with their widowed mother. For twelve months he stayed near New York working on bridge-building, tunnel-work, road-building, railroad construction, etc., making from $2.25 to $2.75 a day. Hearing wonderful tales of the amount of work and the high wages in California, Tony came out last March, leaving his brother in New York. For two months he stayed in San Francisco and could get no work. Finally a friend wrote him that he could get work at Hume and with two others he came, having worked here now for one month and saved $45.

Tony is unmarried, and says that practically all Italians who work as he does from place to place are also unmarried, as a settled life is impossible. He likes this country and believes that English and American people are all right. Remembering, doubtless, experiences with traction foremen, he thinks little of the Irish, who "make work like Hell," says Tony.

When the immigrant's work and the place in which it is done are as strange to him as the language and customs of the people among whom he has come to live, faith in a promised land is indeed a necessity to give hope that he will survive in the new environment. And if a proper adjustment of immigrant and industry is to be made, so that he may become an integral part of the American industrial population, something more than faith is needed. Adequate assistance in finding his place in American industry is also necessary.

CHAPTER III

EFFECTIVE PLACEMENT SERVICE

WHEN the nation was faced with the task of welding millions of drafted men from every walk of life into a competent and effective army, Secretary of War Baker thus described the problem: [1]

> We are taking men from the forests of the northwest and the cotton fields of the south, from every trade and occupation, from every economic and social status of life and grouping them advantageously. We are not getting the men of the same size in the same place, but all sizes in all places. We are getting this agglomerate of men, selected variously and by chance, as it were into great groups. We have no time for men to group into those groups evolved by association, but we have to have a selective process by which we will get the round men for the round places, the strong men for the strong tasks, and the delicate men for the delicate tasks. We have got to evolve a process by which that sort of assortment will take place. Always heretofore in armies that has been a matter of chance, it has been a matter of individual judgment of commanding officers . . .

Have not we essentially the same problem in the millions that have come to us as immigrants from every land to join our industrial forces?

THE PROBLEM OF DISTRIBUTION AND PLACEMENT

We take men from industrially developed countries like England and Germany, from backward nations like Turkey, Syria, and Armenia, from the handicraft industries of Scandinavia and northern Italy, from the fields and villages of Russia, Greece, and southern Italy, and from the mountain occupations of the Bal-

---

[1] *The Personnel System of the United States Army*, vol. I, p. 680.

kan countries. From every walk of life they come—
peasants, laborers, mechanics, tradesmen, scholars and
professional men—to join America's industrial army.
We do not get the peasants on our farms, the mechanics in our skilled occupations, and the tradesmen in
our shops and stores. They, too, are "an agglomerate
of men selected by chance." They, too, have to be
grouped advantageously, fitting men to tasks and tasks
to men. Nor can we wait until years of evolution will
eliminate the unfit and new generations grow up fit for
their tasks. As in the army a process of assorting and
developing men immediately is needed, and this can
not happen by chance or through the individual judgments of the immigrants themselves or of the commanding officers of our industries.

The industrial depression through which we have
just passed made the need of a national system of
placement agencies particularly evident, and the period
of prosperity which we are now entering will again
emphasize it.

President Harding's Conference on Unemployment
in the fall of 1921 found that the presence of great
numbers of unemployed was leading local authorities
and philanthropic organizations to establish free employment bureaus in an effort to find work. Many of
these duplicated existing agencies and in most cases
the administrators of the bureaus were quite without
experience. The Conference, therefore, issued a manual
of instructions to local and state authorities explaining
how to organize such bureaus, and how to operate them
and avoid duplication. A temporary organization in
Washington, headed by Arthur Woods, was established,
and through this central office, a unified policy was promoted throughout the country, and the methods and
practices of the local employment bureaus were to
some extent standardized.

EFFECTIVE PLACEMENT SERVICE

Now that depression has given way to prosperity again, the cry of shortage of labor is heard from many quarters, and many employers' organizations are asking that less restrictive immigration laws be enacted. But while shortages are apparent in certain kinds of labor, there are still abundant supplies in other occupations, and a more effective distribution of the available supplies becomes particularly important because we do not know how long the present business activity will last and whether it will not soon be succeeded by another depression. How can the demand for admission of more immigrants be listened to, until there is assurance that the immigrant labor supply here has been as fully utilized as only a national placement service makes possible.

DISCONNECTED EMPLOYMENT AGENCIES

Public opinion in America has been quite alive to the need of the immigrant for assistance and protection in his search for work. Most of the industrial estates have licensed and regulated and inspected the work of private labor agents and attempted to prevent the abuses to which the immigrant is subject at their hands. In every large city there is some philanthropic organization to help him find work. And in recent years most cities have had free employment bureaus, which are designed to put the wage earner, native and foreign born alike, in touch with opportunities for employment. The Federal Government also established in 1907 a Division of Information in its Bureau of Immigration, with branch offices in New York and other cities to render the same service.

All these, however, have been far less effective than they might if there had been a common policy which guided them in their work. Each has worked more or less independently, pursuing a policy of its own, which was usually determined by the superintendent of the employment office, who might or might not be familiar with immigrant problems.

Nothing can show this more clearly than the contrast in the work of district branches of the public employment bureaus in Chicago. In that city three district bureaus, under federal control, were organized to give service to foreign-born men and women.

A visit to a Bohemian and Polish quarter found an attractive young Bohemian woman in charge of the women's division of the district's office. She had a radiant interest in what she was doing; and she knew the range of employment possibility for Bohemian and Polish women throughout the city's industry. She spoke Bohemian with the applicants when necessary, but still did not lose a chance to stimulate them to learn English by using it herself, and showing them that with the language they could improve their earnings or conditions of work. She knew the traits and desires of the workers; her own home in the city had always been in the neighborhood of theirs. She understood the thrift of Bohemian and Polish husbands which sends wives forth for jobs; and this was a guide to her in determining the necessity for the night work which married women request.

A visit to the Polish quarter found a Russian-born woman in charge of employment who knew Polish countries first hand, and who spoke Polish, as well as several other European languages. Like the Bohemian woman referred to, she had informed herself intelligently of industrial opportunities and conditions for people of the nationality her district office cares for; and she had the same sympathetic understanding on the ground of closely related racial stock. She had been the women's resource in unfortunate industrial experiences. In a case where a woman had lost a hand in a pie factory and had received no compensation, an inquiry brought out the fact that the Polish lawyer to whom she gave the case had collected and kept the money. In some instances the women reported money difficulties with little Polish private employment agencies of the neighborhood, which the woman in charge of this office tried to have adjusted. She was energetic to promote citizenship among the workers also. Of 1500 applications for citizenship taken at the office in five months, 650 were women's. She tried to convince them of a connection between the intelligent participation of citizenship and the development of earning capacity. The district work here had been carried on about a year; and one record month attained a registration of 1081 women applicants—all Polish, and of the neighborhood.

A visit to the third district found an employment office located in a community wholly foreign, including people of Lithuanian, Polish, and Bohemian birth. The person in charge of the women's division was, in this case, an Irish woman. In contrast to the cordiality and interest shown at the other offices, this visit opened with her glance at a clock, whose hands showed half-past three. The office closed at four, she said, and there was "a bit to do 'till then." A quick suggestion from the visitor that a more convenient time be set for the interview, was met with the answer, "No, you might as well stay. Each day brings its own."

This is told only to show that the subject of the industrial fortune of the foreign-born women of the neighborhood did not find an answering spark of feeling, or light up the expression of this Irish woman, as in the case of the other two women, who were of the same Slavic stock as the people whom they served. She said there was so little to do in the women's division that she gave some assistance to the men's. She "couldn't say" whether many foreign-born women were employed in some great manufacturing plants a few blocks away—although it was afterward learned that several thousand foreign-born women are there. She seemed to have no love for either her work, or the people; and she made the unsympathetic generalization that "these foreigners only want to work and save to take money back to the old country." The contrast between the two offices first visited, and this office, indicated personal differences to some extent, but the important indication is that persons who share the old-country experience and the language of the foreign-born women applicants, have all the advantages on their side for understanding, sympathetic, intelligent work in these women's behalf.

One of the main difficulties in developing a public placement system for immigrants has been the fact that it might work to the injury of American workers. Employers might prefer the immigrants and thus American standards would be lowered. No doubt there is some danger that this might happen, but the danger is greater still when immigrants are admitted into the country and then are left to their own devices to find work, or to the devices of such employers as are seeking cheap labor at any cost. Careful guidance, under an organized system of placing immigrants in industry, can avoid the dangers and be of incalculable value to the nation as well as to the immigrant. Once the immigrant is admitted, if we wish to make him a part of our American citizenship, we must give him an opportunity for profitable employment equal to what Americans get. A placement service for immigrants alone, however, might well prove dangerous to American workers. An employment service, therefore, must be organized to handle American and immigrant workers alike without discrimination.

EFFECTIVE PLACEMENT SERVICE

Many of the elements, the parts, that need to go into the building of a national placement agency are already available; and we have had enough experience with them to know what are the proper methods and policies to pursue. There is needed the combination of the various parts and the establishment of a uniform national policy in coöperation with states and cities.

Free employment offices maintained by public authorities have been in existence in this country since 1890, when Ohio exacted the first state law establishing such offices in five cities. After that every period of industrial depression and extensive unemployment was followed by the enactment of state laws and municipal ordinances creating such offices, until at the outbreak of the World War public employment bureaus were in existence in 25 states and 64 cities.

When the United States entered the war a United States Employment Service was created in connection with the Department of Labor, and this extended the offices to cover every state in the Union and the District of Columbia, until it had in active operation about 350 such offices. Many of these were state and municipal bureaus supported in part by funds from the Federal Service. The Director General of the United States Employment Service reported in 1919 that each working day of the eighteen months from January, 1918, to June, 1919, approximately 10,000 persons were placed in jobs of all kinds at a cost to the whole country of about $1.34 per placement.[1] After the armistice, however, Congress refused to allow more than $400,000

---

[1] Annual Report of Director-General, United States Employment Service, 1919, p. 54.

for the Service, and most of the states now pursue their own policies, as they did before the war.

The development of the United States Employment Service was due primarily to the labor needs of the war industries. Until 1917 public employment bureaus had been looked upon primarily as agencies for relieving unemployment and protecting wage earners against the abuses of private labor agents. The war showed that such bureaus are as necessary to industry in a period of shortage of labor as they are to the unemployed in times when there is a surplus of workers. The main work of the United States Employment Service was to mobilize the available supplies of labor and to distribute it properly among the war industries. It was an organized national placement service made necessary by our war needs. Supplies and munitions could not be produced in the quantities needed and on time, if individual workers were to be left to find the work for which they were most needed, and individual employers were to be free to attract and solicit labor without regard to the needs of other war services, or without regard to whether their enterprises were essential to the prosecution of the war or not.

It is exactly this same kind of service that is needed to secure the proper placement of immigrants in our industries, if the workers who come to us from foreign lands are to be assimilated properly by our industries in accordance with our national industrial needs, and not left to congest and maintain un-American standards in industries already oversupplied with labor, or to drift into occupations where their skill must be scrapped and where they may be used for the private purposes of individual employers.

How was the task of distributing and placing labor in accordance with war needs accomplished? In the methods used we may find the means of placing immigrants properly in our industries in accordance with national needs in times of peace.

In the first place, all the existing public employment bureaus were brought under the federal system, and new offices were established in coöperation with the states and municipalities. All of these were asked to register the available labor and the orders for help sent in by employers. The offices in each state were united into a single system under a federal director of employment, who maintained a central clearing house for transferring labor from office to office and throughout the state. These federal directors reported to the Director-General of the United States Employment Service, who maintained a central clearing house in Washington for the transfer of the surplus labor of one state to others where that labor might be most profitably used.

This, in outline, shows the machinery of distribution and placement of war workers, which must be maintained for immigrant workers also if we wish to assimilate such workers with the American industrial population and have them serve our national interests properly.

THE EMPLOYMENT SERVICE AND THE IMMIGRANT

Among the 5,000,000 wage earners placed in positions by the United States Employment Service during the eighteen months' period referred to, there were no doubt several million foreign-born workers; but no special organization or technique was developed for handling immigrant workers. This was due partly to the fact that immigration had practically stopped during the war, and partly also because the business methods of handling all the workers by the Employment Service left much to be desired. Very few of the employment offices had separate departments for handling foreign-born laborers, and the number of interpreters employed in the offices generally was negligible. The results of the experience of the United States Employment Service in placing immigrants are, therefore, mainly negative.

This is all the more surprising since the entire United States Employment Service owes its origin to the law creating the Division of Information in the federal Bureau of Immigration. The law was enacted in 1907, for the purpose of gathering information with regard to opportunities for employment in all parts of the Union and furnishing this information to immigrants and others who might apply. It was designed mainly as a means of distributing immigrants properly throughout the country; but in this purpose it failed almost completely. For many years only one small office was operated by the Division in New York City, and the amount of business it did was negligible.

When the war shut off immigration and left the immigrant inspectors with little to do, many of these were assigned to do placement work for which few of them had training or aptitude. Branch offices of the Division of Information were opened in a number of cities, but with the exception of Chicago these may be said to have been only nominal employment offices. In Chicago, however, a placement bureau of considerable efficiency was developed under the immigrant inspector, which concerned itself mainly with sending men to farms and women into household service. In January, 1918, the Secretary of Labor ordered the separation of the Division of Information from the Immigration Bureau and its expansion and operation as a separate bureau of the Department of Labor under the title United States Employment Service. The greater part of the personnel of the Division of Information was transferred to the Employment Service.

The Division of Information had conceived its duty to be the gathering of quite general information regarding opportunities for employment from rural post offices and similar sources, and the placing of this information in the hands of such people as applied at its offices; leaving the immigrants pretty much to their own devices in finding their way to whatever specific jobs may have been available. An efficient employment service, however, requires active business methods to induce employers to place definite orders for help with the employment offices, with responsible statements of the kind and number of workers wanted, the wages paid, and other conditions of employment. Then the officers of the employment bureau must seek applicants of the kind desired and see that the employers' orders a e filled promptly with workers who meet the specifications. Such a service the Division of Information never had and the United States Employment Service only in part attained.

From the experiences of the Division of Information, the federal Employment Service, and the public employment bureaus maintained by states and cities, however, we are in a position to know the methods of organization, business policies, and office technique which are necessary to distribute and place immigrants properly in American industries, so that a speedy adjustment of both may be secured.

BUSINESS METHODS OF PLACEMENT AGENCIES

Placement work is a highly technical business which requires trained employment managers, who must have the closest contacts with employers and workers alike. The business can not be carried on at long range or by "mail order" methods. This means that the idea of collecting general information about industrial opportunities by mail and distributing it to workers by means of bulletins or posters must be discarded. Immigrants do not know how to make use of such information, and Americans who do often find that crowds have preceded them to the jobs, more than enough to supply all demands. Any employment service operated directly from Washington must from the necessities of the case have these defects, and, therefore, the employment offices must be primarily local agencies, in touch with all the opportunities for employment in the industries of the locality, and capable of mobilizing all the local labor supplies, including the immigrants who permanently or temporarily have made the locality their home.

That most public employment offices have been largely ineffective in finding places for immigrants in American industries is made evident by the existence of the great numbers of private labor agencies dealing with immigrant labor. Although the public offices give their services free of charge, while the private agencies require the payment of fees and are subject to all the abuses we have mentioned, nevertheless the competition of the public agencies has had little effect on the business of the private agencies. The latter seem to prosper ever more and more.

The experience of the Milwaukee Employment Bureau, however, serves to indicate how such a bureau may be made effective in placing immigrants. During the first years of its existence it had little effect whatever on the labor market of the city. Its business was conducted in a small dark room, up a dingy flight of stairs, and one man attended to it all, his work consisting mainly in securing odd jobs for casual laborers. Although one of the main reasons for its establishment was to remove the abuses of private labor agencies, the latter felt its competition not at all. In this its experience was typical of the early days of most public employment offices in other states. Said a private employment agent: "Before the public office was established I had to handle a lot of these short time jobs to accommodate some of my customers, and for this reason I had a lot of 'down-and-outs' hanging around my office whom I did not want. The public employment office has relieved me of all that business now."

In 1911 the Milwaukee office was reorganized by the newly-created Industrial Commission of Wisconsin cooperating with the city and county of Milwaukee, both of which contributed to its support. A large loft was rented for the office, separate departments for men and women organized, and an employment committee consisting of representatives of employers, workers, and public authorities was appointed to direct its affairs. This committee, in conjunction with the state civil service commission, selected a competent superintendent for the office and several assistants, and the business of the bureau began to grow immediately and to change its character. In the course of about two years it had taken away the business of the private labor agencies handling American workers, and almost all of them, with the exception of those placing domestic servants, went out of business. The public office was meeting the needs of the English-speaking workers and their employers in the city; and many laborers were also distributed throughout the state.

It was noticed, however, that few non-English-speaking workers patronized the office, and little impression was made on the business of two private labor agencies in the city, whose specialty was furnishing "foreign laborers" for railroad construction and other heavy work. The public office thereupon selected an interpreter, in the same careful manner that the superintendent was chosen, and he was put in charge of a separate department for placing foreign laborers. Some of the clerks in the office could also speak foreign tongues, and it was the boast of the office that its staff could speak eighteen languages. Signs in various languages were placed in the windows, contacts were made with consuls from various countries resident in the city, and in a comparatively short time great numbers of immigrant workers were attracted to the office and placed both in and out of the city.

The immigrants' department had to do a lot of work not required for English-speaking workers, such as giving written instructions for traveling, helping read and translate letters, sending money orders abroad, etc.; but this was only applying to a special class of applicants the same general principle of rendering the service needed which held in the office generally. The result of this service soon made itself felt, and two or three years later the private agencies in the city which had been handling immigrant workers gave up their licenses.

The problem of placement is, however, a national problem, and, for immigrants particularly, distribution according to national needs is as important as common labor was during the war. The national government must direct the distribution and placement of the immigrant in accordance with national purposes; but this, it has been found, the government can do best by assisting and encouraging state and local authorities in maintaining employment offices, and by directing and supervising their work in line with national employment policies developed by a federal employment authority, rather than by establishing federal offices in the localities where there is a need for employment bureaus.

EFFECTIVE PLACEMENT SERVICE

The local employment offices need to be in close connection with one another, and this has been most efficiently secured where all the offices in a state are organized by a state law under a single directing head, who conducts the local offices in accordance with a unified state plan and maintains a central clearing house for transferring orders for help and workers from office to office.

A unified employment service can thus be built from the bottom up, by uniting the state employment systems under a national director in Washington, who would enforce national policies and arrange for the transfer of workers from state to state through the state directors. In the early days of its existence the United States Employment Service was advised by experts with many years of experience in the state and municipal employment offices, to adopt this method of organization and follow its procedure. The advice was ignored at first, but the public criticism of the Employment Service and the force of the circumstances of placement work led to the approval of the plan toward the end of the war.

The federal laws for vocational education and road building have pointed the way for the congressional legislation necessary to insure such a national placement service. These laws create boards whose business it is to determine the national policies of industrial education and good roads. They set the minimum standards and the approved methods which must be maintained by schools and state highway commissions. The schools and road building, however, are conducted by state and local authorities, and the federal officers have only supervisory authority. The laws provide that states may accept the acts by enactments of their legislatures, and if they do this and their authorities maintain the minimum standards set by the federal board, they receive certain financial assistance from the federal government.

The United States Employment Service was never authorized by an act of Congress. It was established by the Secretary of Labor in an administrative order under his powers as war labor administrator. If we are to have an adequate placement service for immigrants it will be possible to maintain it only as part of a general employment service for all workers; and, to insure permanence and success, this will necessitate congressional action to establish, after the manner of the highway and vocational education laws, a federal administrative body, with authority to supervise and aid states which adopt the law and operate local employment offices in accordance with placement policies devised or approved by the national authority.

The plan outlined in this chapter will be most approved by those most familiar with the difficulty of finding for the newly arrived immigrant, the place best suited both for himself and the country which opens its doors to him. Its adoption will meet many obstacles. In both Chambers of Congress, there is a constant opposition to legislation extending federal power over subjects now in the control of the states. For many years one President after another has asked Congress for legislation extending the power of the federal government so that it would give protection to the life and property of aliens in the states, as provided in our treaties. Such legislation is undoubtedly constitutional, and it is necessary to protect the honor of the United States pledged by its treaties; but so far such a statute has not been enacted.

CHAPTER IV

THE EMPLOYER AND THE IMMIGRANT

WHEN the immigrant enters the doors of an industrial establishment as an employee, he presents the same problems to the industry that he does to the nation as he passes through the port of entry. How can the stranger be absorbed into the industrial community? And what methods and policies of management are best calculated to make him develop a feeling of unity with the native-born and Americanized employees?

EMPLOYERS' VIEWS OF AMERICANIZATION

Among managers and employers we found a general feeling that industry must assume some responsibility for Americanization; but practically all of them identified this with the teaching of English and the naturalization of aliens. A few, however, questioned the responsibility of industries in this respect. The President and General Manager of a mining corporation wrote: "In our opinion the Americanization of foreign-born employees is not the business of the manager of privately owned industries, excepting in so far as their position as large taxpayers gives them influence with local government or school authorities."

And the policy of a large locomotive works was stated as follows: "Being situated in the heart of a large city with every facility of schooling and amusement, we have not considered it necessary or advisable to teach our employees English or civics. We coöperate in every way possible with the established institutions for the teaching of these matters, and we have officers who give advice to employees when they need it."

While most employers committed themselves to a policy of "Americanization," few were clear as to the nature of the responsibility in this respect that industry ought to assume, or as to the methods by which an amalgamation of immigrant and native-born workers might be brought about. And there was apparently little realization among them of the relation between the methods of industrial management and the assimilation of immigrants.

AN ENLIGHTENED POLICY IN A MILL TOWN

A river overhung with trees goes winding through this little town; wood and open country extend beyond its boundaries. A few streets of neat houses, three small churches, a store or two, a schoolhouse and the gray stone mill are all its properties. One could not say the mill is in the town; it is the town, for no one, except the priests and ministers and the public school teachers, lives there who is not mill connected. And nothing is owned there, with the exception of the churches and school, by others than mill officials and those whom they employ.

This mill has never had a strike, and it has lived for forty years. It has seen its early American, Irish, and English workers succeeded by French Canadians and Poles, who are the dominant nationalities now. About ten years ago foreign labor had become a definite problem of management. At this time the mill introduced a woman whose duty it should be to straighten out the complications arising from the "tenements" maintained for the employees. The company was dismayed at the conditions which were growing out of immigration, and foreign-born families straight from Europe were pouring in, making things worse daily. The company houses erected for the purpose of controlling living conditions were themselves beyond control.

This woman found that the families who rented the tenements took boarders, and the company had no idea who lived in the houses nor how many. It did know there was extreme overcrowding and that living conditions were very bad. Her first realization was that nothing effective could be done unless she could communicate with the people. She began at once to acquire a Polish vocabulary of words likely to be needed. It was a difficult matter to get at the truth about the tenants, and it took months. The census of houses showed that in some of those rented by the company for a nominal rental of six or seven dollars a month, the tenants were taking so many boarders that they more than cleared the rent, and that they were not only "making money on the company," but were giving nearly free housing to workers in out-of-town mills who had no connection with this mill. But the worst feature was the wretched way of living. After a true list of occupants of each house and their relationship to the family were obtained, some new regulations were issued by the company which ever since have held the situation in check.

Through the tenement visiting the first steps were taken to bridge the separation between mill authorities and the foreign-born employees, especially the women. The "welfare worker" always used her visits to be on the lookout for opportunities to establish friendly help. The first chance came in the form of roaches. She worked with a Polish woman for two days to get rid of them and success came in the end. The woman's gratitude spread through the community; and, also, the method of eliminating the roaches. It was bound to be true among the Poles that an improvement instituted in one family spread to all the rest.

Semiannual house cleanings were established by the welfare agent. She told the women that it was American to clean house before Christmas and in the spring. Their acceptance of this was a custom she credits not to herself but to their religion. The cleaning times she suggested happened to coincide with an old-country Polish religious custom—to prepare their homes for the celebration of Christmas and Easter. So successful was she that the mill now suffers from the absence of women at this house-cleaning time. They stay out before Christmas and Easter to do the work.

In time, the company's representative made the discovery that dampness in Polish houses and the tendency of paper to come off the walls were due to the continual flow of steam from the kitchen stove. The Poles boiled their food, and boiled it for hours. The use of the oven was scarcely known. Cabbage soup, boiled meat, and pastry bought at the store, were about all the food items they knew. A start in cooking was made one day when she went to a Polish woman's house to teach some simple American additions to the usual menu. The first lesson was not a success, because of the inconvenience of running to the store for what might seem ordinary ingredients. The recipes of the second lesson went well, however, and it was always true that an idea that "took" with the women spread from house to house. After this some of the women were persuaded to attend classes in cooking and canning, which have been going on ever since.

The teaching of English to the men began early in her work. This grew naturally out of the tenement inspecting. She saw men, in the evening, studying from little books which had Polish and English words in parallel columns. She knew that a spoken language is learned by sound, rather than by sight; and her instinct for teaching made her want to help these men to learn in a right way, less discouraging to them. So she and an assistant went to Springfield to learn the Roberts system, and then started two classes. It was always hard getting the women, because their husbands could not see why they should want to learn anything.

When, because of lack of room, it seemed necessary several years ago to hold the adult English classes in the school, the natives of the town objected and talked of starting a petition to prevent this. They did not want their children to use the same seats and desks the next day. In this instance they were overruled in their objection. And gradually the attitude of the natives has undergone change, stimulated by the mill corporation's policy. There is now very little of such feeling in the town. The mill met the situation by helping the foreign born to change, making associated living possible. The town people have become aware that increasing numbers of Poles are property owners; also that, when Polish families take possession of a neglected place, they immediately begin to make repairs, and to "fix up" the yard.

The present welfare worker at the mill finds that it is easily possible to pormote activities of various kinds. Once the start is made in a town so largely mill-owned and controlled, there seems to be nothing to block the progress. The real problem now is how to do these manifestly good and needed things, without devitalizing the people. Does it not, perhaps, sap their initiative to know that the company always stands ready to meet, or even to anticipate, every important community need? The thoughtful superintendent of the mill has not failed to consider this idea. When asked if he did not think that incentives for active citizenship must be provided, he replied that he realized the truth of this, but he believes that American ways of living will lead to community participation. If this was not completely convincing to the visitor, there was surely no lack of conviction regarding the fine quality and spirit of the work which this mill has done, and is continuing to do.

One result of this company's policy has been a low labor turnover, that is, a comparatively small shifting of the labor force. Few quit and few have to be hired. This means that newcomers need be taken only a few at a time, in digestible quantities, to take care of normal expansion. And the company can hope that the standards of the present working force will prevail and be extended to the new immigrants as they come.

THE POLICY THAT ALIENATES

In the mill town the immigrant population was given special consideration. It was put under the tutelage of the employer's representatives until such time as it could conduct its own affairs, when the policies used in dealing with the native born could be extended to the foreign born without evil results.

The exact opposite of this we found in Akron, Ohio, where a large industrial corporation had developed excellent labor management policies in dealing with its native-born and other English-speaking employees, and provided many of the so-called welfare services for these, but neglected almost entirely its non-English-speaking workers.

This corporation had a rule not to employ anyone who was unable to speak English and who had not declared his intention of becoming an American citizen. But when the expansion of its business required additional workers, this rule was waived. And we were informed by the employment manager that in addition to its regular employees there were about 400 immigrant workers who lived in what he himself called "the lousy house," which turned out to be barracks and bunks for the "foreigners." These men were secured through interpreters, who acted as their gang bosses and ran the commissaries. They did their own cooking, the company paying the cooks. They did not associate with the other employees in the recreation facilities provided by the company, and its welfare work did not reach them.

These men were living in a "labor camp," although employed in a large city where home life was possible. Such camps are often used by city industries needing large supplies of common labor, but the camps of railroad and construction workers employ the greatest numbers of immigrants, and the labor policy of neglect is to be found most typical in these.[1]

A railroad camp commonly consists of a coal car, a kitchen car, one or two dining cars, a commissary and provision car, and several sleeping or "bunk" cars. With the exception of the coal car they are all ordinary box cars fitted up to suit the particular purpose. In camps occupied exclusively by foreigners there are seldom any separate kitchen or eating cars. A group of from six to ten foreigners will cook, eat, sleep, and store their provisions all in one car.

Railroad laborers distinguish two kinds of camps: the "white man's" and the "foreigner's" camp. A "white man" is a laborer of any nationality who speaks English, eats American food, and travels alone. "Foreigners" are those who speak no English, travel and work in gangs under the leadership of an interpreter, and board themselves in their native fashion.

Immigrant labor employed on railroad work in Wisconsin is mainly Greek and Italian. Greeks are the most numerous. There are also a great many Bulgarians, Hungarians, and Austrians. The Austrians do the heavier construction work.

[1] *Labor Camps in Wisconsin*, published by the Industrial Commission of Wisconsin, 1913.

ADJUSTING IMMIGRANT AND INDUSTRY

Foreign laborers are secured by railroad companies almost exclusively through private labor agencies. The labor agents keep in touch with interpreters, and when they have a call for laborers they arrange with one of the interpreters to get a gang together. The common arrangement is that the interpreter receives $60 to $75 per month to act as "straw boss" on the work, his main duties being to interpret the orders of the foremen to the gang. He collects from each member of the gang the fee for the labor agent. . . .

What the amount of this fee is depends very largely on what the immigrant knows. If he has been in the country several years, knows a little English, and understands that his labor is in demand, he pays less for his job. If he is recently arrived and his only opportunity for employment seems to be through the interpreter, he pays more. The actual fees that came to our notice varied from $1 to $9 per job. "There's no money in 'white' labor," said one of the most successful labor agents. "It is on foreign gangs that I make my money." But the labor agent contends that he does not get all of the fee that is collected from the laborers. Part of it is kept by the interpreter and the rest must very often be shared with the official of the railroad that does the hiring. While we were in the office of a labor agent an interpreter came in who said he had a gang of 50 Greeks who wanted work and he was ready to pay $4 per man, $2 for the agent and $2 for the road master or whoever did the hiring. . . .

As already mentioned, foreign gangs board themselves. The company furnishes cars, coal, and water, and the men do their own cooking. Each car is furnished with a cooking stove, a table, and benches. Shelves overhead, nails in the walls, and the floors serve as storage places for provisions. Most cars occupied by foreigners do not have individual sleeping bunks. The common practice is to build a platform across each end of the car about three feet above the floor. On this a double blanket (or a straw mattress) is placed and four or five men sleep together on it. Sometimes the floor underneath the platform is used as another bed, but ordinarily provisions are stored there. Eight to ten men are supposed to live in one car. In some, however, only six were found and in others there were twelve and fifteen. . . .

Following are typical notes of an inspection of one of the camps: "Surroundings of camp very bad. Odors plentiful. Everything left over from food seemed to have been thrown out of the cars without any care whatever. Both front and rear of camps bad. Within ten feet of camp is ditch full of water drained from swamp near by. This full of garbage, old clothes, etc. Thick scum on water. Plenty of flies."

72

THE EMPLOYER AND THE IMMIGRANT

CHANGING ATTITUDES

The Delaware Americanization Committee describes a labor camp in a company town in much the same terms as the report on Wisconsin camps just quoted, and concludes:[1] "This condition which is typical of foreign labor camps in all parts of the United States, seems to be due to two causes combined: the company thinks the men do not want anything better and the men think they can not get anything better." The same conclusion was implied by the United States Immigration Commission when it regretfully reported that Southern and Eastern Europeans in America were willing "seemingly to accept indefinitely without protest certain wages and conditions of employment" and were reluctant "to enter labor disputes involving loss of time," . . . and when it complained of their "ready acceptance of low wages and existing working conditions."[2]

But this submissive attitude of the immigrant has been changing, and with it has come a corresponding change in the employer and in the public generally. In years gone by, when American workers struck, immigrants were brought in to take their places. The Americans considered it a mark of distinction to belong to trade-unions and immigrants were condemned for not joining unions and for acting as strike breakers. In recent years, however, this situation has been reversed. Immigrants, having been in the main unorganized and underpaid, formed unions and struck. Native workers refused to strike and even took immigrants' places, and division between native and foreign born was intensified by anti-alien agitation.

---

[1] Annual Report, 1920, 1921, p. 25.

[2] *Abstract of Reports*, Vol. 1, p. 530.

ADJUSTING IMMIGRANT AND INDUSTRY

During 1919, when cost of living was rising by leaps and bounds, immigrant wage earners in great numbers followed the example of native-born workers, and attempted to maintain or to raise their standards of living by means of labor organizations. They struck for higher wages, for shorter working days, for recognition of their unions, and for a voice in determining their conditions of employment.

The reaction of American industry and to some extent of the American public to this movement, has amazed not only the immigrant, but Americans as well. Instead of welcoming the effort of the immigrant worker to raise his standards to that of the American worker and thus make amalgamation easier, a campaign of vilification of the immigrant was begun. His strikes and his unions were condemned as alien, Bolshevik, revolutionary. A deliberate effort was made to divide American employees from the foreign-born and to raise antagonism between them. During the great steel strike the steel corporation issued a statement that the American employees were loyal; only the foreign-born took part in the strike. The strike itself was declared to be not for improved conditions, but for control of the industry by the workers, a syndicalist movement.

Clothing manufacturers in Cleveland, Rochester, and Philadelphia, whose industries were built up by immigrant labor and some of whom were themselves foreign born, advertised for "American help" only, when their employees went out on strike, and charged their labor difficulties to foreign agitators. Textile mills in New England, which have had strikes every two or three years, now discovered that it was the "foreign element" that was making unreasonable demands, and through the press the well-to-do citizens were aroused to the menace of the foreign born in their midst.

THE EMPLOYER AND THE IMMIGRANT

So it was throughout the country. Newspapers carried scaring headlines that striking immigrants were using violence to keep loyal American employees from working. Soldiers were called to quell riots. Raids on the strikers' headquarters resulted in seizure of radical literature. Strikers were charged with being in a Bolshevist conspiracy to overthrow the government and confiscate industries.

In Rochester a union of 12,000 members, having contracts with all but one of the leading manufacturers of the industry in the city, was condemned by a committee of the state legislature investigating radical activity as alien and syndicalist, because it is an industrial union rather than a craft union and is not affiliated with the American Federation of Labor. The condemnation was made on the testimony of one man, at the instigation of the firm whose employees were on strike, and the union was given no opportunity to be heard. Newspapers took up the cry and uninformed Americans were arrayed against foreign-born neighbors.

But this cry against the immigrant seems only to have marked a transition period, when great masses of immigrants were changing their attitude toward their status in American industry, and employers were forced to change theirs. The cry which was heard throughout the country during 1919 and 1920 died away the following year, partly because of the depression but partly also because of a more widespread realization of what leaders among industrial managers had been pointing out for several years—that the immigrant wage earners must be given a new deal; must be treated as belonging to the industries in which they work, as citizens with rights rather than outsiders who were merely brought in to do disagreeable and heavy labor which Americans would not do, or who were willing to accept wages and working conditions that were unacceptable to Americans. The bitter strikes of 1919, with the foreign born taking a most prominent part, made it evident that the immigrants were expecting a new deal from American industry, and many employers who would not voluntarily follow the lead of the foresighted managers who pointed the way, were forced into line by the pressure of their rebelling employees.

A NEW DAY FOR THE IMMIGRANT WAGE EARNER

The International Harvester Company in all its plants, the Standard Oil Company at Bayonne, New Jersey, the General Electric Company at Lynn, Massachusetts, The Midvale Steel Company, all of whom employ a large number of foreign-born wage earners, had taken the lead in developing employee representation plans and industrial councils, which attempted to furnish those immigrants opportunities for presenting their grievances and to offer them, together with their native-born fellowworkers, a voice in determining working conditions. This was soon followed by a very rapid spread of shop committee plans of various kinds, more or less sincerely devoted to the same purpose; and many industrial establishments which had been devoting themselves to so-called welfare work employed special welfare workers who spoke foreign languages and knew foreign peoples to give attention to the needs of their immigrant employees.

The war, the shutting off of immigration, and the fluctuations in cost of living brought about the changes in the attitudes of the immigrants and the employers; and the influences of these forces may be expected to continue long enough to make permanent the new labor management policies which so many American industries are developing for weaving the immigrant wage earner into the texture of the American industrial population.

Many immigrants learned in the army to eat and live like Americans. Many others worked in war industries under protection of government regulations. The enormous increase in demand for labor, which continued after the signing of the armistice well into 1920, together with the recent shutting off of immigration, made the law of supply and demand work in favor of the wage earner. Unskilled laborers were in a position to take advantage of this condition much better than skilled workers or salaried employees, for they could fit into new places more easily. So the wages of the unskilled, in whose ranks the foreign born are mostly found, rose faster even than the wages of the skilled, and the immigrants were able to get a new taste of American life. They had bought liberty bonds and savings stamps, and were praised as one-hundred-per-cent Americans. To this, the testimony is overwhelming that they responded with loyalty and ambition. They wanted to be real Americans, to act like Americans, and to live like Americans. And now American employers are realizing that they must adjust themselves to the new demands of the immigrant workers.

The recent drop in cost of living and the industrial depression have tended to force wages of the unskilled and therefore of the immigrants down faster than those of the skilled and native-born workers. But this has not changed the attitude of the forward-looking employers to the need of maintaining the status of the immigrant worker on a higher level than he occupied before the war. The depression and widespread unemployment have threatened the living standards of all classes of workers, and the common danger has apparently developed a bond of sympathy between the native and the foreign born, which is overcoming the antagonism engendered during the strikes and conflicts of the period of 1919 and 1920. Moreover, the new immigration law, restricting immigration in any one year to three per cent of each nationality in the country in 1910, has made employers realize the necessity of managing properly and conserving the immigrant labor that is available, if it is to be kept loyal and productive when industrial activity is again resumed.

We have, therefore, a more widespread recognition of the need for developing enlightened methods of labor management and labor maintenance with respect to immigrant workers as a permanent policy for American industry. How this is to be done may be gathered from the experience of those employers who foresaw the need and pioneered the way, some of which is described in the succeeding chapter.

The spirit with which this work is to be done and which many employers are coming to realize as necessary may be gathered from the following editorial in the *Christian Science Monitor* of April, 1919:

. . . Too often the employer groups have dealt with their foreign-born employees only as "the help," the means of carrying on the business; they have had no conception of the possible results of allowing the abyss that yawns between the ordinary thought-processes of employee and employer to continue unbridged, or they have thought of that abyss only as something that, at its worst, would mean nothing else than a more or less costly interruption of the business by a strike or a walkout.

The meaning of America must be brought home to employers such as these. They, as well as the foreign-born employee, must become intimately conscious of the American idea. They must be led to realize, before any further social and industrial explosions are required to point the lesson, that in America the advantages of freedom and liberty cannot forever be enjoyed by a few at the expense of the many. Employers and employees must come to see and acknowledge that under the American idea each benefits and prospers only as opportunity is afforded for the benefit and prosperity of all. Liberty under the American idea does not consort with

THE EMPLOYER AND THE IMMIGRANT

exploitation, any more than it fosters anarchy. In America, the key to all right activity and organization is and always has been, commonweal, which is to say the welfare of all in common. And Americanization, under whatever agency, will fall short of its proper effect unless it brings this fact home to native born and foreign born alike.

CHAPTER V

MANAGEMENT OF IMMIGRANT EMPLOYEES

THE time has come when the nation may depend upon the employers to help in adjusting their immigrant employees to conditions of American work and living, as well as to adjust their own labor policies to meet the special requirements of such employees. In the methods and policies which many industries have inaugurated and which we shall describe in this and the three succeeding chapters, there may be much to criticize from the point of view of trade unionists and others who define "industrial democracy" in terms different from those of industrial managers. With this conflict of opinion we are not here concerned. Our purpose is only to point out those labor policies of American industries which tend to fuse the immigrant and native-born workers whom they employ, just as in later chapters we shall describe the trade union policies which have a similar effect.

"AMERICANIZATION CLASSES"

One of the first needs that every intelligent manager notes, of course, is instruction in English for those employees who do not understand the language. This has led to quite a widespread organization of classes in industrial plants either directly by the management or in coöperation with public authorities or civic organizations. But teaching English has not been the only work of these classes. Instruction in civics and American history has usually gone with the language lessons, and preparatory work for naturalization examinations has also been quite common. When industrial managers speak of "Amercanization" work, they usually have activities of this character in mind; and most of the larger industrial corporations have experimented with this work in one way or another.

We shall discuss these classes with more detail in a later chapter. Here it is sufficient to note that where the employer has himself equipped the classes and furnished the instructors the work has not usually been as successful as where public educational authorities furnished the teachers and were responsible for the instruction, with the employer coöperating by giving class room space in the plant, allowing time off to employees who attend classes or offering other inducements for attendance. The tendency throughout the country seems to be for the public educational authorities to take over the work of instruction in the factory classes.

Most of the states having a large foreign-born population have established divisions of immigrant education in connection with their State Departments of Education; and these take the initiative in organizing classes and inducing employers to coöperate. They make studies of the subject matter and technique of instruction and they have devoted themselves to the training of competent teachers for the work. Under this stimulus the classes for factory workers conducted by public educational authorities have been more permanent and successful, while the classes organized and conducted entirely by the employer have been dwindling in number. This may be due partly to the unsatisfactory character of the teachers the management is ordinarily able to furnish but also, no doubt, to some suspicion that the instruction itself is colored by the ideals of government and citizenship that the management may desire its employees to have. Whatever may be the cause, it is a fortunate development that responsibility for instruction in the language and traditions of the land is being assumed by public authorities, because the impartiality of the instruction must always be as important a concern as the efficiency of the teaching.

After all, teaching the English language, the principles of American government, and the traditions of America is not the business of the employer. Nor is the promotion of naturalization his concern. He may assist in all these matters, but it is not through such formal instruction that the employer can be most helpful in "Americanizing" his immigrant employees. It is rather in the methods of managing these employees during their daily duties in the plant that the employer can do most to promote American citizenship among them.[1]

. . . For the immigrant learns of America not only through what we teach him about it, but through what he sees and experiences for himself. Nothing we can ever tell the new arrival about American liberty, and justice can quite eradicate his memories of the needless suffering caused by some minor official's stupidity at the port of arrival, of a real estate agent's sharp practice, of lonely evenings spent in squalid surroundings, or weary days filled with the fruitless search for work. The foreigner judges America by what he finds here, and he nearly always finds the worst first. When this has happened we cannot give him a belief in American institutions by merely describing them to him—we must demonstrate that they are facts, operative in his daily life.

The employer may do much to make these facts operative in the immigrant's daily life by the kind of labor management policies he adopts for the handling of his foreign-born employees.

---

[1] *Report of Delaware Americanization Committee,* 1921, p. 8.

MANAGEMENT OF IMMIGRANT EMPLOYEES

AMERICANIZATION THROUGH MANAGEMENT

In recent years labor management has become the subject of scientific study, and a new profession has been developed to apply the results of this study, which is variously known as employment or labor management, personnel or industrial relations management. The new science has developed a more or less definite set of principles, and the duties of the employment executive have been excellently described by S. R. Rectanus, former President of the National Association of Employment Managers:

The unit of business is the individual breadwinner, and the stable element is the breadwinning, the working member of the American family.

The only business organization which can be permanently effective is the one which is planned, controlled, and guided to give the workingman, the creative being, the fullest opportunity to develop his talents, apply his energy, stimulate his interest, satisfy his ambition, attain satisfaction and contentment.

At least a portion of the opportunity of the Employment Executive in this plan is to advise in the recruiting, selecting, placing, introducing, promoting, transferring, and quitting of these men in their work relations. In the performance of his daily duty he will secure information and make observations which will permit him to contribute sound, logical evidence to the General Manager who must determine the labor policies. It will permit him to contribute to the planning of improvements in pay and rewards, training, safety, sanitation and production. An extensive but exacting opportunity, for it requires that we advise our fellow human beings in some of their most delicate and important decisions.

Clearly, if industrial managers generally applied the principles here enunciated to their relations with immigrant and native-born employees alike, more would be accomplished in fusing all into a common American citizenship than could possibly be done by formal instruction in factory classes. Unfortunately, however, while personnel managers speak of their policies and methods as if these were applied to all employees, in practice they have often been led to make a distinction between immigrants and American or Americanized employees. Those who speak broken English or no English at all, those whose physique, manners, habits, and attitude appear alien, are often treated as a class apart to whom the principles of employment management, of careful study of the individual worker, could not be applied. While the distinction in treatment between immigrants and other employees is not usually so clear as in the case of the 400 immigrants set aside in the "lousy house," which we cited above, this case serves well to illustrate the difference in policy and attitude that used to be common, even in industries which in other respects pursued a most enlightened employment policy. The plant referred to, for example, was one of the pioneers in establishing a separate labor department for the proper handling of its labor policies.

But the principles of personnel or labor management once established in a plant can not for long be restricted to only a part of the labor force. Thus we find that step by step as more and more establishments are employing trained personnel managers, to organize and direct their labor policies in accordance with the modern enlightened ideas, the management and treatment of immigrant labor forces is also improving. The personnel or labor manager attempts to watch the individual career of every worker, to see to it that he is transferred and promoted as he learns more of the business, that his wages are raised as his efficiency increases, that his grievances are heard and considered, that he is guarded against abuse and injustice by foremen and straw bosses, and that he is given some voice in determining the conditions under which he works. These are the methods by which

industrial relations are being improved, but these same
methods, when extended to include the non-English-
speaking with all the other employees, also offer one of
the most effective means of adjustment between the
immigrant worker and American industry.

PLANT LABOR DEPARTMENTS

To carry out the policies of the management with respect to labor, most of the larger industrial corporations now have a centralized authority commonly
known as the labor or industrial relations department,
with a trained manager or director in charge corresponding to the managers in charge of sales, production, etc. Many smaller plants in which the labor
policy can be more directly controlled by the general
manager have similar centralized employment or service departments for handling the details—hiring, discharge, and the "welfare" services of the management.

As long as employers never really formulated a labor
policy for their plants there was no need for such departments, and foremen or other subordinate officials
handled their workers as they individually saw fit.
This lack of policy resulted in enormous losses caused
by constant quitting of dissatisfied workers and hiring
of new ones. The shifting of the labor force, or "turnover" of labor, as it was named, attracted little attention as long as immigrants were entering the country
in great numbers and there was plenty of labor to pick
from; although it was quite common for plants to
hire during a year three and four times as many workers as were normally required to carry on production.
But when the outbreak of the war in Europe shut off
the immigrant labor supplies, "labor turnover" became a serious concern of American industry, and "Employment Departments" began to appear, primarily

for the purpose of improving "hiring and firing" methods. "Welfare" and Safety work, which had appeared sporadically up to that time, were now also greatly stimulated by the shutting off of immigration and by the workmen's compensation laws which state after state was rapidly enacting. These efforts were usually grouped under a "Service" department which was soon joined with the employment department. From this employment and service work, the present labor or industrial relations departments rapidly developed, for the need of a comprehensive policy to deal with all labor relations soon became apparent.

The Westinghouse Electric and Manufacturing Company, of East Pittsburgh, Pa., thus describes the aims of its labor department:

To discover the existing sources of labor supply, and to employ mediums through which the necessary labor may be obtained.

To size up applicants successfully and place them to the best advantage to both employer and employees.

To get new employees to feel at home in their new plant environment and to assimilate them.

To assist the management in endeavoring to establish correct labor policies.

To obtain an effective method of receiving and handling complaints of employees.

To assist in maintaining proper shop discipline.

To carry out personal service (welfare) activities and advocate recreational movements.

To assist in the transfer of employees when necessary.

To assist in combatting labor turnover.

To assist in maintaining the proper efficiency record of employees. . . .

HIRING IMMIGRANT WORKERS

The practice of permitting foremen to hire help for their departments is usually the first to be restricted or abolished whenever centralized labor departments are established. Aside from the inefficiency of the method and the misfitting of men and jobs, this practice affected immigrant workers in a peculiarly vicious way. It developed a form of tribute levying on the foreign-born employees by their foremen which reached amazing proportions. Under the title of "Job Selling in Ohio," the Industrial Commission of that state published a report in 1916 which described in detail how foreign-born workers throughout the state had to pay fees to foremen to secure employment, to hold their jobs after they were employed, and to get increases in wages. There was hardly a plant in the state employing foreign-born labor in large numbers where this graft did not prevail to some extent.

That Ohio is not the only state where the system of permitting foremen to hire labor resulted in job selling and levying tribute in various forms on the foreign-born worker, is evident from the following statement of the Massachusetts Bureau of Immigration: [1]

The prevailing industrial unrest together with the difficulty of creating an understanding between employer and employee, can sometimes be traced to the fact that those coming in direct contact with the foreign-born workmen have too often, because of the indifference of the employers, been able to exploit these foreign-born in matters of securing and holding their jobs. The elimination of this type of exploitation will do much to convince the foreign worker that he can find in America an opportunity for fair play. Unless Americanization work has this basis of just treatment for one and all in the Commonwealth no propaganda work can have permanent success.

Even when the employer is anxious to eliminate this abuse, he finds it very difficult to do it, as long as foremen have the power to hire and discharge employees. Officials of a large plant in Pittsburgh said they spent three years in fighting this form of graft and they were not sure then they got rid of it, until they established

---

[1] First Annual Report, 1919, p. 21.

a centralized employment department which alone had power to hire and discharge workers.

But whether an immigrant worker is hired by a foreman or by an employment manager, there are methods of doing it which will tend to alienate him and methods which will be helpful to him and the industry alike. The contrast between these methods is thus described in a book prepared by a number of industrial managers.[1]

Tony Czelak obtained his first job in this country by the side-door method. He was walking down a street of shops, wondering how long it would be before he could make it understood in this land of golden opportunity that he wanted a job and was a willing worker, when he saw a sign that a fellow Pole had told him meant work. He turned in at the door. The first man he met was a white-collared shipping clerk, who wore his hat on the back of his head and chewed a moist cigar.

"Want job!" said Tony. That was about all the English he knew.

"What the hell can you do?" ejaculated the shipping clerk; and Tony, without understanding what the words meant, bared his teeth and a bulging biceps at the same instant. The shipping clerk liked Tony's smile, and hired him on the spot.

They became great friends. Tony learned to swing coils of wire on to a hand truck, and he got so he could calculate to a nicety the weight of a load on his truck even before he wheeled it to the scales and watched the shipping clerk shift the rider back and forth until the beam came into balance. There weren't so very many people in the shop, and the shipping clerk could always count on Tony to work nights and Sundays if necessary, to get out heavy shipments. Tony stayed in the shop five years.

One day he got nervous because his friends told him of the big money they were making elsewhere. He talked it over with the shipping clerk.

"I'd like to give you more money," said the latter. "I need you here. But the big boss says nix on raises now. Maybe you can get more somewhere else. Think it over if you want to try it, and let me know."

Tony did think it over, and finally decided to take a flyer in

---

[1] *Management and the Worker*, published by A. W. Shaw Co., Chicago, pp. 167–169.

job-hunting. He applied the next morning at a factory where there was reported to be great prosperity and great need of men at good wages. He was ushered into a dingy little office where in a small space were herded 50 other applicants. A uniformed guard pushed him into a seat, growled at him to "keep in his place," and presently a girl gave him a sheet of paper and a pencil and told him to "fill that out." Tony was not strong on writing the English language, though he had picked up enough information to be able to decipher the orders in the shipping clerk's office readily enough. So when he read the paper that had been given him, a long list of questions apparently concerned with his vital statistics, he was beyond his depth. He calmly put the sheet in his pocket.

After an hour or so of assiduous "keeping in his place," his turn came and he was summoned to the desk of a chap who appeared to be a cross between fourth-bookkeeper and errand boy.

"Where's your application?" he asked Tony.

Divining that the sheet he had stuck in his pocket was meant, Tony fished it out. The chap unfolded it and said disgustedly, "Can't you read?"

"Yah! I read," Tony replied.

"Can't you write?"

"Nah!" Tony shook his head and smiled cheerfully. "You fill him out!"

Superciliously the youngster did so; and when the ordeal was finished Tony was taken to a foreman out in the plant who looked him over like a butcher appraising a steer, told him he might start in next morning, and gave him a red card to present at the gate for admission.

Tony reported promptly. His pay was a dollar a day more than he had been getting. But the labor policy plainly hinted at in the employment office was realized too well in the shop. Tony was bulldozed and driven and sworn at without humor, for three months. He asked for other work and was told to "get the hell out if you don't like it here!" And finally Tony did. Confronted by an unintelligent labor policy, quitting was the only thing he knew how to do.

Again Tony hunted a job. This time he was met differently. There was courtesy in the employment office. There were plenty of documents to be filled out, and lots of questions to be answered — all appearing like so much "red tape" to Tony; but the operation was conducted pleasantly, and Tony did not object. When he was finally given a job, he found the same pleasant attitude reflected by his foreman.

Tony is still on the job, and is doing just as good work as he did for his first friend, the shipping clerk.

To insure proper selection, the employment departments use specially qualified interviewers who talk privately with each applicant for employment and who test the quality, the ability, and adaptability of the applicant. Psychological as well as mechanical tests have been developed. With its larger social outlook the employment department tests applicants not only for technical skill and productive ability but also for team work or coöperative ability. And this to the immigrant means that he is selected with an idea as to the possibilities of adjusting himself both to the work and the workers of the plant which he enters.

Mr. Richard A. Feiss of the Clothcraft Shops in Cleveland describes the system of selecting help in his plant as follows:

The interviewing of applicants is important and requires considerable tact, judgment, and experience. As judgment is essential and as judgment is influenced by immediate impression, in this establishment no one is employed on date of application. Postponement of selection tends to bring all applicants in their proper relationship in the mind of the one who has the responsibility of their selection.

Application records are classified as to sex, age, and apparent suitability. When a position is to be filled one or more applicants are sent for. A definite time is set for their appearance. At this time selection is made for immediate employment, and the fitness of the applicant is more definitely determined.

There are two kinds of fitness to be considered, provided a person is suited for industry at all: one is fitness for the position; the other is fitness for the organization. Of these the latter is by far the more important.

Fitness for the organization is chiefly a question of character. Every organization has a distinct character of its own, which is often recognized as being a tangible business asset. It is essential, therefore, that every member of the organization have a character sufficiently developed or capable of development to be in harmony with the character of the organization. This is the basis of *esprit de corps*.

The interview of the applicant by a trained head of the Employment and Service Departments is the basis for predetermining as far as possible both the fitness for a position and for the organization. In judging fitness for a position, past experience, where there is any, is sometimes a guide. At the best, however, it is a guide of only doubtful value. At the Clothcraft Shops investigations and experiments have been carried on for the purpose of determining individual limitations by psychological tests. The tests that are being developed consist of general intelligence tests, including a test for ability to follow instructions and a series of tests for dexterity.

The applicant's fitness for the organization, while more important, is more readily predetermined by the interview. The interview at the time of employment is very thorough and designed to explain to the prospective employee the character of the organization and its policies, and the responsibilities of the organization to the employee as well as the responsibility of the employee to the organization.

This is the system of hiring interviews that employment managers have set up as their ideal, and while it is still very far from being universally carried out in practice, the many plants that have established centralized hiring departments during the last four or five years are making rapid progress in this direction. These systems of hiring and selecting employees offer the means of preventing immigrants from becoming industrial misfits and casual workers, such as is illustrated in the following case, which appeared before one of the arbitration boards in the men's clothing industry.

Daniel Szmolia, a Ukrainian peasant working as a pocket maker, was discharged for poor workmanship. He came into the office of the arbitration board which was to review his case, a picture of perplexity. Heavily built, broad faced, slow of movement, and slow mentally, he could not understand why he was no longer wanted. He had worked at the occupation for three years and now suddenly he was "no good," as he put it. The foreman explained that the man was willing enough, but try as he would he could not do the work properly. Instructors could do nothing with him and he was warned over and over again that he would have to do better, but neither instruction nor threats of discharge brought any improvement. There was nothing to do but to let him go.

One glance at the man's large hands and short fat fingers was enough to convince the chairman of the board that he never would learn to do the intricate work of pocket making. His physical and mental processes showed that he was equipped by nature for rough, heavy labor and was accustomed to waiting for the results of his work to grow. Manipulating cloth under the needle of a sewing machine was the last thing one would expect such a man to be able to do.

"How long have you had this man?" the foreman was asked.

"About nine months. He came to us when we were short of pocket makers and were glad to get anyone. We kept him on pockets as long as we could not get anyone else, then we tried him at sewing up shoulders and backs, but we have had to do all that work of his over again also. It seems he can't sew a straight seam."

There was no place in the factory for Daniel Szmolia and the employment manager had to let him go. His place was on a farm or at other heavy laboring tasks, but in all probability he would apply at other clothing factories and work a few months at a time as he had been doing for three years. Someone had taken him into a tailor shop when he came to this country, taught him to sew on a machine, and now it was the only work that he knew.

Here we have a typical experience of an immigrant, who comes to us untrained for industrial work and who is led into an industry where he must necessarily become an incompetent misfit, because the employers who first hired him had no hiring system designed to secure a proper adjustment between the job and the immigrant worker.

BALANCING NATIONALITIES

It used to be a common labor policy in industries which employed immigrant labor in large numbers to "balance nationalities." This was the name given to the practice of hiring immigrants of many nationalities, to prevent any one nationality from dominating a department or a plant. Originally the policy was designed to prevent racial unity under the leadership of a "padrone" or labor solidarity in a union whose purpose might conflict with the wishes of the management. Racial animosities and lack of a common language kept the employees divided, and concerted action for higher wages or shorter hours, such as were common among native-born skilled workmen, could thus be averted. When dissatisfaction arose among the foreign born and they learned enough English to reach a common understanding, they could easily be displaced by new nationalities and thus the system was maintained.

But this policy always had certain disadvantages. Racial animosities and lack of a common language not only prevented united action against the employer; they also resulted in confusion and lack of understanding of orders and instructions of the management. Foremen would swear and fume at the stupidity and perverseness of groups of foreign born that had carefully been put together to prevent the very same common understanding necessary to carry out orders and instructions. Strikes and dramatic outbreaks against the management might be prevented but only at the price of destructive lack of coördination which effectually prevented team work on the job.

Modern labor management, however, considers team work and plant morale a first essential, and the crude mixing of nationalities as formerly practiced is generally condemned by personnel managers for its effect in retarding production as well as for perpetuating racial differences.[1]

"In addition to fitting work and workers, an important duty of the employment department is to fit workers to each other, thus inducing profitable coöperation. Workers who are most likely to work well together should obviously be placed together. On the other hand, special effort is required not to place together groups of different nationalities that are prone to quarrel. Another important point is to place employees in departments where they are most likely to get along with the foreman. An Italian would be only too

---

[1] *Management and the Worker*, p. 201.

likely to try to break the head of a Czechoslovac foreman! It does not usually pay, again, to build up entire departments from one nationality."

But the practice of mixing nationalities may sometimes serve a useful purpose, as we found in a plant in Chicago, where it was intelligently used by an employment manager to break down clannishness and racial prejudice. The different nationalities he found needed to learn to understand each other as much as they needed to understand Americans, and by seeing to it that a sufficient number of native-born or other English-speaking men were placed in every group, he succeeded most quickly in making English the common language of the group and developing a spirit of cooperation and friendliness among all its members.

INDUCTING THE IMMIGRANT INTO THE SHOP

The hiring methods and policies described above represent only the beginning of what industrial managers are doing to facilitate the adjustment of the immigrant and American industry. It is after the immigrant has already been hired that the practical process of adjustment between him and his industrial surroundings, his fellow employees, and his overseers really begins. To this problem personnel managers are giving increasing attention. They are inquiring very critically into the methods by which new employees are brought into shops and they are devising methods of improving that introduction.

Illustrating his remarks with the recital of unfortunate experiences of a Polish immigrant given his first job in an American plant, an employer addressing a large national convention of employment managers asked:

MANAGEMENT OF IMMIGRANT EMPLOYEES

How do you introduce a new worker to the parties he should know in the plant as he comes to work? The watchman at the gate or factory entrance is the host usually, is he not? The introduction means generally handing the new man a time card and telling him to follow the crowd; possibly informing him that he will find his place on a certain floor of the "B" building. How does our new man learn of the best paths of travel through the plant, where the toilets and washrooms and the tool cribs are located, where to go to secure what instruction he may need, how to work the time system so as to cause no unnecessary work to the time-keeper's office, etc.? Honestly, now, does he not learn most of these things by bothering other workmen asking questions of them? Many times, out of a spirit of deviltry, he is given wrong answers, and thus both his time as well as that of his joking informer are taken from production and therefore from wages earned. How happy a home would many of us have if we took no better care to introduce new friends to our families? Is it wrong to assume that we are taking new members into our families whenever we have new workmen enter our shop? Should we, then, not plan for their being introduced just right so that there be no unnecessary embarassment? ... One of the largest single contributing forces to labor turnover is the willing quitting of the worker because of his knowing he does not know his work, and is, therefore, in danger of being fired. Rather than wait for the time to come when the boss shall discover his ignorance and consequent poor workmanship, the worker quits, knowing he stands a better chance for employment elsewhere by this means than were he to be discharged. How few times has this man been taken in hand as a human and dealt with as such by another truly human, thereby being trained or instructed in the work that is to be undertaken. . . ."

Plants which have studied their experience with employees who quit work have universally found that the greatest numbers leave within the first few weeks of their employment. It is quite common to find that half of all who quit have been employed for less than a month. With the immigrant the main reason for this is his own uncertainty as to whether he knows the work and will make good. He may be a first-class workman, but he lacks confidence in his own abilities. He doesn't know whether he knows his job or not, and this is a great source of trouble not only to the industry and to the workman, but to the country as well, for it multiplies the difficulties of adjustment.

The non-English-speaking worker is particularly in need of some intelligent system of introduction to his workplace. His inability to read signs and bulletins and inability to understand instructions and get information is not only a constant discouragement to him and a serious interference with his efficiency, but it becomes an actual menace in increasing factory hazards to himself and to his fellow workers.

Some of the introduction methods already developed to overcome the immigrant's handicap in this respect include a "*protégé*" system, whereby the new immigrant worker is assigned to an English-speaking employee who knows the work and the shop, and who looks after the newcomer until he adjusts himself, in much the same way that seniors in colleges take freshmen under their wings at the beginning of the school year. Other plants have "Americanization Committees," consisting of a number of representatives of each racial group employed, and the immigrant is instructed to avail himself freely of the services of the members of the committee who speak his language for any information he may need, or on any matters he may desire to bring to the attention of the management.

The employment manager of the Timken Roller Bearing Company of Canton, Ohio, describes the following as the method of introducing new workers in his plant:

When a man reports for work there is much for him to learn—whether he be a common laborer or skilled mechanic, and we find it a very good policy to have a guide show him the location of certain conveniences, the clocks, first-aid room, the proper entrance to use, and the restaurant.

After the man is on the job, we have a recreation man who breaks the new employee into this phase of the work. The new man is invited to attend the ball games, theater parties, evening school, Americanization meetings, and such things. He is given a small book containing information about the plant and also a copy of our latest issue of the shop paper, which gives him a sort of "I belong here" feeling.

Our foremen devote some time to explaining the shop rules and when they find any doubt as to the men not being posted or not clearly understanding the conditions of their employment, the man is either taken to the Employment Department or a representative of the department is sent out to see him, and it is his duty to stay on the job until the man is satisfied and understands. Much of this work is in connection with premium earnings, absenteeism, advances in pay, or holding back pay and tiding over stranded men. It is our method of humanizing industry and instilling and maintaining the personal touch which of late many of us have forgotten or overlooked during the drive of the past emergency. Quoting from a recent shop paper: "Shop morals can thus be developed, but it cannot exist unless the employee feels that he gains a real benefit from his relationship with the management."

Not only the management itself, but the coöperation of fellow employees, is needed to make the newcomer feel at home in his work place, and the following editorial from a plant paper published by a Cleveland corporation shows one method by which this coöperation is enlisted. This appeal is typical of many which appeared in plant periodicals, particularly during the war.

When you go into a country or a strange place you are grateful to the man who extends to you the hand of fellowship, to the one who makes you feel at home.

Remember the new employees on the job. They are strangers within our gates. . . . You can do more in five minutes to establish the right spirit while their impressions are forming than you can in many days after they have formed their opinion of you and your company.

In case the newcomers are foreigners, there is even greater obligation to treat them as guests, and make them feel welcome.

It is the privilege of every American at this time to make the strangers from other lands feel that we appreciate their help in winning this war.

Treat them with the same courtesy and kindness that you would desire if *you* were a stranger in a foreign country.

Your personal contact with foreign fellow workers can *Help to Unite all Races in America* to win this war.

PROMOTION AND TRANSFERS

For the non-English-speaking immigrant, who necessarily must start at the bottom of the industrial ladder, an open road for advancement is particularly important. A personnel director for a corporation operating four plants in Detroit thus describes his system:

We aim to write job specifications, and something about transfers in connection with each job. If there is a class of work which, after we have studied it, we regard as unduly burdensome, disagreeable or tiresome, or monotonous, we intend to write in the job's specifications a statement of the length of time which we will require workers to stay on that job, formally, without asking for a transfer. We will set a determined period, after which time request for transfers will be honored as soon as convenient. There will be another class of operation in connection with which we recognize an occupational disease, such as sand blasting, or anything which requires contact and exposure with lead poison. For those operations, with the aid of our medical department, we shall set a time, at the end of which the operative will be examined to see if it is necessary to transfer him, and we shall transfer him as soon as possible, and if we can't find a job in our plant for that man, we will make an effort to place him in another plant.

By means of transfers from one department to another some employment managers hope also to give a man the same cycle of operations which formerly he could perform within the scope of a day's work, and thus compensate him to some extent for his loss of artisanship caused by subdivision of labor and specialization.

But most employment managers are studying and

experimenting with transfer systems primarily to provide opportunities for advancement to ambitious and capable employees. Said a manager of a packing house corporation:

> There is nothing more vital than this question of promotion and transfer. It is what everyone of us has been looking forward to since we started in this work.
>
> The plan which we are trying to work out now in our own organization is based on three things:
>
> 1. The card which contains a record of every employee, with his complete history.
>
> 2. A rating scale by which he is rated by his superior officers.
>
> 3. Certain mental and trade tests.
>
> This card, in addition to giving us the full history of the man, is so noted at the top by little tabs, that we can instantly put our hand on any man of specific qualifications that we want for any particular job. In the past . . . our great problem has been not so much to get men as to make the utmost use of the men which we have. . . . This card enables us to pick out the man . . . when we want one with any particular quality and judging him in connection with others to decide whether he is better fitted for the position we have in mind than some of the others. It also enables us to avoid the mistake of letting a man get side-tracked or get lost in the numbers of the organization. It has frequently happened in our experience . . . that men have applied to us for certain definite stated positions, and without knowing about their other qualifications, we have put them into that particular job. Many years after, in looking for some men specially qualified, we have passed those men by because we didn't know anything about them, but we believe now with the adoption of this system that is going to cease and that we will be able to put our hands on them when we want them. We believe that it is going to have a tremendous result. . . . When you come right down to it the transfer, which usually means the promotion of any employee, is really the thing that concerns him most vitally.

Mr. Richard Feiss says: "At the Clothcraft Shop, the road is not only open, but every possible aid is given for advancement. Practically all positions in the organization, including clerical and executive positions, are filled by those who by reason of sheer personal merit have come up from the ranks." When

there is an employment and service department, as
there is in this plant, which studies the record of each
individual, no matter how unskilled the work he is
doing may be—and this is done for young and old,
men and women, English and non-English-speaking—
then it is plain that an effective agency has been created by the employer for giving to the foreign born
the same opportunity for advancement on the basis of
merit that the native born have, and for working the
immigrant into the industrial organization as an integral part of it.

COMPLAINTS, GRIEVANCES, AND DISCHARGES

"What is one to do with these foreigners?" said a
sincerely well-meaning plant manager. "Sometimes
the Polish workers—usually women—get together in a
corner of a room gesticulating and jabbering in their
language, and nobody in authority is able to understand a word of it! Then one of them who can make
herself understood may come up to the foreman, or to
me, and say, 'The workers want so and so.' Mean-
while the workers stand around as expressionless and
stolid as this radiator beside me. The leader who
comes forward is soon spotted as the one who has
been doing most of the talking. She may tell what is
wanted and I might say, 'Well, we can meet you half-
way. We will do this much.' Then more gesticulating
and more foreign language talking, and set faces, and
stubborn resistance. Nothing but all, will do—no matter what the mill owners' inconvenience in the matter."

And, in his very next sentence this man answered
his own question. He had had a clear illustration of
what would work among these women—and yet, he
had never thought to apply it. He said that, on an
occasion similar to the one described a Polish woman

secretary from the International Institute of the Y. W. C. A. spoke to the disturbed group of women, in their and her language; and her ability to reason with them and to make herself understood quieted them and settled the trouble.

But many are applying the results of such experiences. In a large shoe factory we found a special woman appointed for every floor and large department to handle such situations. Each of these women had a little room or alcove adjoining her group, so that she was always available; and she frequently took occasion herself to go out among the machines and tables where the women in her charge were working. Her position, in title and special function, was allied with the employment department, and her little room was in a sense a branch of the central employment office. This company appeared to be successful in working out the plan so that the relation between the welfare worker and forewoman or foreman of the department, was coöperative and uninvolved. In other plants where one person is in charge of women workers, with or without assistants, the custom prevails of taking daily trips through the plant, and of being present in lunch and rest rooms at noon hours, so as to come within the reach of every worker, every day.

At the Hog Island shipyards, representatives of the Department of Industrial Relations were stationed at convenient points through the shipyards, whose duty it was to receive and investigate complaints. They were instructed to avoid snap judgments, and told that they must assume that there are always two sides to every question referred to them, and that a thorough investigation must be made of every complaint. And after such an investigation of a complaint of any sort, no matter what the decision might be, a complete explanation was given to the worker. Speaking to a group of employment managers the superintendent of employment of this plant said:

> Another very important function of employment department work can be called "Labor Control" and deals with the worker on the job. You must be so set up that every employee in your whole organization feels that he not only originally entered the organization through you, but that at any time he is welcome to come to you with his grievances or troubles, provided he first takes up his case in the regular line prescribed by your rules, such as with the foreman in case of complaints about the work, etc.
>
> You are his court of appeal! No matter whether the troubles are in regard to his work on the job or personal difficulties outside of the job, the worker's trouble is your trouble and you stand as the bulwark guaranteeing a square deal for him both inside and outside of the gates. To this end, particularly in large plants, unless you are so organized that the worker can obtain ready access to you without considerable loss of time and consequent loss in his pay envelope, you are losing an influence which I insist will do as much and possibly more toward stabilizing your force and reducing your labor turnover than the proper initial selection.

While thus benefiting the employer these systems of hearing, investigating, and adjusting complaints are of incalculable value to the immigrant worker and to the country. For they assure him protection against injustice where it means most to him, and they help him in the trouble he is bound to get into during the process of adjustment to industrial conditions that are strange to him. Where mere descriptions of American institutions will have little meaning to him, these demonstrations of American justice and fair play operative in his daily life offer an effective means of giving him a belief in American institutions.

With these methods of handling complaints and grievances also must be coupled the control over discharges that the new labor departments of industrial plants have assumed. Where there is an employment manager or a labor department, foremen are rarely permitted to discharge employees summarily. Usually the foreman may suspend a worker out of his own department, but he has no authority to discharge him from the plant. The worker is sent to the employment department, which investigates the suspension, and if it is found that an injustice has been done to the employee he is reinstated. If there has been only a misunderstanding between the foreman and the worker, they are brought together to talk it over with the assistance of the employment manager. And where the worker has been at fault through ignorance rather than intent, he is usually transferred to some other department.

CHAPTER VI

TRAINING THE IMMIGRANT WORKER

"THE task of management does not end with getting the man for the job," say the personnel managers. "The man must also be trained for the specific tasks he is to perform; otherwise management has done only half its work, and methods must be found to induce in him the desire to produce to the best of his ability; otherwise, management has done only half its work." [1]

This is the attitude of modern labor management from the purely business point of view. But the realization that efficient management requires a technical education department of some kind in industrial plants, to teach unskilled and semi-skilled men their jobs, as well as skilled mechanics, promises to be particularly valuable to immigrant wage earners. For these are to be found mainly in the less skilled occupations, and training for the job is the most direct way of adjusting the immigrant to the conditions of American life.

AN ADJUSTMENT THAT INDUSTRY HAS TO MAKE

The immigrant has many adjustments to make, in order to accustom himself to American industrial methods and needs. But industry must also adjust itself to the immigrant. The development of automatic machinery and mechanical devices has been one adjustment that American industry has made, in order to use effectively the great masses of unskilled labor that flocked to this country after 1880. And now American employers of this labor have begun to

---

[1] *The Way to Greater Production*, A. W. Shaw Co., pp. 1-2.

104

realize that they must make another adjustment in order to develop the skill latent in this great labor force, and also to make immigrant wage earners feel at home as integral parts of the American industrial citizenship.

Our immigrant labor supply has been used by American industry in much the same way that American farmers have used our land supply. For many years both land and labor appeared to be inexhaustible, and both were worked wastefully without intensive care and with little thought of conservation. But just as the disappearance of free land has led farmers to conserve their soil and to put a considerable investment into maintaining and improving it, so the restrictions on immigration brought about by the war and by legislation have led employers to conserve the skill and strength of their labor and to put a considerable investment into training and improving it. The development of agricultural colleges and experiment stations was stimulated by the need for land conservation, and the development of personnel management courses in universities and special schools, as well as the growth of experiments with advanced labor policies, was largely brought about by the need for labor conservation.

IS TRAINING OF UNSKILLED WORKERS NECESSARY?

The older immigrant labor supply was composed principally of persons who had had training and experience abroad in the industries which they entered after their arrival in the United States. English, German, Scotch, and Irish immigrants in textile factories, iron and steel establishments, or in the coal mines, usually had been skilled workmen in these industries in their native lands and came to the United States in the expectation of higher wages and better working conditions. In the case of the more recent immigrants from southern and eastern Europe this condition of affairs has been reversed. Before coming to the United States the greater proportion had been engaged in farming or unskilled labor, and had no experience or training in manufacturing or mining. As a consequence, their employment in the mines and manufacturing plants of this country has been made possible only by the invention of mechanical devices and processes which have eliminated the skill and experience formerly required in a large number of occupations.[1]

This assumption on the part of the Immigration Commission that machinery and mechanical devices make skill unnecessary was a common belief and practice in American industries before the war. As a matter of fact, however, enlightened employers many years ago saw the falsity and the wastefulness of it. It was profitable because apparently there seemed to be an inexhaustible supply of labor in Europe, and out of the ebb and flow of hundreds of thousands of immigrant workers enough individuals managed by their own ingenuity to acquire sufficient skill to keep up the customary production. When, however, production had to be increased for war purposes, and immigration was temporarily shut off, then it appeared evident to all that training was essential and most of the large industries began energetically to train all the workers that came into their plants.

What the assumption that the development of machinery makes trained labor unnecessary has meant to our industries and to the immigrant laborers may be gathered from the following quotation from a report issued in 1918 by the section on industrial training of the Council of National Defense:

Of 7,910 wage earners, mostly skilled, who applied to the New York State Employment Bureau in November only 172 were machinists. Of 2,500 reputed machine operators recently laid off in one city, it is reported by the resident state employment agent that most of them were so "lacking in adaptability" they could not be

---

[1] U. S. Immigration Commission, *Abstract of Reports*, vol. I, pp. 494–495.

used advantageously in nearby factories. The agent in another city says: "One out of ten alleged mechanics applying for skilled positions is a first-class man; the others cannot fill the positions offered."

Men like these are being taken into the industries without special training and with sad loss in efficiency. They are good men, victims educationally of national and industrial neglect of training facilities. Will not a thinking nation see to it that provision for training is now made in our big factories and elsewhere?[1]

As pointed out by the United States Immigration Commission, it is the immigrant worker who has become our typical machine operator. He comes most commonly from a farm or from common labor, and is unfamiliar with modern machinery. He is bewildered by the very sight and noise of the machine he is given to operate. It is only after many trials in perhaps a number of factories that he becomes proficient at one machine. Because foremen assume that there is nothing to teach about it, he finds himself later "lacking in adaptability" for other machines in other factories when he happens to lose his job.

Even when the immigrant is a skilled worker, he and the industry alike often suffer from lack of proper training and adjustment to his job. A Bohemian presser in a clothing factory could do only fifty coats in the same time that others were doing about seventy. The employer made every effort to get him to do more, but to no avail. The man worked hard, harder in fact than the others who were doing more work, but though willing, he seemed stupid and unable to grasp the simple details of his job. Finally, the employer attempted to reduce his wages in proportion as his production was below that of the other pressers. At this point the union interfered in his behalf. Officials of the organization could not deny the justice of

[1] "How to Overcome the Shortage of Skilled Mechanics by Training the Unskilled," p. 18.

107

the employer's claim that he was worth less than the other men, but they did not want to see his wages reduced. They worked with him and sympathetically showed him how he might save his strength and improve his work. In the course of a week or two his production jumped to sixty-five coats, and it would only be a short time before he would catch up with the others. The only difficulty in this case was lack of proper instruction.

SUCCESSFUL TRAINING OF WAR WORKERS

During the war the influx of women into industries to which they had hitherto been unaccustomed presented a problem very similar to that of the immigrant worker entering American industrial life. The works manager of a large machine company in a Western city thus describes his problem and the method he adopted of dealing with it:

When the writer took charge of the works in January, 1916, it was the practice to bring the new employees directly into the shop, set them at the machines and have them learn the work at these machines in the shop. I noticed that when the new girls came into the shop they were very nervous—badly frightened—and that they did not get over this timidity for several weeks. They were set to work at either large or small machines, the like of which they had never seen before, and naturally were too nervous to do their best. I found that not only was their progress in learning slow, but that they also took up the time of the employees surrounding them in order that they might learn from these employees and thus naturally they learned all the faults of these other employees. Their percentage of scrap was also very high.

I therefore started the mechanical training department. In less than ten days' time we turned out from the training department girls who could operate heavy hand turret lathes, on work requiring great precision. The production from the machines in the training department was, of course, much greater and more accurate than the production from the same machines under the old method of training the employee in the shop. These trained girls, when entering the shop, would attack their machines with vigor and confidence and it did not take more than three weeks for them to reach a high average of production. Upon beginning the work in the shop itself, the girl employee became a part of our system of organization, by which we have set a male job boss over each group of seven or more women. This job boss has been selected with great care in order to see that he is not only a skilled mechanic, but also a man of good character. It is the job boss's duty to see that the efficiency of his group of women operatives is kept up to a point that will ensure an excellent rate of production and pay. His particular duty is to continue the training in the shop of those operatives who are last out of the training department. . . .[1]

When the War Department was confronted with the need of mechanics and repairmen in great numbers and had to use all sorts of men untrained to these tasks, it used the same method. First, the men were selected carefully and assorted to the tasks for which they were likely to be best suited. Then, in addition to the military camps, training schools were established in connection with all the important mechanical schools and colleges, for the purpose of training men to various industrial tasks. The results were as surprising in the cases of these men as they were in the cases of women who, it had been assumed, were unsuited to work in certain industries.

The thing works in a way that I would never believe! In our training in the War Department we handled 140,000 men, trained them in 67 different trades . . . Seventy thousand of those men got over to France, and the composite opinion that came from the Commanding General was that these men were competent, able and resourceful. Now I don't mean to say that every man who was trained in two months was an all-hand mechanic, but he did know how to manipulate jobs on one or two tools and understood the principles which underlay the work.[2]

---

[1] *Council of National Defense, Report of Section on Industrial Training,* April 10, 1918, pp. 8–12.

[2] C. R. Dooley, Educational Director for War Department Committee on Education and Special Training.

ADJUSTING IMMIGRANT AND INDUSTRY

A short period of intensive training developed efficient mechanics not only out of unskilled laborers, but also out of men and women who had formerly been used to "soft" tasks only. It was found that:

General office help, such as clerks, bookkeepers, etc., can likewise be trained to do work requiring mechanical skill.

Many of our most skillful operatives are men and women well along in life; while the young worker is more vigorous, the older one is usually more careful and steady and not so given to change. Their continuous work on their jobs brings their average production up to that of the younger and more vigorous. Thus the older men, who are now occupied in non-mechanical trades and offices, can take the places of the younger men and this method will make them sufficiently skilled in mechanical trades to turn out the more precise munition work.[1]

APPLYING WAR TRAINING METHODS TO
IMMIGRANT WORKERS

The training methods developed by industrial plants during the war were concerned mainly with the great numbers of women who were being brought into the factories, and had to be adjusted to unaccustomed tasks. But the United States Training and Dilution Service, a bureau in the Department of Labor which was created to promote this training, pointed out:

In none of this training has the fact that women were the students any peculiar significance. No reason appears to militate against an equal success in training men. General realization that women have no industrial horizon has led employers to think of organizing training for the women who seek to enter the industrial field. Many employers have not yet recognized the need of men for exactly the same assistance to qualify for new industrial employments. Everything of the advantage training gives to women in industry is duplicated by those plants giving similar training to men. Since the war's abnormal demand for labor has ceased, it would seem that

---

[1] Council of National Defense, Report of Section on Industrial Training, April 10, 1918, pp. 8–12.

TRAINING THE IMMIGRANT WORKER

necessity for calling women from the homes to the factories may no longer exist. But the benefits which in this emergency have been found to inure in adequate training are sexless benefits.[1]

"If we can train women so successfully for industrial work as most of us have done in our factories," said an employment manager of a large industrial corporation in Buffalo, "then surely we can train men, even if they are foreigners." The speaker was unconscious of the humor in his remark, but he was trying to emphasize the need of training immigrant workers by the industries which employ them and the costliness of the neglect of this training.

"VESTIBULE SCHOOLS"

For the adult immigrant, male or female, the method known as "vestibule training" is particularly promising. This method

has had considerable success as a means of rapidly fitting inexperienced employees for factory work. The "Vestibule Schools" . . . take only from three to ten days to turn a school teacher, an office worker, a store salesman, a housemaid, a porter, a farmer, or anyone with normal alertness and strength, into a competent machine operator. With an additional three or four weeks of regular shop experience, these operatives have often far outdone self-taught workers in both quantity and quality of output.[2]

It is of just such inexperienced people that our immigrant labor supply has in the main been made up. For them a long period of apprenticeship to learn a skilled craft is out of the question. They need to become swiftly self-supporting, and American industry needs them mainly for specialized machine operations and other less skilled work for which this method of training is peculiarly adapted.

[1] *Training Bulletin No. 4*, p. 5.
[2] *The Way to Greater Production*, pp. 5-6.

111

ADJUSTING IMMIGRANT AND INDUSTRY

The method of vestibule training is described as follows by the United States Training and Dilution Service:

Vestibule schools are conducted directly by the employers. The students of the vestibule school have previously been hired by the operator of the school. They do not pay tuition. This is perhaps the distinguishing mark of the vestibule school. The school itself may be an imposing building, or a room set apart in a factory, or, as in many instances, a mere section of a factory building, or possibly only a few of the machines regularly employed in the productive operations of the factory set aside during a portion of the time for training use.[1]

The organization of a vestibule school is described by the works-manager of the Recording and Computing Machines Company, of Dayton, Ohio, as follows:

The training department is located in a well-lighted room, away from the factory, and placed therein were all of the different types of machines upon which training was necessary. There were also benches and fixtures necessary for the learning of assembling and inspection. I placed at the head of this school one of my most expert mechanics and operators, being particularly careful to select a man who was a gentleman and who could get along well with the women. I selected women for teachers, so that when the new girl employee would come into the training department her very first experience would be meeting with women teachers. Invariably this woman employee immediately made up her mind that if these women could do the work, so could she. The women teachers were selected with care, thought being given not only to their skill as operatives, but also to their capacity as teachers.

A large ladies' garment manufacturing company employing mainly immigrant men and women has set aside several rows of machines in one part of the shop and this is known as the "school." Every new employee, no matter how experienced or inexperienced he may be, is first put to work in this school. A competent instructor is in charge whose business it is to

---

[1] *Training Bulletin No. 4,* p. 3.

teach every newcomer the particular methods of doing the work that this house considers to be the best. Tailors and seamstresses come from foreign lands. They have to be re-trained to American methods and they must learn to operate power machines, to which they are usually unaccustomed. Garment workers with experience in other shops where the work is done differently might have trouble in adjusting themselves to the manufacturing methods of this house. These, too, are taught the new ways of doing their work in the school, and when they get to their places in the shops they are thoroughly familiar with their tasks. Both they and the foremen are sure that they are fitted for their work, because all new employees are carefully tested in the school and assigned to operations which the instructor found they could do best.

The details of instruction, encouragement, and careful supervision may be gathered from the practice of the Burroughs Adding Machine Company:

As the young women pass through the Employment Department they are placed in this Training School under the supervision of a competent instructor and are thoroughly grounded in the operation performed in that particular department. While in this school their characteristics are studied and as they acquire proficiency and their ability develops, they are assigned to more intricate and important work in the other departments throughout the factory. The selection for these assignments is determined by their physical condition and their mechanical development and aptitude. The instructor explains thoroughly the nature of the new employment, points out the advantages accruing to the employees because of their increased earning capacities; introduces them into the new department, points out in detail the various operations conducted therein, and painstakingly explains the scope of their new duties.

The following day they are started at their new operation, and by frequent observation, instruction, and encouragement improve to a degree where they become expert in the one operation. In this manner girls are gradually developed from the simpler burring and filing operations until we now employ them in departments performing varied operations.

ADJUSTING IMMIGRANT AND INDUSTRY

A school program worked out by a large tool manufacturing plant may serve to illustrate how essential the instruction given is to every beginner, and how thoughtless of the newcomers have been our industries when they neglected to give this instruction, but let them be "broken in" by making mistakes on the job:

First Day

8 A.M.–12 M. Our students when entering the school on Monday morning are addressed by the works manager. Following the address they are escorted by the instructor to the various assembling departments so as to give them the vital need of accuracy; then there is a general trip through the factory showing them the raw material and the progressive methods of manufacture.

1 P.M.–2 P.M. Following the dinner hour they return to their respective places and are taught the differences in iron, steel, and alloys. In connection with this course we have issued a pamphlet called "Supplemenary Instructions and Memorandums." This was made up as a memorandum of what they are taught each day.

2 P.M.–3 P.M. This period is taken up in defining the mechanical terms, such as turning, drilling, reaming, chamfer, etc.

3 P.M.–5 P.M. This period is taken up in teaching them fractions and decimals, which is most essential in our factory. In connection with fractions all are taught to read a scale graduated to 64ths and 100ths.

Second Day

7 A.M.–10 A.M. They are now taught to read blue prints. This we do by getting some finished part and a print of same in this manner letting them compare with print; also with explanation on blackboard.

10 A.M.–12 M. We have chartered a sufficient number of inside and outside calipers, scales, and gauges from our tool stock room, and use these in teaching how they are used and why.

1 P.M.–5 P.M. The remainder of the second day is spent in teaching the students how to use micrometers. We have also chartered a sufficient supply of these from our tool stock for this purpose.

Third Day

7 A.M.–12 M. The forenoon of the third day they are put throughout the factory with the inspectors and are made familiar with the use of gauges, scales, micrometers, etc.

TRAINING THE IMMIGRANT WORKER

1 P.M.–5 P.M. The afternoon of the third day they are taken to the several training school machines and a thorough descriptive explanation of each machine is given. The following days they are put on a machine and are taught how to operate this particular machine. In connection with this practical training they are taught how to sharpen drills, use files, etc.

To follow up the progress made by students after they are transferred to the factory, we use a follow-up sheet, to compare the average wage earned with that of the skilled men. We have also a form for interviewing students about twice a week to help them until they are able to take care of their work without aid. The learners have proved that they can, with from five to twelve days of intensive training, bring their ability as machine hands to a standard of accuracy controlled by a .0025 inch limit.

SOME RESULTS OF TRAINING

The Packard Motor Car Company in 1914 lost a good many of their expert varnish rubbers and they could not get skilled men to replace them. They tried to break in men directly on the operation but found too much work spoiled by the green hands. The experienced men did not have the time or the inclination to instruct properly those who were unskilled. This led to the establishment of a school for training varnish rubbers and was the beginning of the company's efforts to train unskilled workers. Says the vice president in charge of manufacturing: "The result of this experience was so highly successful that we carried it to all of the other branches of body manufacture, and a school for training unskilled help became a permanent part of our institution."

At the Norton Grinding Co., which was one of the first to try vestibule training, a man who was successfully operating a horizontal milling machine had less than two weeks before been a Turkish bath attendant. At this same plant the night foreman of toolmakers came up through the training room and developed into one of the best toolmakers in the plant. He had formerly worked in a paper bag factory and had had no machine shop experience whatever before entering the training room.

One factory that had trained its operatives was compelled by business conditions to lay off 2200 people. But their earnings had so increased under the training and they were so much better adapted to the work in this plant, that a single advertisement six weeks later brought more than 2100 of them back, "somewhat to the embarrassment, be it noted, of the companies with whom these workers had been less fortunately employed in the meantime. At another time it laid off indefinitely nine hundred, and some three months later easily secured the return of all but nine." [1]

These satisfactory results are especially important to the immigrant worker. They increase his skill and earnings and broaden his opportunities, and to the extent that he becomes a satisfactory worker he has successfully adjusted himself to his American job. A manager in charge of training in a clothing factory tells us, for example, that the second generation of immigrants makes the best operators on machines but the foreign born do best at hand work. Without the tests that a training department is able to give, many shops have broken in immigrants on machine operations with the resulting inefficiency, low wages, and discouragement, when a careful system of instruction in other plants has made of the same kind of people most efficient hand workers.

Many immigrants come over skilled in trades that have little or no value here. They cannot find work in the trades they learned abroad, and they are shut out of opportunities for maintaining their status and

---

[1] *National Association of Manufacturers, Report of Committee on Industrial Education*, May, 1918, p. 12.

standards as skilled mechanics. They naturally resent being compelled to work as common laborers when they have spent years in learning a trade and have the pride of skill. A training department is of special value in such cases. These workers are likely to be above the average in intelligence. Their hands and eyes are trained, and the vestibule school enables them in a short time to become proficient in new occupations where they can make advantageous use of their skill. Thus are opportunities opened up to immigrants and permanent additions made to the skilled labor force of our industries, where otherwise these men would feel that their status had been lowered by coming to America.

This is also true of educated immigrants with university training but no industrial experience. An industrial relations expert with many years of experience in industry tells us:

I recall once seeing a foreman trying to patronize a Bohemian who turned out to be a degree man of the University of Prague. I have heard Italians singing fluently opera strains, to hear which the average American foreman couldn't stand the entrance charge; and I can recall many instances when I ran up against university men in ditches, wheeling barrows, and pounding sand. In fact, the well-educated but non-English-speaking alien by his very lack of industrial experience is reduced by our rough and ready labor administration to the lowest levels of manual drudgery.

Such people may be quickly discovered in the training department and soon brought into responsible positions, where they will be of greatest value to themselves and to our industries.

It is not intended, of course, that immigrants on landing in this country should be sent to schools by employers to become skilled tradesmen. This is not their need and it is not the need of American industries. The purpose of the training in industries largely manned by foreign labor must be the same as that of the training work carried on during the war, to make advantageous use of the mass of labor that is available but unused to the industries in which it was needed. Said a maker of gear-cutting machinery: "We do not attempt to develop competent machine operators in the training school. We try only to give them the fundamentals required, so they will not find shop work and shop surroundings entirely strange. The training is continued in the departments to which they are sent, where they gradually learn to set up their machines, grind their tools, etc."

A good deal of the problem of training immigrants is not so much the teaching of skill as teaching familiarity with American industrial methods generally. Many operations are quite simple, so that little training for skill is needed; but many immigrants cannot endure immediate entrance into the rush and noise of our shops. Also many will not go straight to unfamiliar industries where labor is lacking and take the risk of failure. Instead, they will go to overcrowded immigrant trades. Proper distribution will be easier when immigrants know that special preparations are made for their reception and introduction through a training department. Such a department also makes the transition easier from European to American industrial methods. Just as many women were led to undertake work in factories by the knowledge that they would be taught before being put on the production floor, so many immigrant workers may be led away from the overcrowded fields of common labor to more skilled and better-paying jobs in the factories.

TEACHING ENGLISH FOR PRODUCTIVE EFFICIENCY

The new view of management, that it is necessary not only to select employees properly, but also to train and adjust each worker carefully to his job, gave a new purpose to the work of the so-called "Americanization Classes" mentioned in the last chapter. American industry had come to realize that immigrant workers needed a knowledge of the English language not only for their own benefit, but primarily for the sake of industry. Non-English-speaking workers hold back the productive efficiency of the establishments in which they were employed.

D. E. Sicher & Co., manufacturers of muslin garments, found that their non-English-speaking employees turned out less work than the average of the rest of the employees. The firm organized classes to teach these workers English in the factory. During the first year after the classes were organized their production increased from 10 to 40 per cent; and instead of four or five instructors to teach the girls the work, only two were needed. A textbook for industrial managers recently published opens with a citation of this experience, and points out its lesson to managers in the following words: [1]

Sheer illiteracy so hampered 10 per cent of the 500 women employees of a New York concern that they were actually unable to approach a normal standard of efficiency. This fact appeared when the management made a close study of production. It resulted in the establishment of a school, which the management undertook to maintain in coöperation with the city board of education. Fifty-five girls were enrolled to receive 45 minutes' instruction each morning on the company's time. A careful record was kept of the work and wages of these girls, and after four years it appeared that they had steadily increased their hourly wage rates. In addition, less supervision of their work was required than formerly.

There was nothing spectacular in this increase of efficiency, and nothing particularly novel in the methods used. It is cited as just a plain, workaday instance of one result that may commonly be expected from practical training methods in business.

---

[1] *The Way to Greater Production,* p. 1.

ADJUSTING IMMIGRANT AND INDUSTRY

Further,[1]

The non-English-speaking worker is recognized as a potential source of disturbance or waste, largely because it is difficult to convey to him the intentions of the management when there are just instructions regarding safety, health, and other conditions of employment.

The responsibility of American industry for teaching English to their foreign-born employees that modern managers feel is well expressed by Mr. Harold McCormick of the International Harvester Company.[2]

A working knowledge of English is as essential to the employee's service as to his citizenship. Without it he cannot be taught to protect himself adequately against exploitation of his ignorance on the outside. Lacking that knowledge, he cannot fully grasp either the industrial or the social opportunities of his adopted country and must be denied much of the opportunity it offers for self-development. The teaching of English to alien-born employees is, therefore, a primary and fundamental duty resting upon all American employers—a duty whose competent discharge is bound to bring full compensation to all the parties and elements in interest.

DEVELOPMENT OF ENGLISH INSTRUCTION IN FACTORIES

As long as learning the language was considered mainly a matter of the immigrant's own concern, the non-English-speaking worker was expected to attend evening classes conducted by public authorities, if he had ambitions that way, and few industrial establishments felt they had any responsibility in the matter. It was the Y. M. C. A. which began the work of urging employers to establish classes in English at the places of employment, but the idea appealed to comparatively few employers prior to 1916. It is significant that when Ida Tarbell published her book *New Ideals in*

---

[1] *Ibid.*, p. 24.
[2] *National Efficiency Quarterly*, Nov., 1918. Quoted by Daniel Bloomfield, *Labor Maintenance*, p. 147.

TRAINING THE IMMIGRANT WORKER

Business, in 1916, in which she surveyed all the most important experiments with scientific management of employees, she scarcely mentioned factory classes for immigrant workers. So few were the classes that in her chapter on "The Factory as a School" she found no occasion to mention them.

But since that time practically all of the larger industrial establishments which employ immigrant workers have established factory schools of some kind, and there are few even of the smaller plants which have not offered facilities to their non-English-speaking employees in one way or another to learn the English language.

The supervisors of immigrant education of the state of Massachusetts describe the spread of factory classes in these words: [1]

The idea of teaching immigrant employees in the place of their employment was first broached at the time of the inception of the Ameircanization movement in 1915. In reality, many such classes were in operation before this year, and in this venture the Y. M. C. A. may be looked upon as pioneers. Probably the first factory classes in the country were conducted at the plant of the Boston Woven Hose and Rubber Co., in Cambridge, by Harvard students working under the direction of the Cambridge Y. M. C. A. This was in 1906. (Parenthetically, it may be noted that this work, begun in this plant 16 years ago, has been kept up without interruption to the present day. This year, for the first time, the Y. M. C. A. and the industry have turned the classes over to the Cambridge public schools.)

During the decade following this first experiment, the idea took hold in other cities, usually under Y. M. C. A. auspices, though, in some cases industry itself conducted the work. There were classes at the Hartford Machine and Screw Factory in Hartford, Connecticut, in 1907. In 1910 classes were organized in the foundry of the Westinghouse Air Brake Company in Pittsburgh. In 1912, the Fall River Cotton Mills engaged in the enterprise under Y. M. C. A.

---

[1] John J. Mahoney and Charles M. Herlihy. "Industry and the Non-English-speaking Employee"—An unpublished report.

leadership. The Ford English School, started in 1913, and conducted by the company itself, attracted widespread notice for several years. A few years later, the Massachusetts Bureau of Immigration, under the energetic leadership of Mr. Bernard J. Rothwell, began a very vigorous movement to interest industrial executives in the factory-class idea. . . . This was in the midst of the war, when the country was keen for Democracy and uplift, and had not yet wearied of Drives. The Americanization movement had been launched in 1915, and by 1918, the factory-class idea had been "sold," *as an idea*. Factory classes sprang up on all sides, flourished for a brief period, and in a discouragingly large number of cases, died. It was the time when everyone relied on enthusiasm, and practically nothing else, to get this job done. Anybody could teach. Make everybody 100 per cent American, and do it overnight! Speaking English will win the War! And so on."

Early in 1919 a movement to standardize practice and improve teaching began. Several national and state conferences were held, and a consensus of opinion developed that industries must coöperate with public school authorities in conducting factory classes. A number of state laws were enacted to carry out this purpose, and in many communities the concrete methods of coöperation were worked out in conferences between school authorities and representatives of the industries. With this development classes became more stable and a systematic development of English instruction in industrial plants is now taking place.

THE METHODS OF THE FACTORY CLASSES

Special methods of teaching English to foreign-born factory workers were also first developed by the Y. M. C. A. Mr. Peter Roberts, who was a pioneer in this work for the Y. M. C. A., prepared a book on the subject and the Roberts method of teaching became popular in the factory classes. School authorities and others have also devoted themselves to the special problems of teaching English to adult immigrant wage earners; the use of the children's textbooks for this purpose is now a thing of the past.

The most common method in the factory schools is to begin with conversations. This is followed by simple compositions of a few sentences in oral and then in written form. The topics are chosen from the work and the habits and necessities of the shop. Safety rules, health measures, foremen's orders, instructions in manufacturing operations, and the general regulations of the shop are studied and drilled upon, until the pupil acquires not only a knowledge of the common terms in most frequent use in the shop, but a vocabulary for his ordinary conversations. Intermediate and advanced classes are also common, and these add American history and civics to the shop subjects for study.

Some employers tried to make attendance of non-English-speaking workers at the factory classes compulsory. This policy aroused resentment, and it was not found to be very successful. The character of the instruction, the general interest aroused in the classes by announcements, notes in pay envelopes, personal talks, and especially by the opportunities for advancement opened to those who learned the language, proved to be more effective means of securing attendance.

The meeting time of the factory classes is usually just before and just after the working day. Frequently half the hour comes from the company's time, for which the employee is paid, while the other half is on his own time. A good many firms have offered payment for the time spent in the classes as an inducement to attendance, but experience has shown that the most effective inducement has been increased earning capacity after attendance at the classes. Some of the largest companies have had classes in session continuously from 7 A.M. to 11 P.M., workers going to them as the shifts changed, and also a few being permitted to go from each department at various hours.

The Ford English School started with teachers who were all Ford employees volunteering their time. Many other employers attempted to select and pay their teachers, often hiring them from the Y. M. C. A., Y. W. C. A., or from local schools. But as we noted in the preceding chapter, this practice is giving way rapidly to a coöperative arrangement with public school authorities by which the latter supply teachers for the factory schools. We shall have occasion to discuss these arrangements further in a succeeding chapter.[1]

An excellent example of the work of these classes is that of Armour & Co. described by Mr. C. A. Livingston:[2]

> Any afternoon at the Chicago plant of our company—and the same thing, pretty much, goes on at some of our other plants—you can see an interesting gathering in one of the rooms of the employment department. Twenty or thirty workmen in their shirtsleeves, just come off duty on the day shift, are seated on benches; they are laboriously copying on paper such sentences as "This is a black coat" and "The coat has a collar." . . . These are foreign-born workers, learning the language of their adopted country after eight hours of hard work in the cattle-pens, the skinning rooms, and the canning plants of the stockyards. . . .
>
> The instructor comes to the plant daily from the Chicago Board of Education. . . . This teacher is a Slav by birth, an American by development; like many educated Slavs, he speaks an appalling number of languages. And because he has been through the mill himself, he has a sympathetic understanding for these men who, under greater handicaps, are starting on the long hard grind which he knows from personal experience. . . . You can't take a man from a bench and put him in charge of an English class, so Armour and Company has found out, no matter how well he may speak the language. . . .

[1] Chapter XIII, The Government's Responsibility.
[2] *The Way to Greater Production*, pp. 91–96.

TRAINING THE IMMIGRANT WORKER

The men come to class whenever they can; sometimes they make it three times a week, sometimes only once. But whenever they can be present, directly after work hours, they find the class and the teacher waiting for them. Learning does not progress here at such a rate of speed that these fellows cannot catch up if they find it necessary to miss a time or two; if it did it would defeat the purpose of the class—the greatest good to the greatest number. . . .

The complete course of study is 30 lessons. "There is little hope of teaching a man English if you can't get him well started in 30 simple lessons," explains the executive in charge of the work. . . .

Lessons in citizenship are taken up as soon as the men have a fair understanding of English. Citizenship is taught by what the instructor calls the dramatic method. Five lessons each represent a year of the naturalization period. The students go through naturalization proceedings, with witnesses, giving evidence of their residence in this country and attending to other details. One of their number acts as a judge. After they have been "naturalized" they become "citizens"—for classroom purposes.

The class is next organized into wards—a ward in each aisle in the schoolroom. Aldermen and a mayor are elected, and debates and conversations conducted which bring out the various duties and privileges of American citizenship.

"The plan gives everyone in the class something to do," explains their teacher. "We get them to working, to talking, making speeches. The rest is easy. They learn from one another."

In Brockton, Mass., a group of employers joined forces with the Y. M. C. A. in conducting factory classes. Here not only is instruction in the English language given, but this is combined with instruction in shop practice. Methods of performing operations are explained in pictures and the simple readers and textbooks used in the classes are concerned with stories and methods of the shop instead of the ordinary reading lessons. Factory rules and announcements are studied in the classes, and the common terms of direction for the manufacturing operations, of command, warning, praise, and criticism, constantly repeated and explained in the classroom, soon teach the immigrant the language of his work place.

CHAPTER VII

AMERICAN WORKING CONDITIONS FOR THE IMMIGRANT

"Father, does everybody in America live like this? Go to work early, come home late, eat and go to sleep? And the next day again work, eat and sleep? Will I have to do that too? Always?" A little Jewish girl[1] asked this question a short time after coming to this country. The experience of the wage-earning members of her family was on her mind.

This was sweat-shop experience, where the hours of labor were entirely unregulated and each worker remained in the shop as long as his strength endured to eke out a meager wage. It is not difficult to see that immigrants cannot become Americans when they work and live under such conditions; but this is not so promptly recognized in the establishments where hours of labor are standardized, even though the standard workday may be unreasonably long.

HOURS OF LABOR

Legislation was necessary to reduce the hours of labor for women, and most of our northern industrial states now limit these to eight and nine per day. But those employers who had the vision to study the problems of labor management and to establish separate departments for dealing with these problems, saw the importance of a proper working day and leisure for all their employees, and they quickly reduced the hours for men to the same standards.

---

[1] Rose Cohen, *Out of the Shadow*, p. 74.

AMERICAN WORKING CONDITIONS

Says an Ohio manufacturer: [1]

It is our aim always to be ahead of the law and the demands of labor. Our hours now are less than the maximum prescribed by the state law, and we intend shortly to reduce them still further. Why? Because we watch our people very closely and if we detect signs of over-exertion, we investigate the cause. Our organization is keyed up to the top pitch and we would not be able to maintain this level if we tolerated for a moment any condition that detracted from effectiveness. So, if we find our people can't hold the pace throughout a certain period, we shorten it to the point where they get along better.

At the present time the number of hours worked weekly in this plant is 50, as against a prescribed maximum of 54 for women. We contemplate lowering the hours to 48.

How such employers are led to reduce the hours of labor may be illustrated by the experience of the Fayette R. Plumb Company of Philadelphia:

We became thoroughly convinced during the war from the results given to us by Great Britain that there was such a thing as fatigue and we finally considered reducing our working hours to see if we could do something to eliminate absenteeism and to decrease our labor turnover. Here again we did not approach it with an attitude of simply posting a notice, but we sold the idea to our workmen. We told them that we did believe there was such a thing as fatigue and that if they worked shorter hours and had a greater rest period they could do as much work in a short time as they did in the longer time. At that time we were working $57\frac{1}{2}$ hours a week and we cut our working time to $52\frac{1}{2}$ hours a week. The response was immediate. Results achieved were so satisfactory that we felt we had not gone far enough and we eventually cut our working time to $47\frac{1}{2}$ hours a week.

Occasionally in a large plant long hours are worked without the knowledge of those who direct the policy, but when the management has the means of discovering these conditions, it promptly remedies them; as in

---

[1] *Working Conditions, Wages and Profits*, A. W. Shaw Co., pp. 14–15.

the case of the International Harvester Company, cited by Mr. Harold McCormick:

> One example of what our employee representation plan has done to improve conditions of the workingmen is this: We never knew that we had a body of men—about 100 in number, who worked for us seven days a week, twelve and one half hours a day. We didn't know it. We got it through the employee representatives . . . one of them kicked and it was stopped.

Under the leadership of the United States Steel Corporation, which has lagged behind the country in employment management work, the steel industry still maintains the twelve-hour day[1] for a large portion of its employees; and one of the main demands of the steel strike of 1920 was the abolition of this long working day. It was the foreign born who were the strikers, as the corporation itself pointed out; and the contrast between its policy and that of the International Harvester Company, in handling the problem of hours of labor, strikingly illustrates how the employer may be a help or a hindrance in the adjustment of the immigrant to American industrial life.

WAGES

"My people do not live in America, they live underneath America," said a Ruthenian priest in 1907. "A laborer cannot afford to live in America."[2] This was a reflection of the policy of treating immigrant labor as an inferior and subordinated industrial class, which is to be content with lower wages and lower living standards than the rest of America. Just before we entered the war a manager of a group of foundries located in different states told us he employed mostly foreign-born laborers who received $15 a week. When

---

[1] In 1923 the U. S. Steel Corporation changed to an eight-hour basis.
[2] Emily G. Balch, "A Shepherd of Immigrants," *Charities*, vol. XIII, p. 195.

asked if they could live and support families on that amount, he answered: "You don't understand these people. They don't need any more; they save money, and don't expect any more."

In one of his books describing immigrant life in America, Abraham Cahan, Editor of the Jewish *Daily Forward*, tells of an immigrant who, as he landed in New York, was met by a prosperous-looking gentleman who addressed him in his native tongue and offered him employment at tailoring. Later he learned that the man who accosted him was a cloak contractor and his presence in the neighborhood was anything but a matter of chance. He came there often, in fact, his purpose being to angle for cheap labor among newly arrived immigrants. Angling for cheap labor in this fashion has been very largely abolished by government regulation, but similar means of recruiting labor from among newly arrived immigrants are available in the want columns of foreign-language newspapers, in private labor agencies, and in *padroni* or gang leaders of various nationalities.

We saw in a previous chapter the difficulties into which immigrants were led by attempts to get new supplies of workers at cheaper rates. These trying experiences are spared the newcomers by those establishments which have labor departments charged with administering definite wage policies. In the first place, their study of wage questions has shown convincingly that the inexperience and the cost of breaking in great numbers of new employees make the "cheap" labor really more expensive. Every attempt is made, therefore, to hold the older employees instead of getting new ones, even if these may be secured at lower rates. Secondly, in attempting to make workers and their jobs fit properly, employment managers have found it necessary to develop careful systems of job specifications; and these specifications not only describe the ability and the qualities necessary for the worker on each job to have, but they also specify the value of the job in earnings commensurate with the effort and skill involved, in comparison with every other kind of work that is done in the plant.

The contrast between the old methods of employing immigrants at lower wages than the native born and the new method of paying the price that each job is worth in comparison with all others, regardless of nationality or need of the worker, may be illustrated by two examples: In the first plant,[1]

As vacancies occurred or new jobs were created the general manager adopted what he considered the wise means of getting "cheap labor," and picked men from the town's newly acquired immigrant population. This policy speedily had two results: it virtually emptied the plant of the old experienced working force; and it introduced new problems with which the manager was unfitted to grapple. There were, in the end, strikes, which the manager fought through, as he saw other employers in a like plight fighting them. . . ."

In the second plant, a large corporation manufacturing paper products, the employment manager tells us:

I have found in our industry it is entirely possible to classify all of our jobs, to determine the number of workers engaged in each job, the number necessary to maintain each job's productive strength during the year, and that it was possible to determine whether the labor needed for the different jobs should be obtained by transferring from a job within the plant or obtained by going outside and engaging new workers.

The Employment Department and the Operating Department heads of our Company all sat in a conference and analyzed the job specifications and determined what seemed to be a fair remuneration for each of the jobs, considering the steadiness of employment, skill required, difficulties of the job, the pleasant features, the outlet of the job to more remunerative work, and all the things that ought to be considered in appraising jobs equitably.

---

[1] *The Management and the Worker*, cited above, p. 4.

AMERICAN WORKING CONDITIONS

The employment managers' idea is not to bargain for the cheapest man, but to get the best man for the work and pay according to production. This policy assures to the immigrant wage earner the same rate of pay that the native-born worker gets for the same work; and puts into practice the suggestion that if we want immigrant workers to become Americans they should be treated as Americans.

In fixing the wage policy for the whole labor force, living costs and the possibility of saving are carefully considered. Says the Director of Employment of the American Rolling Mill Company, of Middletown, Ohio:

Wages have naturally been the subject of more than one discussion at the meetings of the management with Advisory Committees composed of representatives of the employees. Our men know that their wages increased 125 per cent while the cost of living index went up 102 per cent. We have studied and discussed living costs. Our study of the cost of living in Middletown was made under the direction and with the help of a group of workers who were interested in that subject.

To let wages lag behind increasing living costs is considered bad labor policy, and some companies developed cost of living bonuses, which increased or dropped with the movement of the index of prices.

At the White Motor Co. in Cleveland the wage policy was described by its vice president and factory manager as follows:

The highest possible wage on a straight time basis without bonuses, premiums, or profit sharing is paid employees. The factors instrumental in establishing the wage-scale are cost of living and amount of production. . . .

Second in importance to wages paid, in the mind of the average workman are working hours. These must also be regulated by the relation of earnings to living cost, and by production, holding the margin of safety between too long hours, which result in inefficiency, and underproduction, which endangers the future operation of the

131

plant. It is the belief of the management that a community derives the highest benefit, social and economic, from maximum production paid for at a maximum safe wage rate, with hours regulated accordingly to afford an opportunity for general development of the man outside the factory."

That such a policy when applied without discrimination to native-born and immigrant employees will build a united working force may well be imagined. But the fact that it also pays the employer in the concrete terms of dollars and cents to pursue such a policy is most significant. For it insures for the future a continuation of the widespread development of scientific labor policies that recent years have witnessed.

According to the manager of the White Motor Co. in the City of Cleveland, where his factory is located, most of the industrial plants had an average labor turnover of about 300 per cent. The White Company's percentage was only 63, and in 1919 it was only 25 per cent. That meant that few workers were leaving and few had to be discharged. It meant, also, that the per man production steadily increased, so that between 1914 and 1919 labor cost went up only 7 per cent, while wages increased 110 per cent. In the words of the manager:

The efficiency of our plant, its size, and the size of our working force, increased steadily through the war period, crossed the armistice without a bump, and went right on increasing. We have no labor problem in the ordinary sense of the term.

Most plants experimenting with wage policies, however, do not pay on a time work basis, as does this company. Piece rates and bonus and premium systems of various kinds are tried, but wherever the intent is not to get the "cheapest" labor but to pay what the work is worth as nearly as that can be measured, the result is the same.

AMERICAN WORKING CONDITIONS

Ida Tarbell, describing the wage payment methods of the Clothcroft Shop says:[1]

Mr. Feiss handles a difficult labor group. Of the 828 persons in the shop in 1914 one half were foreign born. They come as a rule without experience, often speaking no English. They have all to learn. The theory of the shop is that they are worth teaching; and, moreover, that the more they know, the healthier and happier they are, the better "pants" they will make; also the better "pants" they make the better citizens they will be!

Starting with the basic wage in Cleveland in the industry . . . in 6 years—June, 1910 to June, 1916, the hourly wages in the shop have increased 69 per cent, the weekly 49 per cent.

During the same period production increased almost 60 per cent, thus showing a decrease in costs.

SAFETY, SANITATION, AND OTHER PHYSICAL CONDITIONS

More important even than wages and hours of labor is the adjustment of the immigrant to the physical conditions of his work place. Accidents in the course of employment are usually higher among non-English-speaking immigrants than among all other employees.[2]

Obviously of all inexperienced men the one suffering the most handicap is the one who is both new to his task and also is unable to communicate freely with the man to whom he is responsible. Study of this condition shows that the accident rates of such workers are higher than of those familiar with the language. That this is not due to some racial peculiarity is indicated by the fact that the English-speaking foreign born have rates scarcely higher than the American born.

In another study made by the United States Bureau of Labor Statistics it was found that accidents in the machine building industry showed both a higher

---

[1] *New Ideals in Business*, Macmillan Co., pp. 214–216.
[2] United States Bureau of Labor Statistics, *The Safety Movement in the Iron and Steel Industry*, pp. 40–41.

frequency and severity rate among the foreign-born employees than among the native-born, as follows:

TABLE VI

ACCIDENT RATES AMONG FOREIGN-BORN AND NATIVE-BORN EMPLOYEES

ACCIDENTS	NUMBER OF ACCIDENTS PER 1000 EMPLOYEES		DAYS LOST PER 1000 EMPLOYEES	
	Native Born	Foreign Born	Native Born	Foreign Born
Death................	0.5	0.9	2.9[1]	5.3[1]
Permanent Disability...	1.6	4.6	0.9	3.4
Temporary Disability...	58.5	96.3	0.5	0.9

The foreign born are not entirely non-English-speaking, but the constant excess of the accident rates of the foreign born, as shown in the table, may clearly be attributed to causes similar to those affecting the accident rates of the non-English-speaking workers in the steel industry, referred to above. This conclusion is strengthened by the accident experience of a group of Polish workers which it was possible to isolate from the other foreign born. In this Polish group, consisting of 4798 300-day workers, is found the greatest proportion of non-English speakers and also the greatest proportion of those engaged in common labor. The accident frequency rate of this group was 115 cases per 1,000 workers and the severity rate 13.5 days lost per worker. These are distinctly higher than the rates for the foreign born as a whole (101.8 and 9.6 days).

The steel industry and machine building are the only industries in the country for which we have careful studies of this problem over a period of years. Both studies prove that the immigrant employee who does not know English is injured oftener and more seriously than the English-speaking employee.

Fortunately, however, in this respect of the adjustment of the immigrant to the physical conditions of

---

[1] Days lost before death.

his employment, more progress has been made than in any of the other matters relating to the industrial management of the worker. It was the Workmen's Compensation laws, which all but about half a dozen states have now enacted, that stimulated the widespread development of the "Safety First" movement in industry by transferring the burden of accident cost from the worker to the industry. As state after state enacted these laws the membership in the National Safety Council, an organization of industrial managers to further the prevention of accidents, also grew, and the reduction of accident rates has been the universal experience of employers who have undertaken this safety work.

But the reduction of accidents is not the only contribution to immigrant adjustment that the safety movement is making. It has been one of the most effective causes of spreading English teaching through industrial plants. Employers are constantly giving the frequency of accidents among the non-English-speaking employees as the reason for their support of factory English classes, and most of those who have had such classes say they are convinced that the factory classes reduce accidents, even though statistical data may be lacking to prove this.[1]

A western employer also stresses the importance of instructing foreigners in English. "In our concern," he says, "34 per cent of the workmen are foreigners; and of this 34 per cent there are many high-grade workers, men who are rapidly becoming good Americans. These workers, however, were furnishing us 80 per cent of our mishaps. That was because of their inability to comprehend safety orders. We attacked this by organizing a fellowship club with over 1000 members. At the meetings the men all get together and the aliens quickly learn English. Our percentage of accidents among foreign workers is steadily decreasing and we count on an even better showing in the future."

---

[1] *The Way to Greater Production*, p.25.

ADJUSTING IMMIGRANT AND INDUSTRY

Mr. C. W. Price, formerly Safety Director of the Industrial Commission of Wisconsin and General Manager of the National Safety Council thus summarizes the results of the safety movement:

One outstanding fact is that we have absolutely demonstrated that we can eliminate three fourths of all accidental deaths and serious injuries in industry.

The second most significant fact is that accident prevention has offered the first legitimate common ground on which employer and employee can meet with mutual interest and understanding, and with profit to both.

According to the experience of hundreds of industrial plants in which accidents have been reduced in amounts varying from 50 to 75 per cent, it has been found that not more than one third of what was accomplished was made possible by any mechanical guard or mechanical equipment.

According to this leader of the safety experts of the country, it was educational work among the workers and the foremen in the plants as well as organization of numerous safety committees in the plants, that was responsible for two thirds of the reduction in accidents. This bringing together of employees with foremen and managers, to investigate and discuss accidents that had occurred and to devise means for preventing repetition of such accidents, also brought management and men together on common ground and led to closer contacts. With the immigrant so largely concerned in the matter of accidents it is obvious that the safety educational work, the service and experience on committees with American fellow workers, and the close contacts with management, have offered a means of fusing native and foreign born in industry, than which there could be hardly anything more effective.

"Give a workman some active part in safety work, some recognition, some responsibility," says Mr. Price, "and you will secure his interest. This has been the experience of all companies which have properly organized workmen's inspection committees." Committees usually consist of from three to five workmen and their membership is changed frequently, so that all employees may get the educational advantages of investigating accidents as they occur, fixing responsibility, and devising preventive measures. Thus the immigrant worker is first taught English to lessen his liability to injury, and then is brought into the fold of the plant-wide safety organization by the common tasks of accident prevention.

The safety movement led quickly to interest in other physical conditions in the plants. Sanitation, ventilation, temperatures, factory lighting, fatigue, and occupational diseases all become subjects of study, and a further impetus to this movement was given by the new idea of management, which emphasizes that conditions must be right in the factory in order to get the right results from employees.

Twenty thousand dollars a year is spent in one plant for achieving perfection of cleanliness in shop conditions; and the cleaning is of the sort for which some other companies incur no expense, letting each worker take care of his own area as best he can. When other companies have said that this plant is so well off it can afford such expenditure, the man who has been superintendent for thirty years has replied: "We are well off, just because we have done this kind of thing." The plant represents a branch of the cotton textile industry wherein the perfect condition of machinery is of high importance. Spoiled or interrupted work is prevented by keeping close watch of machines at all times to see that no dust or waste collects in them. The workers are expected to show the kind of intelligence that prevents trouble. The superintendent believes that order and cleanliness not only keep up the standard in the workers' production, but that an effect is produced which they carry home into their manner of living. He points to this as the company's best service to the immigrant. His employees are French Canadians, Portuguese, and Poles.

A New York employer finds that by providing proper atmospheric conditions employees increased their output 10 per cent. Another, studying losses due to colds contracted by employees from poor ventilation, figured the loss at $24 a cold. And a Baltimore employer discovered that defects in the heating and ventilating system of an otherwise model factory building caused $27\frac{1}{2}$ per cent of the working force to suffer illness during two successive winters. But when the defects were discovered and corrected, the percentage of illness dropped to 7.[1]

Examples like these are published and circulated among industrial managers through the management and engineering magazines, and thus the work of improving working conditions for immigrant and native worker alike goes on.

MEDICAL SERVICE

A common responsibility assumed by the new industrial management is the furnishing of medical service to employees. This has been made the subject of special study in the volume of these studies entitled *Immigrant Health and the Community*, and we mention it here only to note that through this service many employers have been able to teach foreign-born employees the health habits they must acquire if they are to survive in an industrial environment; as well as the habits they must discard, which may have been reasonable enough in the agricultural villages of Europe, but are unsuited and dangerous here. The value of medical

---

[1] *Working Conditions, Wages and Profits*, pp. 2-3.

service to the foreign born is not so much in the furnishing of the service by the employer, but rather in the method of its administration. One company finds that its South Italians will not accept its offer of medical aid, because as a people they "fear strange doctors"; but another company dealing with this nationality says that "the Italians fairly rush the medical service," and that they try to get their whole family doctored by dramatically describing the symptoms and pains of an ill one at home, pretending that they are themselves the poor sufferer.

The effect of this kind of service is well illustrated by a story told by Ida Tarbell:[1]

> They tell a story of a Polish miner, at Ishpeming, Michigan, who was obliged to spend some weeks in the company's hospital. His home had been the despair of the company's nurse, so dirty and crowded it was. But when the man returned from the hospital the place was immediately transformed. "Clean and nice all the time, now," he told the nurse when she exclaimed at the change. "Clean and nice like the hospital, feel good."

HOME VISITING

The home visiting which companies are promoting through nurses, service workers, housing supervisors, and other representatives of the employment department, often becomes a family matter, although the occasion of the visit is usually absence of an employee from work. In cities such visiting is done sometimes to make a contact with the non-English-speaking parents of young girl employees, who may not even know the company's name, much less its location. Some employers, notably the Clothcraft Shops in Cleveland which have for a number of years had the custom of having the homes of all new girls visited, are convinced that the attempt to reach the parents of the

---

[1] *New Ideals in Business*, Macmillan Co., p. 27.

foreign born is rewarded with greater stability and regularity on the employees' part. In suburban places and in the smaller towns, where the factory or mill may be a prominent feature of the town, and employers and employed come close together in their living as well as their working lives, the most energetic and inclusive visiting seems to be done. The city employer does not feel the urge to inquire into and improve what he does not see; while the country employer, who cannot escape seeing, is likely to be driven to improvement for his own peace of mind, and because of the obviousness of the connection between living standards and workmanship.

LUNCH ROOMS

The attitude of foreign-born workers toward their work, as well as toward the company, has been appreciably improved through the medium of the lunch room. A woman service worker in a clothing plant spoke, in illustration, of a Polish woman who gets up in the morning, and hurriedly dresses her children and gets her family fed. Perhaps she only takes time for a drink of coffee herself, and hastily throws some food together for her luncheon. On she goes to the factory, where she sews busily at her work all morning. At the noon signal she thrusts across the back of her chair the coat she has been working on, opens up her news-paper-wrapped lunch and eats it quickly and silently, perhaps thinking about things that worry her or not thinking at all. She is almost glad when the signal for power comes, when she grabs the coat and takes up her work again; and so it goes on until the end of the day. But, with the coming of the lunch room, with food planned for hot days or for cold days, and the mental as well as physical interruption, all is changed. She leaves her work place for a time, and sits at a table with space enough for comfort. And besides having food she likes for a trifling expense, she may even be drawn into talking and laughing with others at the table. The psychology of it is that she goes back to her work new, and she may feel comradeship in place of isolation.

Lunch rooms in industrial plants of any size may now be said to be the rule rather than the exception. In these, employment managers and service workers, who are paying attention to the problems of their foreign-born employees, find many opportunities of working the reluctant immigrant into the spirit of their native-born and Americanized workers.

While visiting a lunch room in a Chicago plant employing about 1000 people, we noticed an immigrant in an obscure corner eating with his back to the room, so no one could see the lunch he had brought with him. He was setting himself apart, conscious of the strangeness of his food and the manner of his eating. Unfortunately some employers have assumed that this must be a permanent condition, and either they provide no lunching facilities whatever for their foreign-born labor, or they do not encourage immigrants to patronize the facilities provided for American employees. This is often caused by the resentment which native-born Americans feel, or claim to feel, if the foreign-born use the restaurant or cafeteria. But many employers have found the means of breaking down this division among their employees. Their service workers encourage the foreign born to sit at tables with other workers, and eat and talk with them. Thus, gradually, the immigrants are led to acquire a taste for American food and a consciousness that essentially they are no different from the others.

From the point of view of efficient management employer-conducted lunch rooms . . . have proved

not only a convenience to workers but also a direct
means of safeguarding their health, and thus increasing their productivity. But for the immigrant wage
earner it has a larger usefulness in bringing him into a
commonness of kind with his fellow workers.

The lunch room has been further useful as a means
of demonstrating the idea of democracy. The plant
which is chosen to illustrate this is living out its democracy in other ways. If this were not so, it would
not, probably, accomplish much through the lunch
room. Here the cafeteria serves, in the same room at
the same time, all persons connected with the company in any capacity, whether administrative or mechanical. The dining room in this case is a kind of
many-windowed corridor connecting two factory buildings. It is like the sun parlor on an ocean recreation
pier; while it is filled with light, it seems to be so
shaded as to give the smiling, pleasing buoyancy of
sunshine, without its harshness or glare. To the visitor
it seemed that the free expansive qualities of air and
sunshine had something to do with the ability of people
of many kinds, seemingly, to use this room in comfort,
together. A smoking room for men adjoined one end; a
girls' rest room with player piano flanked one side,
actively enjoyed by girls of evident foreign birth.

RECREATION

The Delaware Americanization Committee tells of the
change wrought in a group of laborers by a little organized recreation, and the effect of the change in
their attitude toward their place of enjoyment: [1]

On Friday nights, when there was no school, the Committee held
open house in the shanty. Never were dominoes and parchesi and
lotto played with such untiring zest. Sometimes there was music,

---

[1] *Report of Delaware Americanization Committee*, 1920–21, p. 25.

and always at ten o'clock one of the tables was laid with white napkins, cocoa was served in china cups from the big pot on the stove and a plate of buns was handed around with perfect dignity by Felix, Chairman of the Social Committee. ("It's even nicer than a party," says Felix, "to sit eating together like family.") And these boys, who reveled in the daintiness of that repast and washed the dishes between times with such scrupulous care, were the same "hunkies" who put up with almost anything in their mess house because they and everybody else took it for granted that it was the best that could be had.

It is interesting to observe that, in making possible the creation of that little home center for its foreign laborers, the Worth Company has unconsciously guarded its future against the high rate of "turnover" for which the employers of the community held their alien labor chiefly to blame during the war. That little group of homesick young chaps is scattered now. Some have returned to Spain or Italy, others have gone to seek work in the coal fields of Pennsylvania; but they all said the same thing when they went: "When the Worth Company has work again we will come back *quick* to Our Shanty."

At "Fashion Park," a men's clothing factory in Rochester, whose employees are mainly Italians, the Fashion Park Band gives expression to the musical talent of some of its workers, and unites all the workers in appreciation of its concerts. It is the pride of the plant and also of the Italian community of Rochester, for it gives many performances for the public generally. Through enjoyment of efforts of this kind and recognition of talents, the native born and workers of other nationalities are brought into close sympathy with the Italians, and a basis for closer contacts is made. The labor department of this company also organizes baseball nines among its employees, and teams in other athletic games, in which the foreign born are encouraged to take part; and interest is stimulated by games arranged with teams from other plants in the city.

The immigrant nationalities in our industries do not excel in outdoor sports and it is difficult to enlist their participation. But when they are encouraged by invitations, their interest in trying to learn the rules of the game in baseball and football is as exciting as that of young boys. On the other hand, American workers have been found to evince great interest in the folk dances, songs, and pageants, which the immigrants delight in exhibiting, with the slightest encouragement from intelligent service workers.

The reputation of the foreign-born women employees for not being "good mixers" breaks down, in a Connecticut plant, in connection with "sings." The song periods find general interest and enthusiasm in this plant where Italians, Irish, English, Russians, Lithuanians, Poles, Albanians, French, Portuguese, and Spanish are represented among the foreign-born employees; but the Italians and the French are the most appreciative. The periods are of further benefit, the company finds, in helping the women to master the English language, and in assisting them in the class work which the educational department conducts.

PLANT PERIODICALS

Very many employers have in recent years undertaken the publication of plant papers or house organs. The purpose of these periodicals is to add to that common feeling among the employees which makes for morale and loyalty to the organization of which they are a part They print news and the gossip of all the departments, births, deaths, marriages, and other "personals," which serve to emphasize the common interests of all the people in the plant. They are much like small town newspapers in this respect, and serve much the same purpose of uniting the community.

For those foreign-born employees who can read English, however little, the plant paper offers a most excellent method of developing unity of mind with their native-born fellow workers. They are interested in the personals, the biographies, and the news of the plant, and this interest gives a foundation to build on.

A number of these plant papers have tried the experiment of printing sections in foreign languages but most of them have avoided it upon the theory that it would encourage the immigrant in his use of his native language. While there may be some danger in this direction, the greater danger is that the immigrant will have nothing to bind him to the working community of which he is a part. By reading about his American place of employment and its views and its problems, even though he reads in a foreign tongue, he is gradually acquiring an interest in things American and learning to understand his fellow workers. This in itself is a stimulus to learn English, so that he may read the rest of the paper and understand better what is going on. Some plant papers have been used as texts for English lessons, with translations of articles also published. This is an excellent means of teaching English to foreign born and at the same time making them feel at one with the rest of the employees.

We have mentioned the use made of the plant paper to urge American workers to give greater consideration to the new employee, especially the immigrant, but in general the possibilities of these periodicals in reaching the foreign-born employees have still to be worked out.

WELFARE SERVICES

It is interesting to walk through a plant with a woman service worker who is really the friend of her group of employees, and to whom the company gives some leeway to make her recommendations effective. In the course of such a walk, for example, an American girl asked for transfer to a department in which she had formerly worked and where she thought she had been better adjusted; two colored women asked advice in health matters; a group of Polish girls secured the service worker's promise to attend the wedding that night of one of their group; a beach party with other Polish girls was arranged; and a Swedish foreman told of his anxiety about one of the women in his department who had had an operation, and asked to have someone from the company go to see her.

Two foreign-born girls were soldering cans. They were obviously very uncomfortable from the flame before them as well as the hot weather; but this did not prevent their looking up and smiling in friendly fashion. The service worker pointed out that the flame is two thirds enclosed now, whereas it formerly was entirely open. She brought about this improvement, and is studying ways to make the situation still better. Her daily walks through the plants, she said, take note of these things; and changes are coming, though slowly.

In the lunch room in another plant the woman who is placed in general charge of women employees fell into friendly conversation with an Austrian girl near her at the table. In the course of their conversation it came out that on the following Saturday the girl was going to a neighboring town, to get another "job." After a little questioning it was clear that she liked the company, was happy in living at the company boarding-house, and was satisfied with the wages which, she agreed, she might not receive in the new place. The thing she did not like was working in Plant No. 4 which is always warm and, during the past two days of unusual summer heat, had been seemingly unbearable. The service worker persuaded her to postpone the decision about going until the question of transfer could be taken up with the proper persons;

for she knew that this girl was one of the fastest workers in her branch of mill work, and the company could not afford to let her go. This seemed a clear demonstration of the way in which the welfare worker's functions straighten out difficulties that might otherwise miss adjustment because of not being known. The girl would more readily have left the company than she would have taken any steps in the prescribed way— to complain to foreman or employment manager. She knew probably that both these persons could be appealed to, the service worker said, but it was like a foreign-born girl to think it was easier to "just leave."

Industrial companies, also, are waking to the application of this idea—foreign-language assistants in connection with the work for the foreign-born women employees—whether such work be designated personnel, employment, service, welfare, or other. Two interesting experiments of this kind were started within the last two years in stockyards plants of Chicago: These plants employ (in 1919) respectively 2000 and 1000 women, the majority of whom were born in Slavic countries. In each instance a young Bohemian woman of college education and social training holds a responsible position which ties her work into the plant employment department, and all the branches of service and production departments which relate to the women. A day spent in the plant with one of these workers seemed to offer many proofs of her inherent understanding of the employees for whom she works. That the promoters of the plan consider it advisable is suggested by the fact that she was sent recently to organize similar work for women in the company's western plants.

"Working conditions affect profits," the personnel managers say.[1]

---

[1] *Working Conditions, Wages and Profits*, pp.1-2.

ADJUSTING IMMIGRANT AND INDUSTRY

Provisions for safety are mere common sense. Decent housing is essential if workers are to be had in sufficient numbers and of the right caliber. "Welfare Work" of certain kinds and managed in the right spirit may also be conducive to profits. The worker's health must be attended to, or dollars slip into the "loss" column. Fatigue, if it becomes overfatigue, is dangerous to quality and quantity of work. . . . If the right measures are undertaken, and in the right way, the inevitable result is better business.

In this profitableness of improved working conditions we have assurance of the permanence and extension of the conditions and measures here considered; and the importance of providing American conditions of employment can not be overestimated, if we really wish to absorb the immigrant wage earner into the common life of America.

CHAPTER VIII

A VOICE IN DETERMINING WORKING CONDITIONS

OF all the development which modern industrial management has brought about in American industry, perhaps the most promising for fusing immigrant and native-born workers in a common citizenship is the attempt to give employees a voice in labor management by means of elected representatives. Works councils, shop committees, factory senates and houses of representatives, industrial coöperative plans, and other forms of employee representation have become quite familiar institutions in American industries within the last five years. Through these organizations, whatever the name given to them, many employers have attempted to apply the principle that government derives its just powers from the consent of the governed to the rules and regulations of the shop. The orders and discipline of the employer, it has come to be recognized, are for the wage earner laws of at least equal importance with the ordinances of the city council or the enactments of state legislatures. The term "Industrial Democracy" which has for years been common in the propaganda of trade unionists, socialists, and social reformers, has now become popular among employers and managers as a name for these plans of employee representation.

Under various names representation plans have been inaugurated in very many plants throughout the country. The National Industrial Conference Board reported in 1920 that they had found between 200 and 300 establishments in which employee representation

149

plans were in operation, covering over 500,000 workers. Since that time many more have been organized, notably by the packing industries of Chicago and the large milk companies of New York. In February, 1922, the National Industrial Conference Board found more than 700 such organizations. The companies which have these plans are usually those which do not recognize trade unions. Mostly, they are the large corporations employing great numbers of unskilled and semiskilled workers, among whom the foreign born predominate.

AMERICANIZING THE MANAGEMENT

Mr. Paul W. Litchfield, vice president and factory manager of the Goodyear Tire and Rubber Co., who has inaugurated what he calls an "Industrial Republic" in his plant in Akron, Ohio, conceives that "the relations between a political government and the people living under that government are very similar to the relations between the management of an industry and the people working in that industry. In other words: management and government are synonymous terms, one being usually applied to the political and the other to the industrial world." He says further:

It is our problem, as we see it, to Americanize industrial management. We have all heard about Americanization, and many of us think that it applies only to the individual, but when you Americanize the individual and he makes an analysis of his form of government in industry, and finds that it is not Americanized also, you are going to have more trouble than when you started, unless it is Americanized. Management must get confidence, good will, interest, and incentive from its workmen, and to do that they must believe not only in the efficiency of the management but they must also believe equally in the justice in which that management will function for the benefit of all. Management in that sense is the same as government. In other words, it is a selected body to govern in the interests of all, keeping in mind that it should govern in the interests of the majority.

A VOICE IN WORKING CONDITIONS

American workers who have been reared in an atmosphere of representative government, and immigrant wage earners who have been exhorted to love and revere such institutions, naturally contrast this democracy in political government with the monarchy in industrial government, and management finds its orders reluctantly obeyed or openly violated and its power contested in strikes. It was this problem which led the Colorado Fuel and Iron Co. in 1914 to organize its employees into what trade unionists call a "Company Union," and stimulated the copying and adaptation of the plan by numerous other companies since that time.

The trade unions have charged that these plans are not put forth by employers in a sincere effort to give their workers real representation, but primarily to destroy independent labor organizations. Many employers frankly admit that they have organized works councils to avoid or to get rid of what they call "outside" labor organizations; but they say that the legitimate ends of trade unions can be better accomplished by a plant organization.

While most of the constitutions of the representation plans provide that there shall be no discrimination as between union and non-union workers, the companies rarely recognize as the proper representative of their employees the union to which any of them may belong. The idea of these corporations is to avoid the necessity of dealing with a union, and to provide the ordinary methods of collective negotiations and the benefits in adjusting complaints and grievances on which trade unions insist.

Whether the plans are in opposition to trade unionism or not, it is plain that they provide a large measure of collective dealing between elected representatives of employees and the management, and they do give the wage earners some voice in determining conditions of employment and rules and regulations of the shop. Whether the method will be as effective in this respect as collective bargaining with trade unions, the future will determine. But for the purposes of joining immigrant and native worker in a common organization, for participating together in joint meetings, conferences, and dealings with the employer, employee representation plans do offer a fruitful field. And where this is being done in plants employing foreign-born workers, practical schools for citizenship are being established in industry; and they promise to do for immigrant wage earners what school governments have aimed to do for school children in familiarizing them with the institutions of the country.

REASONS FOR EMPLOYEE REPRESENTATION

Quite significant from the point of view of naturalizing foreign-born wage earners as citizens with equal rights in American industry, instead of treating them as a lower class who will work under conditions which Americans will not accept, are the reasons given by employers for affording representation to all their employees.

It was the vice president and factory manager of the Goodyear Tire and Rubber Co. who said that industrial management must be Americanized. The factory manager of Wm. Demuth & Co. which has had its employees organized in the form of a senate and house of representatives for a number of years, puts it this way:

In the first place, employers are discerning more clearly the meaning of loyalty, and now can see that this spirit cannot be obtained through the old autocratic attitude. They are beginning to realize that the growth of their business depends upon the growth of the people in their organization, and that loyalty, like electricity, works only when there is a return current.

Secondly, there is more general recognition of the fact that political democracy or self-government is somewhat hollow.

Cyrus McCormick, works manager of the International Harvester Co., Chicago, discussing the industrial councils of his company, gives the following as the reasons for employee representation.[1]

There are various reasons why employers are turning to employee representation. In the first place, there may be fear of syndicalism, a fear that if legitimate interests of employees are not recognized in this or some other way, or that because of repression they are unable to get things which they believe are legitimately theirs, they will have to resort to revolution in order to secure a new state of things in which they shall be on top.

Secondly, I might compare the growth of employee representation to the growth of democracy. . . . Now up to a very few years ago our industrial system was also benevolent despotism. It was benevolent because large corporations tried to do the best they could to start safety campaigns, to start scientific employment, to start welfare work, give recreation, and the like; but because all this came from the top and had no reference to the opinion of the governed, in other words amelioration without consent of the governed, that benevolence was still tinged with despotism. . . .

A final reason is that employee representation is good business for the company and for the man. Scientific industry has just one more step to take. We have done about everything we could in progressive machinery and assembly. We have secured such experts as we could find to study the technique of our operations, including many things that were never thought of fifty years ago— safety work, for example. We must now endow scientific management with soul. When this is done, industry can claim to be for the benefit of management and men alike and the community as well. When this is done, when industry is endowed with soul, it can at last claim to be fully and finally scientific.

And Mr. Henry S. Dennison of the Dennison Mfg. Co., Framingham, Mass., sees in the similarity between the government of the people of a nation and the

---

[1] *Proceedings National Safety Congress*, Cleveland, 1919, pp. 41-42.

management of workers in industry the reason for giving wage earners a voice in controlling the conditions of their employment.

It may be questioned whether there is the difference between the fundamentals of the problem of industrial management and the problem of political management that some of us think there is. Some of the experiments that are being worked out in industry, even if they seem unsuccessful for a time, must nevertheless rank as experiments in the management of men on a non-autocratic basis. I think that those experiments are going to prove of very great interest and very great value. The technique of democracy—how to manage ourselves as citizens—is not very different from the problem of how to manage ourselves as parts of a producing or distributing agency.

KINDS OF EMPLOYEE REPRESENTATION

Employees' organizations sponsored by employers classify themselves into three kinds, from the point of view of the amount of self-government they allow the workers.

The first group are properly only welfare or shop committees. They are merely advisory committees of the working force selected either by the management or by the employees, for the purpose of investigation or conference with foremen, safety directors, and personnel and service managers. The matters with which these committees concern themselves are primarily safety and welfare work, with a small number trying to extend their activities to include grievances. Complete authority is centered in the management, the committees merely giving advice and suggestions which may or may not be accepted by the management. The powers, functions, and methods of operation of these committees identify them with the service work of the plants rather than with problems of bargaining, of wages, hours, and shop discipline.

A VOICE IN WORKING CONDITIONS

The second group of employees' organizations are "company unions" in form. Representatives are elected by secret ballot of all employees, to take up with the employer or with representatives chosen by the management all questions in which the worker may be concerned. But the employer's absolute control over wages, hours, and discipline is restricted no further than to give the employee the right to be heard. Appeals are provided from the representatives of the management to higher officers of the company, but in all cases of disagreement some officer of the company has final authority to decide.

The third group may be called real "company unions." They not only provide for representation of all employees in the plant by means of delegates elected by secret ballot, but when there is disagreement between representatives of the workers and the management, after all the means for settling disputes within the plant have been exhausted, provision is made for decision of such disputes by an arbitrator connected neither with the company nor with the employees' organization. Joint committees, with the representatives of employees and management having equal voting power, are provided for complaints, grievances, investigation, and for conference covering wages, hours, discharge, and any other question that may arise in the relations between workers and management.

These organizations are unions in every sense of the term, except that they have not the right to strike. But in this they are in the same position as the ordinary trade unions after they have entered into arbitration agreements with employers. The only real difference is that when an ordinary trade-union agreement expires, the workers have the right to strike to force a change in the agreement. In the representation plans there are usually provisions for amendment, but if the management refuses to agree to any amendment, the employees would have no right to force it by means of a strike. Such a strike would in effect be a revolution, but it is conceivable that after a strike of this character the company organization might continue with the forced change, just as the government of Italy continued after the revolution of the Fascisti. [1]

By personal investigation of approximately fifty of these plans, we have found that employees' representation may provide simply an orderly method for the adjustment of grievances; it may include machinery for collective bargaining with reference to wages, hours, and working conditions; it may be the means of eliciting from workers their hearty coöperation, and valuable suggestions regarding processes, organizations, and policies, or it may involve all of these or any combination of them. Its structural features may be very simple and the procedure altogether informal, or these may be highly elaborate. The power possessed by employees through their industrial representation may be that of public opinion—the authority of the representatives being merely advisory to the management—or the management may delegate to the employees final authority in regard to certain specified matters, or authority may be exercised jointly by the men and the management. I wish to emphasize the fact that in no plan which we have investigated have we found the measure of control implied by the term Industrial Democracy.

ORGANIZATION OF REPRESENTATION PLANS

In form of organization these plans vary much more widely than in type. Some are merely informal gatherings of workmen called together by the management to confer with or assist the management. Others provide elaborate systems of election machinery, defining carefully the election constituencies, organizing conference committees and joint general meetings, and providing adjustment committees, umpires, and boards of arbitration. A few permit the employees' representatives to meet alone in their works council, with the

---

[1] E. B. Tolsted of the Independence Bureau, Philadelphia, consulting management engineers.

management represented only on joint committees appointed by the council and by the company to handle specific problems. Still others allow no separate sessions of the workers' representatives, but require all committees to include management representatives as well as elected delegates of the employees. Then there is the so-called "Industrial Democracy Plan" organized in many plants by John Leitch. This establishes a cabinet made up of the executives of the company, a senate consisting of foremen and superintendents appointed by the management, and a house of representatives elected by secret ballot of the whole body of employees.

The wide variation in form is due largely to the methods by which the plans are inaugurated in the first instance. Mr. Leitch has his "Industrial Democracy Plan" all worked out and he sells the plan to corporations which engage him to introduce it into their plants and to supervise its operation. Mr. Leitch describes his method as follows:

We held meetings once a week through five weeks to adopt what I told them was to be the business policy of the whole company . . . from president to the newest learner—and which was to guide all our actions. . . . Then we organized as á sort of constitution, a government on the same lines as that of the United States. The cabinet consisted of the executive officers of the company, with the president of the company as president of the cabinet. The legislative bodies were a senate made up of all department heads and foremen, and a house of representatives elected by the employees themselves. The elections to the house were by departments . . . one representative for each twenty employees. . . .

Then we started to govern ourselves under this new dispensation, with the understanding that all rules and regulations affecting the employees were to be in the hands of the legislature, subject to the confirmation of the cabinet.

A ready-made plan is thus purchased by the company and the employees are induced to accept the plan by a vote after a long series of meetings. Whatever may be said of the democracy of such a method, the educational effect of the meetings both before and after the adoption of the plan cannot be questioned. Mr. Leitch was employed some years ago to install his system in a clothing factory in Baltimore, where most of the employees were foreign born, and the articulate leaders among them desired to unionize the plant but had been unable to succeed. These leaders argued and voted for the adoption of Mr. Leitch's proposal because they felt that, once given the right of discussion in open meeting, they had as much chance of winning the workers to a union as the firm had to its plan. They proved to be more effective educators than Mr. Leitch, for the entire plant is now unionized and the firm makes collective agreements with the organization of employees that includes workers in the same industry all over the country.

The International Harvester Co. made a careful study of the entire literature of the subject and a careful investigation of all representation plans existing in the country before it was ready to offer its employees the right of representation in March, 1919. After a long period of incubation and investigation it presented for the consideration of the employees in its twenty plants in the United States and Canada a plan which the management felt was most suited to its conditions. The workers were given a free choice, to adopt or reject. Nineteen plants adopted it by secret vote elections, in which 97 per cent of the wage earners voted. One Chicago plant rejected it and the plan was not put into operation in that plant. The industrial relations manager of the company says that if they had it to do over again they would probably call for an election of representatives first to help devise the plan, even though the arrangements now in force would have been adopted anyway. Such a method would have more educational value.

The more recently adopted plans have followed the method of having joint constitutional committees, so to speak, with employee representatives to help frame the arrangement for representation, organization, and government. The plan of the Goodyear Tire & Rubber Co. is one of these, and before inaugurating it the company

formed a council composed of some representatives appointed by the management; some were elected by the foremen of the plant and some elected by Australian ballot, from the men of the plant themselves, so that in working out the plan we tried to get something that fitted our particular industry, which would be just and fair, promote efficiency, and be satisfactory to all concerned. We unanimously arrived upon a plan which we submitted to the Board of Directors for their approval. The board received it, together with a secret ballot of the employees of the factory. It received 92 per cent of the votes in the affirmative.

The plan is substantially as follows: We adopted what you might call a shop constitution. It provides first, that the executive functions be placed entirely in the hands of the management, the same as the operation and executive departments are placed in the hands of the President and his elected representatives who run the different branches of the government.

In order that this control should not be autocratic, a legislative body was created, elected by the workmen by Australian ballot. This body has legislative powers to act as a check on unwise or unfair movements of the management. The industrians or citizens were asked to vote by Australian ballot for two houses . . . similar to what we have in our state and national legislatures, one being called the house of representatives and the other the senate, the senate to be composed of twenty members elected for two years ten each year, and house of forty members all chosen annually. . . . At the present time, as that stands, there are about 12 per cent office workers, including clerks and others in the office, 6 per cent are foremen, and 82 per cent are factory workmen.

It will be noted that the organization here resembles somewhat that of Mr. Leitch. But it is only a super-

ficial resemblance; for both houses of the legislature
are elected at the Goodyear Co., and the employees'
right of legislation extends much farther.

The Cambria Steel Company and affiliated companies posted the following notice in its plants in
Johnstown, Coatsville, and Nicetown in September,
1918:

> The Board of Directors and officers of Midvale Steel and
> Ordnance Company, Cambria Steel Company, and subsidiary com-
> panies recognize the fact that the prosperity of their companies is
> inseparably bound up with the general welfare of their employees,
> and propose, with the coöperation and assent of their employees
> and for their mutual interests, to establish a plan for representation
> of employees, which will hereafter govern all relations between the
> various companies and their employees. . . .
>
> We recognize the right of wage earners to bargain collectively
> with their employers, and we hereby invite all employees to meet
> with the officers of their respective companies for the purpose of
> considering and if practicable adopting, a plan of representation by
> the employees which shall be thoroughly democratic and shall be
> entirely free from interference by the companies, or any official
> agent thereof.
>
> It is hoped that every employee will respond to this invitation,
> and meet the officers in the spirit of fair dealing and mutual help-
> fulness.

In accordance with this notice elections were held
and the representatives chosen selected a committee
to work out with the management in Philadelphia a
plan of organization. A draft of a plan had been prepared by the company as a basis to work on. It was
taken up section by section, discussed and amended
and finally unanimously adopted. Later the larger
body of representatives at each of the three plants
approved the plan by secret ballots.

A VOICE IN WORKING CONDITIONS

Election of employee representatives usually takes place semiannually or annually, and the secret ballot commonly prevails. The privilege of voting is rarely restricted beyond a requirement that the voter must have been employed in the plant for a short period. Whether of native or foreign birth, male or female, there is equal suffrage for all. The fact of being a permanent employee is the only basis for citizenship under practically all of these industrial constitutions. To hold office, however, or to serve as representative, there are usually requirements of a minimum age of eighteen or twenty-one, ability to read and write English, a period of service of about a year, and often also United States citizenship.

When an employee has a grievance, or wishes to make a suggestion or request, he is required by most of the plans to take the matter up with his foreman. If the foreman's handling of the matter does not suit him, the worker takes it up with his representative, who is authorized either to bring the matter before a higher official of the management or to present it to a joint committee for decision. If this does not satisfy, appeal may be made to the highest officer of the company, or in some cases, as we have seen, to an arbitration tribunal. Questions of general interest to the management or the workers are usually taken up at conferences of all the elected representatives with officers of the company, which takes place periodically.

Mr. Arthur H. Young, industrial relations manager of the International Harvester Co., describes the procedure in the works councils of his company as follows:

Any employee or group of employees has the right to present to the Council, either through the secretary thereof or any employee

161

representative, any suggestion, request, or complaint pertaining to wages, hours, working conditions, recreation, education, or any other matter of mutual interest; added to this is the right of personal appearance before the Works Council on any matter so presented.

The Council must meet once a month and may meet as much oftener as it sees fit; it may summon any employee as a witness and may secure from the management any information required in its deliberations; it may visit any part of a plant as a body or by committee. The company pays employees for time lost from work while, acting as employee representatives or serving as witnesses for the Council, but the employees may, if they choose, compensate such employees by pro-rata subscription among themselves.

In case of a Works Council deadlock, the question is referred to the president of the company, thus being brought promptly and sharply to the highest executive attention. If the president does not present a satisfactory settlement within ten days, the matter may be referred by mutual consent to impartial arbitration; or if the question is regarded by the president as affecting more than one plant, he may summon a general council from all such plants, with equal representation for the employees and the management. If the general council is unable to settle the matter expeditiously, it may be referred—again by mutual consent—to outside arbitration. Decisions by general councils or by arbitration are binding upon all concerned.

In the Bethlehem Steel Co. plan thirteen committees are provided covering wages, hours, safety, employment, working conditions, pensions, education, health and sanitation, etc., to which any matter requiring adjustment must be submitted. From these committees any case not settled goes to a General Joint Committee, from which appeals are taken to the president of the company.

Under this plan 493 cases were considered between October, 1918, and October, 1919. Of these, 336 were settled in the affirmative, while 81 were negative. Of greater significance, probably, is the relative frequency of the various causes of the employees' grievances, as shown in the percentage column. Nearly 60 per cent of the cases considered referred directly to wages and working conditions.

A VOICE IN WORKING CONDITIONS

The following is a classification, by percentage, of these cases, listed according to subjects:

Wages, Piece-work, Bonus, Tonnage Schedules......	32
Employment and Working Conditions..............	27
Health and Works Sanitation.....................	10
Practice, Methods, and Economy..................	10
Safety and Prevention of Accidents...............	8
Employees' Transportation.......................	7
Housing, Domestic Economies, and Living Conditions.	2
Education and Publications......................	1
Athletics and Recreation.........................	1
Rules, Ways and Means..........................	1
Continuous Employment and Condition of Industry..	½
Pensions and Relief..............................	½
	100

Settlement of Cases

Affirmative...............................	336	68
Negative.................................	81	16
Compromised.............................	43	9
Pending..................................	24	5
Withdrawn...............................	9	2
	493	100

Matters of discipline and discharge are often given special consideration under the plans. In the arrangement of the Cambria Steel Co. a list of offenses which merit discharge without notice is given, and another list for which dismissal may come only after warning. Provision is also made through the machinery of the committees for appeals by any discharged employee. A Boston Department Store leaves the entire judgment in cases of discharge to a committee or jury of employees, while another company provides that a two-thirds vote of employee representatives may overrule the management in case of an alleged unjust discharge and bring about reinstatement.

ADJUSTING IMMIGRANT AND INDUSTRY

WORKS COUNCILS AS AMERICANIZING AGENCIES

A New Hampshire shoe company found that Greek women whom it employed had to get permission from their husbands before they dared to vote for representatives and officers of a shop committee which was organized in the factory. No amount of lecturing about American democratic institutions could have brought home to these immigrant workers so effectively the spirit of America as participation in industrial self-government did in this case.

Where industrial representation is inaugurated and operated in good faith, it offers a practical method of making American institutions operative in the daily life of the immigrant. The nomination of candidates, election of representatives, meetings, conferences, investigations, reports, appeals, decisions, and the discussions of all of these not only afford the immigrant wage earner a most practical school for citizenship, but the subject matter of it all being very often his own complaints, grievances, conditions and terms of employment, he may see and feel justice work out in his behalf. Being recognized as an industrial citizen on an equality with all his fellow workers, he finds himself taken into the fold of the workshop community, and the discrimination, oppression, and grafting at the hands of petty bosses, which have been his bitter experiences in the past, gradually disappear as the machinery of representation brings the abuses out in the open, tries them, adjudicates them, and punishes the offenders.

In the table of cases handled at the Bethlehem Steel Co. it appeared that 68 per cent of the complaints were settled in favor of the employee, while 9 per cent more were compromised. This is almost a universal

164

experience. When we think of all the just complaints
that the immigrant worker may have in his efforts at
gaining a livelihood and all the problems of adjustment he has had to meet in his work place without
help from the industry, we can readily appreciate the
promise that employee representation holds for improvement in the relations between immigrant and industry.[1]

Several years ago, Henry T. Noyes of Rochester stated that his
own company, Art-in-Buttons, Inc., after ten years of periodic
departmental meetings, during which the company and the employees
had been working earnestly for their joint good, found that approximately 90 per cent of all complaints made by the employees
were justified in whole or in part. Mr. Noyes hazarded the opinion
that there must be under the usual form of management a tremendous
aggregate of dissatisfaction incapable of elimination chiefly because
the management knew little or nothing about it. Consequently,
we have not been surprised to find that the existence of a works
committee not only brings complaints to light before they are too
serious to handle, but that it eventually reduces the number and
seriousness of complaints.

Almost invariably foremen have undertaken to reform their
ways when their attitude of petty tyranny was the cause of grievances, and have endeavored to adjust complaints satisfactorily when
first brought to their attention, rather than to allow their negligence
to be the subject of discussion by committees, and thus also by the
rank and file of employees, and eventually the subject of a repri-
mand from the management. This means that complaints are
more and more adjusted out of court; consequently the time of the
works committee is reserved for more important matters.

As long as the right to vote and to become a citizen
under these industrial governments is not denied to
the immigrant, the restriction on office holding which
most of them have offers no serious handicap. It may
even serve as a valuable inducement to him to learn
English and become naturalized, but in any case he is

---

[1] Report of Investigation of Employee Representation by E. B.
Tolsted. *Proceedings National Safety Congress*, 1919, p. 65.

assured the full benefits and protection offered by the arrangement simply by the fact of being an employee. Occasionally an employer has attempted to deny to his immigrant employees the right to participate fully in elections, and the revolt that has followed showed both the appreciation of the immigrant of the benefits of representation and the mistake of such a policy.[1]

In one plant voting was restricted to (American) citizens, but all were, of course, allowed to present grievances. A group of foreigners did not understand this point, and struck because they thought they had no means of presenting their grievance.

Mr. Leitch in operating his plans has had similar experiences with immigrant workers, not because they were excluded from participation, but because they did not understand the plan.

The representative system did not work smoothly. A few of the elected representatives did not attend meetings . . . some because they did not grasp the idea, others because they were afraid they might be called on to speak and thus expose their curious English. But other members did catch the theory of representative government from the start . . .

For instance, half a dozen men who could not speak English walked out. We took it up at a house meeting. One of the representatives explained: "These fellows do not speak English. All that they know how to do when they do not like anything, is to quit. That is the only way they can express themselves."

The House appointed a committee to investigate and traced the whole trouble to some trivial error of allotment in the work; it had not been called to the attention of the head of the department. The committee hunted up the men, talked to them in their own language, and had them back within a few hours.

It was incidents of this kind that led representatives to introduce resolutions requiring the management to establish factory classes in English, so that all workers might be equally able to make use of the machinery of

---

[1] *Proceedings, National Safety Congress*, 1919, p. 69.

the factory government and all might work together in complete understanding.

The Detroit Sulphite and Pulp Co., which developed a system of stock ownership and profit sharing as a means of having employees participate in management, was also confronted with the problem of including or excluding the immigrant worker. The solution adopted by the company illustrates the tendency among employers to extend to all their employees, without distinction of nationality or race, the full benefits of the new devices of industrial management. And the reason for this policy as given by Mr. F. H. MacPherson, president of the company, illustrates well the Americanizing effect it is hoped to accomplish.[1]

Citizenship has not been made a prerequisite to stock ownership. On working out the plan, careful consideration was given to this question, and the decision arrived at that the bars should be left down, so that any employee, regardless of nationality, who had put in the probational period of service, should be permitted to buy stock. We figured that if we could obtain the interest of the foreign-born unnaturalized employee, by taking him into partnership, then in the great majority of cases the matter of citizenship would just naturally take care of itself. And it is working out just as anticipated. Some men who had planned on going back to their families in Europe are now sending for their families to come to America, and others who were going back are now debating what they had best do. If they stay here they will become American citizens and they will be the right kind, because they have a "stake" in the country of their adoption—they are capitalists.

That the feeling of being adjusted, of belonging to the community of workers as one of the family, may come to the immigrant as a result of participation in shop committees and works councils is indicated in the words of a worker who said:

I have been working for this company for seven years. Up to about a year and a half ago, I always felt I was a servant of the

---

[1] *The Management and the Worker*, p. 126.

ADJUSTING IMMIGRANT AND INDUSTRY

family. To-day, I feel that I am a real honest-to-goodness member of the family and that I can sit down at the same table with the rest of the family.

It is this feeling of belonging to the family of employees that the immigrant needs to acquire for adjusting himself completely to American industry, and participation in shop representation plans offers a most effective method of accomplishing such an adjustment.

CHAPTER IX

ORGANIZED LABOR AND THE IMMIGRANT

WHAT the great industrial corporations which refuse to recognize trade unions are trying to accomplish in uniting their employees in a company organization that will develop plant morale, the trade unions are also attempting for the craft or industry as a whole. Neither all the employers nor all trade unions are actuated by this motive, and many in both camps have pursued policies which tended to divide and keep separate the foreign born from the native and Americanized workers. But many trade unions as well as many employers have pursued policies tending to fuse wage earners into a common people, and the very purposes of trade unionism and its methods of organization, as the purposes of scientific labor management and the organization of proper industrial relationships by the employer, tend to bring about a unity of mind and coöperative action between native-born and immigrant workers.

It is not our purpose, nor our task in this volume, to pass judgment on the desirability or undesirability of the purposes which trade unions seek to accomplish, nor on the motives which may actuate them in furthering certain of their particular methods of dealing with employers. Just so, it was not our purpose in the preceding chapter to pass judgment on the motives of employers in setting up employee representation plans and employment departments for handling the human relationships in their plants. These controversial issues, arising out of conflicting interests and difference in point of view between management and working people, appear in all industrial countries whether the people concerned are of one race and nationality or of many. We know that trade unions are here to stay, that they are continuing to grow, and we know that employers will continue to develop more scientific methods of labor management. Our concern is only to point out that in pursuing the purposes that trade unions consider right and proper and American, just as employers in pursuing labor management policies that they consider right and proper and American, unifying agencies have been developed for fusing the native with the foreign born. We are describing the unifying policies and pointing out the policies that tend to divide, regardless of the merit or weakness in the points of view either of the employer or the trade unions with respect to the ultimate results of union shops or non-union shops.

IMMIGRANT ORGANIZERS OF AMERICAN UNIONS

No better proof of the Americanizing effects of trade unionism on immigrant labor is needed than the change in the attitude of the public toward the older craft unions affiliated with the American Federation of Labor. It is assumed that these are essentially organizations of American workmen and that the influx of immigrants threatens the existence and the effectiveness of these unions in maintaining American standards. As has already been shown, the United States Immigration Commission reported to Congress in 1910 that immigrants were undermining American trade unions and many unofficial writers have taken the same position.

Yet in 1884 the State Department of Labor of New Jersey characterized the trade-union movement as a foreign importation, and its policies and practices as un-American methods developed by immigrant workers to protect themselves against economic evils which they suffer in this country.[1] And in 1893 a writer in the *Century Magazine*[2] charged that trade unions were composed of foreign workmen who kept American boys from learning trades and becoming mechanics.

That most of the national unions which went into the building of the American Federation of Labor in the eighties and the nineties were composed mainly of foreign-born wage earners and were organized and led by immigrants can hardly be doubted.[3]

A distinguishing characteristic of the trade unions of this time was the predominance in them of the foreign element. The Illinois Bureau of Labor describes the ethical composition of the trade unions of that state during 1886, and states that 21 per cent were Americans, 33 per cent German, 19 per cent Irish, 12 per cent Scandinavian, and the Poles, Bohemians and Italians about 5 per cent. The strong predominance of the foreign element in the American trade unions should not appear unusual, since owing to the breakdown of the apprenticeship system, the United States had been drawing its supply of skilled labor from abroad.

"In all trades except plumbing," said Colonel Richard T. Auchmuty, the pioneer worker for industrial schools, in 1889, "we find that the best workmen, those who command the steadiest employment, are of foreign birth." [4] And he charged the unions with maintaining this situation, the same charge that was later made by the writer in the *Century Magazine* just quoted. As far back as 1825, when the Boston House Carpenters struck for a ten-hour day, the organization

---

[1] Quoted in Hourwich, *Immigration and Labor*, p. 331.
[2] *Century Magazine*, vol. 46, p. 151.
[3] Commons, *History of Labour in the United States*, vol. II, p. 315.
[4] *Ibid.*

of the workers was charged with being of foreign origin by the "gentlemen engaged in building." [1]

In 1878 J. P. McDonnell, born in Ireland, and F. A. Sorge, a German, formed the International Labor Union, which was "the first deliberately planned effort in this country to organize on a comprehensive scale the unskilled wage earners." This proved a vain attempt. But, at the time when McDonnell was vainly attempting to build up an organization of the unskilled, Adolph Strasser and Samuel Gompers succeeded in creating, in the reorganized International Cigar Makers' Union, a model for the trade unions of the skilled. Strasser had taken part in the labor movement of Germany and came to the United States in the seventies, and Gompers was born in England of Dutch-Jewish parents.[2]

Both Strasser and Gompers were active in the formation of the Federation of Organized Trades and Labor Unions in 1881 and its successor, the American Federation of Labor, five years later. With them were associated many other Irish, Scotch, English, and German leaders. At the second convention of the federated trades it was necessary to elect a German secretary as well as an English secretary, and Hugo Miller of the German-Typographia was chosen for the place. Miller was also a delegate to the first convention of the American Federation of Labor, as was also B. Davis, representing the United German Trades of New York. Of the forty-two delegates at this convention a majority were clearly foreign born. Gompers and Strasser of the Cigar Makers were there. James Duncan, born in Scotland, represented the Granite Cutters. The waiters' and the furniture workers' unions of New

---

[1] Perlman, *History of Trade Unionism in the United States.* Macmillan, 1922, p. 8.

[2] *Ibid.*, pp. 306–7.

ORGANIZED LABOR AND THE IMMIGRANT

York were made up mainly of German immigrants and they sent delegates of their own nationality; the carpenters and the New York boatmen sent Irishmen, and there were other men from England, Scotland, and Ireland.[1]

After the formation of the American Federation of Labor in 1886, it drew native American workmen rapidly to its ranks. So completely were native and immigrant fused in its constituent organizations that by 1909, when the United States Immigration Commission made its investigations, it was generally forgotten that the unions had been formed by immigrants, and the Commission found them to be bulwarks of Americanism and American standards, which were threatened by the more recent immigrants.

But while immigrant leaders and immigrant members played such an important part in organizing American trade unions, it must not be assumed that trade unionism is a foreign importation. The Irish immigrant came from districts with little knowledge of trade unionism. Yet they were "the most effective organizers of the American unions. Most remarkable of all, the individualistic Jew from Russia, contrary to his race instinct, is joining the unions." [2] The Germans and the English leaders did have some trade union experience abroad. But it was American conditions that gave birth to American unions.[3]

The American unions, in fact, grow out of American conditions, and are an American product. Although wages are two or three times as high as in his European home, the immigrant is driven by competition and the pressure of employers into a physical exertion which compels him to raise his standard of living in order to have strength to keep at work. He finds also that the law forbids his

---

[1] American Federation of Labor, Proceedings, 1886.
[2] Commons, *Races and Immigrants in America*, 1908, p.153.
[3] *Ibid.*

children to work and compels him to send them to school. To
maintain a higher standard and to support his children he must
earn more wages. This he can do in no other way than by organizing a union.

THE ORGANIZABILITY OF IMMIGRANTS

Although the finding of the United States Immigration
Commission that immigrants were weakening and dis-
rupting American labor organizations has been questioned,[1] it must be admitted that the rapid influx of
new labor did tend to weaken the existing labor organizations. But that this was a temporary result of
the necessity of finding a footing in American industry,
and not due to the racial character of the more recent
immigrants from southern and eastern Europe, is evident from the strong unions of mine workers, garment
workers, and shoe workers, that have been built up by
these immigrants; and from the fact that every other
race of newcomers in industry, including rural native
Americans as well as North European immigrants,
have also weakened labor organizations. English,
Scotch, and Irish immigrants were used to break the
strikes of native workers early in our history. When
these in turn formed unions and struck, German workmen took their places. Bohemians, Scandinavians, and
Jews were the strike breakers of the eighties, and in
later years the south and east Europeans merely repeated the experience of the previous comers.

It was assumed by the Immigration Commission and
many writers on the question, that the recent immigrants are more docile and tractable than the native
workmen and the earlier immigrants, but the experience of the past and the extensive strikes of the foreign
born since the armistice was signed should be sufficient
to show that it is merely the immigrant's helplessness

[1] Weyforth: *The Organizability of Labor*, pp. 163–164; and Hourwich: *Immigration and Labor*, Chap. XV.

in his first years, which is taken for tractability and not a permanent inherent quality. Even native Americans have served to weaken unions and have been dubbed tractable and charged with maintaining low standards.

In Southern cotton mills it is the native elements that prevent organization. The foreign-born coal miners of northern Illinois had to organize the natives in the southern part of the state in order to maintain their organization and the conditions they had won; and many a street railway strike has been broken by country youths of native stock. In recent years the unions in the clothing trades, textile industry, packing houses and steel mills have had less difficulty in enrolling foreign-born workmen and inducing them to strike than they have had in getting the American-born workers. And as far back as 1875 the manager of a Pittsburgh mill wrote:[1] "My experience has shown that Germans and Irish, Swedes and what I denominate Buckwheats (young American country boys), judiciously mixed, make the most effective and tractable force you can find."

The real explanation of the difficulty which has been experienced in effecting organization among our immigrant workers is to be found, it would seem, not in the character of these workers as immigrants but in their character as unskilled laborers; and the principal problem to be solved in organizing them is not so much that of overcoming their opposition to or hesitancy about joining a union or engaging in a strike as that of binding them steadily to the union so that stable and continuous organization may take the place of ephemeral combinations, formed simply for the purpose of obtaining some immediate advantage.[2]

---

[1] J. H. Bridge, "Inside History of the Carnegie Steel Company," quoted by J. A. Fitch, *The Steel Workers*, p. 147. Compare also Commons, *Races and Immigrants in America*, pp. 149–152.

[2] W. O. Weyforth, *Organizability of Labor*, Johns Hopkins University Publications, p. 178.

Dr. Leo Wolman proved conclusively that before the war the great bulk of organized labor was made up of skilled men; and that the trade unions had but little success in organizing unskilled workers and women.[1] But the war and the period of rapidly rising prices following the signing of the armistice brought an enormous increase of unskilled and semi-skilled members of trade unions, and most of this increase was due to the organization of immigrant men and women. The International Association of Machinists by letting down the bars so that semi-skilled and unskilled machine hands might become members of the union brought within its fold something like 250,000 members. The Maintenance of Way Employees grew from a union of 50,000 to over 200,000. By means of the so-called "System Federations" and the Railroad Department of the American Federation of Labor, many semi-skilled and unskilled workers in the railroad shops were organized and distributed among various national unions.

The packing house employees, of which only the skilled men were able to maintain organizations before the war, were almost completely organized by a co-operative campaign launched by the various national unions which have members working in the stockyards. A stockyards labor council was formed to unite these workers into a single body for organizing purposes and for properly representing them in bargaining and negotiations with their employers. A similar coöperating committee of all the unions working in steel mills succeeded in organizing great numbers of unskilled workers in that industry, and its strike call was answered by 130,000 workers, mostly unskilled immigrants. In the shipyards, in the clothing industries both men's and

---

[1] "The Extent of Labor Organization," *Quarterly Journal of Economics*, vol. 30, p. 516.

women's, among the shoe workers, longshoremen, and in many other trades there was a great increase in the membership of existing trade unions, consisting largely of unskilled workers.

In addition, new unions of the less skilled workers, mostly immigrants, have been formed, which give every sign of being permanent organizations. Such, for example, are the United Leather Workers, and the Amalgamated Textile Workers. Many of these organizations have suffered great losses in membership during the present industrial depression and many of their strikes have resulted in defeat. But the organizations themselves have not been disrupted. In the normal course of events a return of prosperity will increase their membership again, and if the policies of the unions which have been successful in holding unskilled immigrant workers are followed, they should be able to merge these more recent immigrants with the older membership in much the same way as the older immigrants in the skilled craft unions were merged with the native born.

If we bear in mind that neither American wage earners nor those of any other nationality join unions automatically, but they must be educated to it; that unionism must be "sold" to working people just as scientific labor management must be "sold" to employers; that organizers must be employed and organizing campaigns planned; that strategic measures must be devised for overcoming the opposition of employers; that funds are required for carrying on strikes as well as for developing enthusiasm and morale; that statesmanlike leadership and expert business ability are needed to build stable and permanent organizations and to negotiate and bargain with employers: if we bear all this in mind, then it becomes plain that organizing and assimilating the more recent immigrants is primarily a problem of efficient union management; more difficult, no doubt, than organizing skilled mechanics, either native or foreign born, but essentially the same problem of union management. The new races react to union experience in much the same way as the older immigrants have done. And just as the unions that were organized and led by immigrants in the eighties and the nineties were recognized as essentially American institutions and powerful Americanizing agencies before a generation had passed, so the experience of the unions that have been successful in organizing and holding the more recent immigrants shows that similar influences are developing a like transformation of the present generation of immigrants.

THE I. W. W. AND THE IMMIGRANT

In the next chapter we shall describe the methods of those unions which have succeeded in organizing immigrant wage earners from eastern and southern Europe, and the policies they have adopted for holding and assimilating these workers will be contrasted with the alienating methods and policies of other unions which have not succeeded in bringing the immigrants into the fold. More unions have failed or neglected to organize the recent immigrants than have succeeded, and with the exception of the recent efforts in the stock yards and in the steel industry, the national headquarters of the American Federation of Labor have not stepped in to do the work which the constituent unions have left undone or failed in attempting.

The unwillingness of some, the failure of others, and the neglect of many more left the field clear for an organization like the I. W. W. This organization, as we shall see, has dwindled in membership and its appeal to the workers has become less and less effective, as wage earners of all classes have found it possible to improve their conditions by successful strikes and union organization. Little has been heard of it in recent months, but under one name or another a revolutionary organization of some kind usually appears to offer a philosophy of hope in a utopian society whenever large bodies of workers despair of improving their conditions under the existing order of things. If the condition of unorganized helplessness in which unskilled workers found themselves before the war should come again, the I. W. W., or the same thing under another name, will no doubt become active and influential again.

The Industrial Workers of the World set itself up in 1906 as the champion of the unskilled, and because native and immigrant unskilled workers alike were unorganized it appealed to both. The American migratory workers of the Far West, the Finns and other nationalities of the Northern iron mines, the Italian silk operatives of Paterson, N. J., and the medley of races in the woolen mills of Lawrence, Mass., all espoused the I. W. W. But this organization did not succeed any better than the trade unions in forming permanent organizations of the unskilled. After thirteen years of existence it claimed only between 30,000 and 40,000 members at its last convention.

It proceeded, however, to formulate the experiences of its failure into a philosophy of revolution. Despairing of gradual progress under the present industrial order, it pinned its faith in a new society. It considered its main mission to be to sow the seed of revolt among the masses and to develop a "militant minority," who are to become the leaders of the revolution. The masses need not be conversant with the philosophy of the I. W. W., we are told, but they must be taught to have confidence in the leaders and to follow without question.

With this objective, strikes for the I. W. W. became an end in themselves and not a means to secure improved conditions, or to build up organizations for maintaining the standards that are won. No matter by whom called or for what purpose, the I. W. W. was willing to assume the leadership of a strike, because its leaders regarded strikes as a means of training the "militant minority," as drill for soldiers of the future revolution. Better conditions were often offered to strikers as a sop to the rank and file, but the idea was to have frequent strikes to keep up the fighting spirit of the workers. Trade agreements and stable organizations, with ample treasuries for protection, were condemned because they often make strikes unnecessary and lead to conservatism. An organized "militant minority" with a discontented working class, ready to strike upon the least provocation—this was the ideal of the I. W. W.

As a propaganda organization it was unsurpassed. Its conventions concerned themselves primarily with methods of agitation and the spreading of its ideas. It was less concerned with getting members than with molding the thought of working people. In this it had remarkable success. Practically all the migratory workers of the West and most of the immigrants whom the trade unions have not reached were influenced by its ideas. They learned from it to distrust the leaders of the American Federation of Labor movements and to hold in contempt ordinary trade unionism.

For its work of propaganda the I. W. W. developed methods and tactics remarkably efficient. Enormous quantities of literature—pamphlets, books, and periodicals in every language—were printed, sold, and distributed where it was likely to have the greatest effect. Capable and magnetic speakers were constantly on the road, and were freely offered as leaders of strikes wherever these occurred. Mob psychology the I. W. W. leaders understood and used in most effective ways. Songs that appeal to the oppressed, cheer the discontented, and sarcastically ridicule the weaknesses of capitalism were written and taught and sung in groups.

All this made a tremendous appeal to the unorganized, unskilled workers, whether native born or immigrant, and I. W. W. sentiment therefore developed most strongly among the migratory laborers of the Far West, who are very largely native born, and among the unorganized, immigrant common laborers of the East. Before this sentiment among the immigrant workers, most of the regular trade unions gave up in despair, although the success of the unions in the mining, clothing, and other industries makes it apparent that the immigrant wage earners, like the native born, want progressive improvement in their working conditions and in their status, not abstract revolutionary doctrines.

The secretary of a national union in an industry three fourths of whose employees are immigrants, when asked what he thought of the prospect of winning the foreign born to his organization, replied that it could not be done with the present generation at all. The president of another national organization explained that his union ceased trying to organize immigrants because they had found they were only recruiting for the I. W. W. Still another official, when asked as to the advisability of issuing foreign language literature explaining trade union principles, replied that this would only give the agitators among the immigrants better opportunities to make the American Federation of Labor ridiculous in the eyes of their countrymen. The suggestion that young, intelligent immigrants, or children of immigrants, be enlisted for educational work among foreign born he felt would be useless, because "foreigners" have no confidence in anyone connected with the American Federation of Labor. As soon as the organizers announced their connection they would be suspected by the immigrants. A high executive of the American Federation of Labor complained that the socialists and radicals had poisoned the minds of the foreigners against him, as well as other leaders, making them believe that he was dishonest and a reactionary. He seemed to feel there was no hope of overcoming this propaganda. And the representative of the Federation in a large industrial state frankly declared he did not want to organize too many foreigners as there were so many radicals among them.

This attitude of the leaders of organized labor made it appear that the I. W. W. had attained a strength that it really never had; and played into the hands of the revolutionary leaders. As a matter of fact, the dogmas of despair of steady improvement and faith in revolution have as little hold on the foreign born as on Americans. Any organization that brings them measurable success in meeting the cost of living, security of employment, and enough income to support families according to American standards, wins their allegiance, although they do like to have these prosaic purposes idealized into grandiose programs of social reform. We shall see in the next chapter how a number of unions have amply demonstrated this.

If the leaders of the ordinary labor organizations could but realize this, and were willing to organize immigrants, they would find the task much easier than they assume it to be. The I. W. W. does not organize. It fears the conservative effect of permanent, successful organization of working people. Success in improving their conditions makes wage earners satisfied with the slower method of gradual progress. The I. W. W.

rarely organizes and prepares for a strike. Immigrants who are forced to strike against oppressive conditions turn to it for leadership when they have no one else to turn to, or when they have learned to be suspicious of other leadership. But they are usually disappointed with the results of I. W. W. leadership; for the revolutionary leaders are interested in propagating their ideas, not in winning concessions from employers.

The dogmatic attachment of immigrant workers to "industrial unionism" is generally pointed to as evidence of their opposition to trade unionism. But industrial unionism is thus confused with the "One Big Union" idea of the I. W. W. The immigrant working, in the main, at unskilled occupations, and under the necessity of changing from job to job, has little pride in craft. He has also suffered from the selfishness of skilled craftsmen whose unions protected their own interests, sometimes neglecting him, and sometimes at his expense. He wants a union of the whole industry where there will be no "aristocrats," where he will have an equal chance to have his interests considered in dealings with employers, and which will enable all that work for the same employer to act together for mutual benefit and for protection of mutual interests. This is quite different from "One Big Union" uniting all the workers in the land, regardless of industry or craft. The latter prevents discussion of problems that concern only people of one factory or of one industry, and makes collective bargaining with employers practically impossible. The one big union as advocated by the I. W. W. is designed as an organization to accomplish social revolution. Industrial unions like the United Mine Workers and the unions of the clothing trades are organized for economic improvement. It is the latter which gains a permanent hold on the masses of immigrant workers.

ADJUSTING IMMIGRANT AND INDUSTRY

As a result of the failure of the I. W. W. to function as an economic organization, the immigrant workers of the Eastern industrial centers who followed it formerly began to abandon it shortly after the war. So strong was their disappointment that at the I. W. W. convention of 1919 out of fifty-four delegates only five were from the East and six were from the Mid-West, the remainder coming from the Far West. The eastern element through its leaders gave to an investigator for this study the following reasons for no longer remaining with the I. W. W.:

During the war it had become an outlaw organization, so that it was playing into the hands of the employer to let the I. W. W. lead their strikes. In all the great strikes the I. W. W. leaders were more interested in furthering its principles, placing the immediate needs of the workers as secondary. It failed to develop local leaders so that after a strike, when the national leaders left, there was no one there to continue the local organization on permanent lines. Even if an effort was made to perpetuate and make permanent the organization that sprang up during the strike, the national organization was not in a position to supply counsel and guidance that would be helpful in dealing with employers. A further failing was that the I. W. W. not only made no provision for funds or a treasury, but actually discouraged it. This meant that local paid officials could not be employed, and the workers had no machinery through which they could transact business with their employer. After a strike was settled all negotiations with the employers were generally discontinued, since recognition was not requested, and since no local machinery existed for the purpose of negotiation and adjustment.

For reasons of this kind immigrant wage earners who are carried away by the appeals of such organizations as the I. W. W. soon come to prefer the ordinary labor. unions, if these are at all effective in meeting their needs as wage earners. We proceed now to a consideration of the methods and policies with respect to immigrant workers which typical trade-union organizations have adopted and pursued.

CHAPTER X

TYPICAL TRADE UNION EXPERIENCES WITH IMMIGRANT WORKERS

THE MINERS

THE United Mine Workers of America was the first of the unions that succeeded in organizing south and east European immigrants into a permanent and strong union. Prior to the organization of this union, the miners in the anthracite fields of Pennsylvania called a strike for increase of wages under the auspices of the Knights of Labor. They were utterly defeated and the organization was destroyed.[1]

The defeat at this time is ascribed with unanimity to the presence of the cheap labor of southern Europe, which could not be controlled and organized according to the methods then pursued. The operators were able to play one section against another section and one nationality against another nationality.

In the bituminous fields, however, local organizations, united in a "Federation of Miners and Mine Laborers," achieved enough strength in the states of Illinois, Ohio, and Pennsylvania to hold joint conferences with the mine operators annually from 1886 to 1893 at which scales of wages were agreed upon. During the entire period of these interstate conferences it had been impossible for the unions to organize southern Illinois, and the arrangement was destroyed by the competition of these unorganized fields of southern Illinois where the miners were predominantly Americans of native stock.[2]

---

[1] Industrial Commission of the United States, 1900, vol. xv, p. 405.
[2] *Ibid.*, p. 407.

ADJUSTING IMMIGRANT AND INDUSTRY

In 1897 a general strike was called in all the competitive bituminous fields, and although the unions at that time numbered less than 10,000 members, more than 100,000 mine workers responded to the call, and the Slavs and Italians joined their American and north European fellow workers almost to a man. The miners of northern Illinois took the lead in this conflict, and because they held out about a month longer than the strikers in other states they were able to settle on more advantageous terms and their organization has ever since been much stronger than the unions in other parts of the bituminous field. It is in this field that the prominent leaders of the miners' union have received their training and experience. Since the strike of 1897 the south European immigrants have been thoroughly organized in the bituminous fields and the United Mine Workers have been making annual agreements with the mine operators, fixing both wages and working conditions in great detail. The only state where it has not met with any measure of success has been in West Virginia, where again native Americans have predominated.[1]

It was in the anthracite districts that the miners union met its greatest difficulties, and developed the methods that are most successful in organizing and holding immigrants in a permanent organization. Shortly before his death John Mitchell told us of these difficulties and how he met them while he was president of the miners' union.

The problem of organizing the immigrant workers in the bituminous fields, he said, was not as difficult as in the anthracite. In the former native-born and other English-speaking miners were pretty much scattered among the non-English-speaking workers; but in the anthracite fields the companies colonized the immigrants, so that one race predominated. Up to 1898 sporadic attempts at

[1] "Slavs in Coal Mining," *Charities*, vol. xiii, Dec. 3, 1904.

organization were made, which brought tangible results in wages and working conditions, but permanent organization could not be maintained. In that year he took charge himself of organizing the anthracite country. The first work was to overcome the prejudice of the native miners. He dwelt upon the importance of organizing the newcomers and treating them as equals. He appealed to the native-born workers to discard derisive names like "Hunky" and "Dago," and if they could not pronounce the foreigners' surname to address them by their Christian names.

While foreign language literature was used to a great extent, main reliance was placed on foreign language organizers and interpreters. Mitchell took it upon himself to select these men and to direct their work. He interviewed each one and made painstaking inquiries into their qualifications and integrity from persons who knew them and were competent to judge, such as priests, leaders of national organizations, fraternal lodges, etc. As a result very few organizers or interpreters betrayed the union, a difficulty that is constantly met in organizing immigrants.

The immigrants were organized first in local unions of each nationality, and an interpreter was assigned to guide and foster each local. Not understanding trade union principles, the immigrants were impatient to strike as soon as they were organized, and a great deal of pains had to be taken to educate them to the importance of being businesslike, and the necessity of building up a strong union by paying dues regularly, so that their strikes and other efforts at improving conditions might prove successful.

Mr. Mitchell felt all along that the impulsiveness and lack of stability of immigrants were not racial characteristics, but due to inexperience and ignorance of trade unionism. By avoiding drastic measures as much as possible, and by counseling the miners carefully at the conventions which were called to formulate the policy that was to guide the anthracite miners, Mr. Mitchell and his associates were able to effect a complete organization of the industry in a comparatively short time.

As late as 1899 the idea of organizing the anthracite miners of Pennsylvania was scouted by all but a few of the leaders of the United Mine Workers. The difficulties in the way of such an organization appeared insurmountable. The differences in race, religion, and ideals of the many nationalities in the region, the variations in the standard of living, the mutual distrust among the races, and the former failures of attempts to form permanent unions, all conspired to make the men distrustful of the new movement. Among the three districts of the anthracite region, the Lackawanna, Lehigh, and Schuylkill, keen jealousy existed, and conditions varied to such an extent as to render it difficult to formulate the grievances in a series of general demands. Many miners grown old in the anthracite fields shook their heads and gloomily predicted that organization would never secure a foothold in the anthracite region.[1]

A strike was called in September, 1900, only after the operators refused to meet the miners in joint conference to work out a scale of wages and a set of working conditions, and after they had been given ten days in which to consider the wage scales and working rules which the miners' convention had formulated. The conciliatory attitude of the union and the refusal of the operators even to discuss the miners' proposal enlisted public sympathy on the side of the strikers, and the operators were finally forced to make concessions. They did this by posting notices at the mines and continued to ignore the organization of the miners. The officers of the union, however, instructed the miners to accept the concessions and resume work, though all the demands were not granted and the union was not recognized. They thought that what had been won would strengthen the organization of the miners and they hoped that within a short time the operators would enter into contractual relations with the union. Practically every miner in the anthracite fields was enrolled

---

[1] John Mitchell, *Organized Labor*, Chap. xli, p. 362.

in the United Mine Workers shortly after the strike, but the operators still refused to deal with the organization.

In 1902 another strike was called, after the operators had again refused to meet the mine workers in joint conference. This was one of the greatest strikes in American labor history. It lasted five months and was finally settled by the intervention of President Roosevelt, who appointed an arbitration commission. It meant a victory for the union, although the principle of the open shop was maintained, and since that time wages and working conditions in the anthracite districts have been fixed by collective bargaining between the miners' organization and the operators.

The success in organizing the various races from southern and eastern Europe, and in winning recognition for the organization, was due to efficient union management, good leadership, and statesmanlike strategy. And this may be illustrated by the way in which some of the difficult situations were handled during the great strike of 1902.

The first critical question that came up was the calling out of engineers, firemen, and pumpmen. To call these men out suddenly would have inflicted great injury on the industry by flooding the mines. The union, however, gave the companies ten days' notice before letting the men strike, and the men were told to strike only if their demands were not granted. Nor were they to stay out after these demands were granted merely to support the miners. By avoiding the temptation to injure the operators, the sympathy of the public was not alienated, as often happens with new unions which follow a less cautious policy.

The next big problem was the demand that came from many local unions of miners that a sympathetic strike of all the bituminous miners be called. A convention of both anthracite and bituminous miners, held in Indianapolis, voted unanimously not to strike, because the bituminous miners had contracts with their employers and the delegates saw the importance of keeping their contracts inviolate. Here again was a great temptation overcome, with many of the strikers suffering pangs of hunger and with the great possibility of success of a sympathetic strike that would soon tie up the railroads of the country. The wise counsel of the leaders was followed, and as a result public sympathy for the miners was still further strengthened.

Then there was the great problem of financing the strikers and their families. When the convention decided against a sympathetic strike, the bituminous miners pledged themselves to contribute $1 or 10 per cent of their wages weekly for the benefit of the anthracite strikers. In this manner over $2,600,000 was contributed during a period of sixteen weeks, and while at no time during the strike was there sufficient funds to provide for all who were idle, by intelligent distribution of aid to those most in need, by careful instructions to relief committees as to the manner in which money should be expended, by circular letters to each local union explaining lack of funds or delays in distribution, the problem of relief was overcome and only for one week during the whole long strike did it seem dangerously to threaten disaffection in the ranks.

Finally, there was the attitude of conciliation and reasonableness. When the offer of arbitration came through the President, the mine workers had practically won the strike. Public sympathy was with the strikers, the funds of the union were increasing rapidly, and the men had remained steadfast in the face of the entire Pennsylvania Guard, called out by the Governor on the theory that miners were deterred from returning to work by fear of violence. Victory was in the hands of the union and it might have dictated terms of peace, but it had fought for the principle of arbitration, and the leaders did not feel justified in rejecting it because victory was in their hands. The union, therefore, accepted arbitration and the miners went back to work.

PACKING HOUSE EMPLOYEES

In the slaughtering and meat packing industry the organizability of the recent immigrant races has several times been demonstrated, but the Amalgamated Meat Cutters and Butcher Workmen did not succeed in developing the leadership and the policies that would enable them to hold all the workers in a permanent organization. During the war a coöperative movement of all the crafts working in the stockyards was started, which made remarkable progress in organizing work and in winning improved conditions and terms of employment. This movement met a setback, however, when the tripartite war agreement between the packers, the government, and the union was terminated in 1921 and the "United States Administration for the Adjustment of Labor Differences" was supplanted by the packing companies' own Employee Representation Plan. It remains to be seen whether the employers or the unions will prove more effective in organizing and assimilating the masses of immigrant workers in the packing house industries.

The story of unionism in the stockyards and packing houses taken in connection with the story of the miners, shows an interesting contrast between trade-union methods and policies which make for assimilation, and those which result in disintegration. Up to 1897 organization and strikes in this industry were sporadic and temporary, but in July of that year the skilled workers in the industry formed a national union under

191

the American Federation of Labor, and in 1902 it was thrown open to the less skilled workers, the recent immigrants. In Chicago, the center of the industry, a Packing Trades Council was formed, representing at one time twenty-two local unions. Each local was organized by departments in the plants. The cattle butchers formed one local, pork butchers another, then sausage makers, canning room employees, oleo, butterine workers, etc.

The skilled workers in each department were organized first, but gradually these extended their numbers to take in the semi-skilled, and finally departments altogether unskilled were organized. Each local union dealt separately with the employers and made agreements at different times covering the work in the departments where its members worked, with the approval of the national organization. In May, 1904, however, the union asked for an agreement covering all departments and all classes of laborers, with a minimum of 20 cents an hour for common laborers, which was afterwards reduced to $18\frac{1}{2}$ cents. It was this demand that precipitated the great strike of 1904. The packing companies, which had previously made agreements to fix minimum wages for unskilled in departments where skilled were employed, refused to do the same for wholly unskilled departments and for common labor generally.[1]

Perhaps the fact of greatest social significance is that the strike of 1904 was not merely a strike of skilled labor for the unskilled, but was a strike of Americanized Irish, Germans, and Bohemians, in behalf of Slovaks, Poles, Lithuanians and Negroes. The strike was defeated by bringing in men from the companies' own branch houses for the skilled occupations and Negroes and Greeks for unskilled.

---

[1] J. R. Commons, "Labor Conditions in Slaughtering and Meatpacking," *Quarterly Journal of Economics*, vol. xix, 1904, p. 28.

TYPICAL TRADE UNION EXPERIENCES

The immigrants stayed out until the last, but the union was defeated. Shortly before the strike was called off, the packers offered to arbitrate, but unlike John Mitchell in the anthracite strike, the leaders of the stockyards workers refused to accept the offer, although arbitration was what they had been demanding. About ten days later the men returned to work on an agreement to arbitrate, but after an hour's work they went out again, charging the companies with discrimination against union members in rehiring. The agreement to arbitrate provided that discrimination as well as other grievances should be submitted to arbitration, so the second walkout was clearly a violation. After this, defeat was inevitable.

After 1904 the union in the packing industry dwindled away. Membership fell from over 34,000 in 1904 to 6200 in 1905, according to a report of the organization, and until 1917 the Chicago stockyards were unorganized with exceptions of some minor crafts. Under the leadership of the Chicago Federation of Labor, however, an organization campaign was begun in the latter part of 1917 which again established unionism in the packing industry; a plan of organization was carefully worked out with the idea of getting every trade that works in the yards to coöperate in the movement. First, the Chicago local unions having jurisdiction over the crafts employed in the industry were interested. Then the national unions were approached and after much urging twelve national unions associated themselves in the effort to organize the entire industry.

A whirlwind campaign with organizers from each national union, foreign-language speakers, and literature was launched, and a low initiation fee established for all trades as well as for unskilled labor. Great numbers were immediately attracted. Those employed in crafts which were under the jurisdiction of national unions affiliated with the American Federation of Labor were distributed among these unions, the others were organized as federal or mixed local unions chartered by the Federation. Separate local unions of women, colored workers, Poles, and other nationalities were formed. A Stockyards Labor Council was organized, representing all the locals, and by the end of 1917 the organization felt itself strong enough to present demands to the packing companies.

The request for recognition and negotiation was denied by the packing companies. The unions then presented their case to the Secretary of War on the ground that a strike would interfere with supplies for the army, and arbitration was requested. The President's Conciliation Commission arranged a settlement by which the dispute was arbitrated, and the employers and the unions each agreed with the government to set up machinery for the adjustment of future disputes. The United States Administration for the Settlement of Labor Differences in Packing House industries was thus set up. This arrangement was in force until September, 1921. Although the unions were not formally recognized by the companies, hours of labor were reduced to eight per day, several substantial increases in wages were made, and grievances were heard and decided by the administrator, who did recognize representatives of the union.

In September, 1921, this arrangement was broken off and the leading packers inaugurated employee representation plans in their plants. The representatives chosen under these plans accepted a wage-cut a short time afterward. The unions charged that the main body of employees was dissatisfied with the cut. They called a strike, which proved to be ineffective.

Whether the unions will be able to maintain their

organizations in the stockyards in the face of the industrial depression and the packers' "company unions" is doubtful. They have accomplished a good deal in forcing an enlightened labor policy in the industry. The packers know that, if the representation plans do not accomplish much the same results that the unions were seeking, they will have to deal with these unions again.

These employers say that their plans provide for collective bargaining and all that unions seek to accomplish that is good, without the evils of unionism. The unions charge the packers with bad faith, claiming that their real purpose is to destroy the labor organizations in the stockyards. Whatever may be the truth in regard to the claims and the charges, it is apparent that some form of unified organization of all the nationalities in the stockyards has come to stay. Whether this organization will be a company union or a national labor organization will depend largely on which of the organizations shows the greater efficiency in handling the problems that the variety of immigrant nationalities presents to the industry.

Thus far the unions in the stockyards have not shown ability to hold the foreign-born workers together as the miners' organization has done. The recent immigrants in the stockyards have not been scattered among departments containing Americans and older immigrant workers. They have been kept apart, by national and race feeling as well as by the fact that each new race came in at the bottom. This segregation makes the problem of organization most difficult, as John Mitchell found in the anthracite coal districts. Moreover, while the leadership in the miners' organizations was taken by American, Irish, and British workmen, who remained in the mines in sufficient numbers to take the more recent immigrants under tutelage and teach them sound principles and policies of unionism, in the packing

industries the American workers have almost entirely
disappeared and the Irish and Germans are following
them rapidly out of the labor ranks. This left few with
knowledge and experience to guide and train the newcomers, which may account for the mistakes and un-
restrained actions of the union when the immigrants
were organized.

The rank and file of the unions, as well as the "house
committees" which were appointed for each department, were often insubordinate. Frequently they violated their own constitutions and agreements by stop-
ping work instead of referring their grievances to higher
officers for settlement with the company. The officials
of the union had not developed the efficient system of
supervision and control which the miners worked out.
After the strike of 1904, the secretary of the Amalgamated Meat Cutters and Butcher Workmen reported
at its convention that over one hundred treasurers of
local unions had defaulted, and that on account of these
the bonding company had notified the union that no
more bonds would be issued except at double the previous rates.

These are problems which all unions encounter in
one form or another. The miners showed that they
could be overcome and that permanent organization
among immigrants could be maintained. The packing
house unions overcame them in part in 1917 and 1918
by the new methods of organization and management
developed under the leadership of the Chicago Federation of Labor. Now that the agreement is broken it
remains to be seen whether these unions can continue
to play a vital part in the lives of the immigrants in
the stockyards.

TYPICAL TRADE UNION EXPERIENCES

IRON AND STEEL WORKERS

An industry in which unionism had concerned itself primarily with the interests of the skilled men and given little heed to the great masses of the unskilled immigrant workers is iron and steel. As in the stockyards, however, the unions in this industry have in recent years realized the dangers to themselves as well as to the immigrants that result from the organizations of native-born skilled craftsmen holding aloof from the great masses of unskilled foreign-born workers in the industry. They have, therefore, also attempted new methods of organizing the immigrants, but also with only partial success.

John Fitch, in his comprehensive study, *The Steel Workers* shows that the Amalgamated Association of Iron, Steel, and Tin Workers began as an organization of skilled iron workers, before the day of the great steel plants and before the development of the steel industry made places for the great numbers of unskilled immigrants. This union never acquired a strong footing in the industry, its main strength in the days of its power being in the less developed iron industry.[1]

The Association has always been an organization of skilled workers and has centered its efforts on securing better conditions for that class of labor alone. Since 1889, to be sure, the constitution has permitted the admission of all men except common laborers, but this has not affected to any great extent the top-heavy character of the organization. Its usefulness has been impaired and its power less than if it had included in its membership all of the workmen in every union mill.

Significantly enough Mr. Fitch found that the same problems of instability, lack of discipline, and race antagonism, which are supposed to be characteristic only of east and south-European immigrants, confronted

[1] John A. Fitch, *The Steel Workers*, published by The Russell Sage Foundation, p. 97.

197

the union of iron and steel workers when its membership was made up almost entirely of Americans and north-Europeans. He writes: [1]

Limited as the membership of the Amalgamated Association has been, much internal dissension has existed throughout its history. This has apparently been due to two main causes. One is the clannishness of the races making up its original membership. These included Scotch, Irish, Welsh, English, and Americans, and there seems to have been a good deal of race antagonism. The other source of trouble has been jealousy among the different trades, a factor still (1910) making for trouble within the union.

The influence of this union was destroyed with its defeat in the great Homestead strike of 1892, and, driven from every important steel mill in the country, it became again practically an iron workers' organization. In 1909 the American Sheet and Tin Plate Company refused to renew its contract with the union and after a strike the union was finally driven out of the last of the mills controlled by the United States Steel Corporation. In November of that same year the American Federation of Labor at its annual convention levied a *per capita* tax on all its members for the purpose of organizing the steel industry. Conferences of labor leaders were held and appeals made to all unions to aid in the organizing campaign. But nothing came of it. The Amalgamated Association of Iron, Steel, and Tin Workers had neither the form of organization nor the confidence of the great masses of unskilled workers to enable it to organize the industry effectively.

It was not until 1918 that the American trade union movement made any effort in this direction. Then it came not from the Amalgamated Association of Iron, Steel, and Tin Workers, but from the same people who had planned the coöperative organizing campaign in the packing industry. These induced the American

[1] *Ibid.*, p. 98.

Federation of Labor to enter upon a similar campaign of organization in the steel industry. The plan was to organize every worker in the industry, and for this purpose a coöperative committee, representing twenty-four craft unions which had jurisdiction over trades in the industry, was established with a paid secretary and a large staff of organizers. Organization districts were established with quarters in Pittsburgh, Chicago, and other centers of the industry.

From the first Poles, Croats, Serbs, and most of the other nationalities came in rapidly, because organizers speaking their tongue were employed and a great mass of literature in their own language describing the purposes of the campaign was circulated among them. Roumanians and Greeks, however, remained cold at the beginning because speakers of those nationalities were difficult to secure. A uniform low initiation fee was provided for all who joined, and applicants were distributed to the unions of their trade where such existed, or were formed into "federal" unions directly connected with the American Federation of Labor where no union claimed jurisdiction.

The organizing campaign was started shortly after the armistice was signed, and the temporary slump in business at the time created some difficulty. Then when business was resumed, the newly enrolled unionists were anxious to strike before their ranks were solidified, and before enough of an organization and a strike fund could be created to make it possible to present demands to the companies. In July, 1919, one of the organizers in Indiana described the situation as follows: [1]

---

[1] This official, who was native born, explained that the Americans did not join the unions. The old workers remember the disasters of previous strikes of the Amalgamated and having but a few years more to work do not want to risk being blacklisted. The young Americans are holding highly skilled jobs, earning high wages, and do not see the need of trade unions.

ADJUSTING IMMIGRANT AND INDUSTRY

The foreign workers have been losing interest for about two months. At the last meeting of one local only about six out of 2000 members attended. When visited in their homes they explained in broken English that they did not think the union could do anything for them. It seems that some organizers had tactlessly promised that by June they would have an eight-hour day with twelve hours' pay. This is what they wanted and were willing to strike for, and they were disappointed in not getting it and not being called on to strike. They were disappointed; a renewal of mass meetings would not bring them back. A strike, however, would bring them all in line, together with others who had not yet joined.

Between August 1, 1918, and January 31, 1920, 156,700 iron and steel workers were organized by the National Organizing Committee. And the committee claimed that another 100,000 joined the unions directly.[1]

---

[1] Report of William Z. Foster, Secretary-Treasurer, National Committee for Organizing Iron and Steel Workers. This report includes only those members actually signed up by the National Committee for Organizing Iron and Steel Workers and from whose initiation fee $1 apiece was deducted and forwarded to the general office of the National Committee. It represents approximately 50 to 60 per cent of the total number of steel workers organized during the campaign and is a minimum report in every respect.

The report does not include any of the many thousands of men signed up at Bethlehem, Steelton, Reading, Appollo, New Kensington, Leechburg, and many minor points which felt the force of the drive but where the National Committee made no deductions upon initiation fees. In Gary, Joliet, Indiana Harbor, South Chicago and other Chicago District points, the National Committee ceased collecting initiation fees early in 1919; hence this report makes no showing of the thousands of men signed up in that territory during the last few months of the campaign. Likewise, at Coatesville and Sparrows' Point, during only a short space of the campaign, were deductions made for the National Committee. Many thousands more men were signed up directly by the multitude of local unions in the steel industry, that were not reported to the National Committee. These do not show in this calculation. Nor do the great numbers of ex-soldiers who were taken into the unions free of initiation fees—in Johnstown alone 1300 ex-soldier steel workers joined the unions under this arrangement.

While the leaders would have liked to postpone the strike, this they found impossible, as the restlessness of the men threatened to destroy the entire movement. The strike was therefore called and the result is well known.

The Steel Corporation by an extraordinary campaign of publicity convinced the public that this was not any ordinary strike for trade unions, but a revolutionary strike for control of the industry by Bolshevists and the I. W. W. But the defeat of the strikers is not so significant as the fact that the American Federation of Labor had at last found a method of uniting immigrant workers and the native-born in coöperative organization for common purposes. Some such organization will no doubt assert itself again, unless the steel industry develops some form of employee representation efficient enough to make the workers in the industry prefer it to the trade-union organizations.[1]

TEXTILE WORKERS

In the textile industry we find an example of trade-unionism which had adopted the policy of looking after the interests of the skilled workers and leaving the unskilled immigrants to shift for themselves. As a result there has been little united action of the native and the foreign-born wage earners in this industry, but instead considerable opposition between the two.

---

[1] The Bethlehem Steel Co., The Midvale Steel & Ordnance Co. with its subsidiaries, and the International Harvester Co., as we have seen, already have established industrial representation plans. During the strike the industrial councils of the Harvester plants, according to the company, kept the people at work in all the plants where they were operating. Only in the one Chicago plant which had failed to adopt the council was there a walkout, and the councils of the nearby plants helped to get these people back to work.

ADJUSTING IMMIGRANT AND INDUSTRY

In Cohoes, New York, the United States Immigration Commission found that "the unions manifest little interest in the immigrant employees until they have advanced to the occupations controlled by the labor organizations"; and similarly in Fall River, Massachusetts, it reported that the unskilled occupations which are taken up by the immigrants are not organized, and the coming of the foreigner does not concern the textile union.[1]

According to officials of the United Textile Workers only about 10 per cent of its members are immigrants from southern and eastern Europe, although over two thirds of the operatives in the large textile centers of the North have come from these countries. The membership of the union is made up mainly of the skilled craftsmen in the mills, and the foreign born of the more recent immigration who are in the union are those who have worked their way into the skilled occupations.

The attitude of the United Textile Workers toward the masses of unskilled immigrants in the industry was well expressed by a member of its executive board in an interview:

On the whole, he said, the foreign elements are Socialists and radicals. They want an industrial union and think everything can be accomplished by a strike. They do not appreciate the value of negotiation. This feeling has been accentuated because of their experience during the war, when departments would stop work and generally get what they wanted. It is difficult to decide what to do with the foreigners. It is not advisable to bring them together, as the United Textile Workers might not be able to handle them when the different nationalities belong to one union. On the other hand, when the nationalities are organized separately, they have no one to lead them and they disintegrate. The problem seems hopeless and the United has practically decided to abandon all hope of ever organizing the immigrants. . . .

[1] U. S. Immigration Commission, vol. X, pp. 123–124.

TYPICAL TRADE UNION EXPERIENCES

It was not long after the southern and east European nationalities came into the textile industry, said another official, before the union realized the futility of organizing them and making permanent unionists out of them. It was easy enough to organize them, but generally the I. W. W. reaped the harvest. It seems that even those foreigners who do not come here as radicals are carried away by the flighty ideals. The best Polish organizer we had was completely carried away by the I. W. W. propaganda in Paterson during the big strike of 1912. The Poles and Italians, this official thought, are the hardest to hold, as their church has little influence over them. But another executive board member blamed the Jews for the attitude of the immigrants toward the United Textile Workers. He felt that they are hopeless and he knew of no way to win them over to the United Textile Workers. The radical organizations cannot hold them either, he said, but these organizations are called on for leaders when they strike. The immigrants, in this official's opinion, do not seem to realize the value of a permanent organization.

In spite of these officials' views, the United Textile Workers have had a fair measure of success in organizing immigrants in Lowell, Massachusetts. In that city there are even separate local unions of different nationalities, yet the organizations have been maintained continuously for a good many years. According to officers of the union, Lowell is a good example of the circumstances under which it is easy to organize immigrant wage earners. The different nationalities were brought in gradually and the employers did nothing to hamper organizations. As a result it was possible to assimilate them and educate them to trade-union principles; but possibly the fact that the immigrants were working themselves into the skilled trades had a great deal to do with both the anxiety and the ability of the union to organize them in Lowell.

When the unions of skilled men were confronted with a strike in Lowell in 1903, they made active efforts to induce the unskilled immigrants to strike with them. These "went out with the members of the unions, but during the nine weeks received no aid from the unions.

203

They have only not gone back, but they are taking the places of the strikers. There are Portuguese doing beaming, Greeks doing spinning, and Poles who have returned in other departments at higher wages." Since the strike of 1903 the United Textile Workers has been quite active among the foreign born in Lowell.

In Lawrence, however, officers of the city central labor body stated that at no time since the immigrant workers have been in the mills in large numbers, has the United Textile Workers made a serious effort to organize them. These officers thought that the union did not want Lawrence organized, for fear it could not control them. Recently in one textile town a Greek doctor offered his services to the United Textile Workers to organize the five thousand Greeks in the mills. The president of the union, after sizing up the situation, concluded that some two thousand of them were infected with I. W. W.'ism and to organize the rest would mean a battle with the I. W. W. He declined the offer and nothing was done.

This policy naturally led to a division between the native born and the immigrants. When the great strike of 1918–19 occurred in the Lawrence mills, the city was divided into two hostile camps. The United Textile Workers had disapproved of the strike and most of the English-speaking employees remained at work, while most of the non-English-speaking went out. The city divided as the mill workers had divided, and became much wrought up over the danger of the alien elements in its population.

By staying out, however, the immigrant workers were able to secure a 15 per cent increase in wages, as well as reduction in working hours to 48 per week; and then they organized a union in competition with the United Textile Workers, known as the Amalgamated Textile Workers. This union spread rapidly, attracted the immigrants of other New England mill towns, and was extended to New York, New Jersey, and Pennsylvania. It used many foreign-language organizers and a great deal of foreign-language literature; but it is also trying to get the native Americans and English-speaking workers into the organization; and for this purpose, native-born trade unionists are employed as organizers.

While the membership and the leaders of this organization are radicals and socialists, they have definitely repudiated the I. W. W. because of its failure to build up strong unions. In Lawrence and Paterson the I. W. W. leaders were called in by the strikers to conduct the strikes of 1912, because the United Textile Workers had alienated the foreign-born workers. But these immigrants were interested in improving their conditions, not in spreading revolutionary propaganda; and when the I. W. W. left them without an organization, they turned away from it in 1919, as they had rejected the American Federation of Labor seven years before. They turned to the Amalgamated Textile Workers.

The foreign-born employees in the textile industry are no different from the immigrants in the mines in this respect. They follow radical leaders when these promise improved conditions, which the conservative leaders are unable to secure. They do not, however, accept the program of the radical leaders and they turn from these as quickly as from the conservatives when radicalism fails to bring them improved conditions. Although the leaders of the Amalgamated Textile Workers are radicals and socialists, they have negotiated with employers and have signed agreements with them in much the same way that the United Textile Workers have done.

The following quotation from an agreement signed

by the Amalgamated Textile Workers shows what they will subscribe to when they are successfully organized.

The parties to this pact realize that the interests sought to be reconciled herein ordinarily tend to pull apart, but they enter into this agreement in the faith that by the exercise of a coöperative spirit it will be possible to bring and keep them together. This will involve as an indispensable prerequisite the suppression of the militant spirit by both parties and the development of reason instead of force as the rule of action. It will require also mutual consideration and concession and a willingness on the part of each party to regard and serve the interests of the other for the common good. With this attitude assured it is believed no differences can arise which this machinery cannot mediate and resolve in the interest of coöperation and harmony.

The agreement of which the above is a part was adopted by a two-thirds vote of the membership of the local unions in New York and it lasted for three years. Recently (1923) it was given up at the request of the union. The members of the unions, while mainly radicals, are not unskilled laborers. The weavers alone, of all the employees in the New York silk ribbon mills, were covered by this agreement. While the Amalgamated Textile Workers made rapid progress in the first year or two of its existence, it has more recently shown it is not any more successful in organizing and holding the unskilled foreign-born workers in the industry than the United Textile Workers.

CLOTHING WORKERS

There remain to be described two unions in the clothing trades, one of which, the International Ladies' Garment Workers, is affiliated with the American Federation of Labor, and the other, the Amalgamated Clothing Workers of America, in the men's clothing trade, is outside the Federation. More than three fourths of all the employees in these garment industries are foreign born, mainly Jews, Italians, and Poles; yet they have developed two of the strongest labor unions in America.

Each of these unions claims about 175,000 members. They are the former sweatshop workers, who now have come to the forefront of American labor organizations by establishing forty-four hours as the standard work week, raising wages above those obtained by most union workers of similar skill, and abolishing arbitrary dismissals by foremen or bosses. These unions, composed mainly of immigrants, have learned much of their unionism from the older American trade unions, but they also have contributed to the American labor movement new ideas of their own, among which is to be mentioned the establishment of continuous judicial tribunals for interpreting the trade agreements which unions commonly make with employers in the industries in which they operate.

After a great strike of cloak makers in 1910, a "Protocol of Peace" was signed, establishing collective bargaining relations between the Ladies' Garment Workers and the manufacturers. Collective bargaining is still maintained and will probably continue permanently in one form or another, although the Protocol itself was abrogated after seven years of existence. It was under this protocol arrangement that the leaders of both the men's and the women's clothing unions learned the constructive policies of American trade unionism, as well as the principles of government in industry, which is making their unions the models for organizing immigrants in many other industries.

The Protocol established a Board of Grievances with clerks and representatives of both parties who acted as adjusters, and later an impartial chairman was employed to decide deadlocks between the two. A tribunal for appeals and for deciding the principles of law underlying the agreement was also created, known as the Board of Arbitration; and Justice Brandeis, who more than any other individual was responsible for the Protocol, was made Chairman of this body. The preferential union shop, judicial and legislative methods of determining controversies, organization of both employers and wage earners, and "efficiency and economy as duty of worker and employer in industry"—these are some of the principles established and worked out under the Protocol. Although this agreement is no longer in effect, others are made from year to year along the same lines. Recently the union in this industry signed a pact with the Ladies' Garment Manufacturers of Cleveland establishing practically the same principles, and in addition, committing the union to scientific methods of determining the workers' output and committing the employers to a guarantee of at least forty-one weeks' work per year.

In 1911, the union of the men's clothing industry in Chicago entered an agreement with Hart, Schaffner & Marx, which established a "Trade Board" with an impartial chairman for hearing disputes and deciding questions of fact and a Board of Arbitration for hearing appeals and deciding matters of law or principle. The preferential shop was also added to this agreement, and "deputies" employed by both sides to investigate complaints and argue cases before the Boards. In addition there were price committees formed with representatives of both parties to deal with the vexing problems of fixing piece rates.

This agreement has persisted until the present time, and so successful has it been in the eyes of the workers that the union was able after long strikes to force similar arrangements by practically all other men's clothing houses in Chicago and in New York. The largest clothing house in Baltimore has been dealing with the union on this basis for a number of years, and Rochester, another large men's clothing center, entered into such an agreement in 1919 without a strike. This growth of the union in the men's clothing industry and the establishment of agreements in all the important markets has been secured by the Amalgamated Clothing Workers of America under the capable leadership of Sidney Hillman, its president, who began his union career as a deputy at Hart, Schaffner & Marx, and then worked as Chief Clerk for the Cloak Makers' Union in New York under the Protocol until he was called to become head of the men's clothing organization.

In form of organization, structure, methods of organizing, control, and supervision by national officials, the two unions in the clothing trades are surprisingly like the United Mine Workers. Certainly there was little communication between them and the mine workers, but their problems of immigrant organization were similar, and they met those problems successfully by similar methods. The clothing trade unions are industrial unions, like the miners' organization, taking in all workers in their industries. The local unions are organized largely by craft, although there are separate women's locals and nationality locals, as well. These last are necessary to get the non-English-speaking into the unions, but they are considered temporary expedients.

The local unions normally have little power, but delegate bodies known as Joint Boards are organized, which are the seats of authority for the city or the branches of the trade they represent, subject to the supervision of the national organization. Thus the local unions of cloak makers send delegates to a Cloak Makers' Joint Board, and the Waist Makers to a Waist

Makers' Joint Board of the International Ladies' Garment Workers. Similarly the Amalgamated Clothing Workers has a New York Joint Board, consisting of delegates from the local unions of the men's clothing workers, and separate Joint Boards for Children's Clothing and Shirts and Blouses. These Joint Boards correspond to the district organizations of the United Mine Workers and perform similar functions.

Both the clothing workers' unions have entered into extensive educational activities of a formal nature, as distinguished from the training the members get through union meetings and activities. They have educational departments with classes in English, economics, trade unionism, literature, and personal and industrial hygiene, and they arrange concerts and other entertainments on a large scale for their members.

The career of the Amalgamated Clothing Workers is particularly significant to the present study, because of its conflict with the native and older immigrants in the United Garment Workers from which it broke off, and the light it throws on the problems of organizing various immigrant races and assimilating them into a single labor organization.

The United Garment Workers, like other unions in the American Federation of Labor, had great difficulty in organizing the immigrants into a permanent and stable organization. Its leaders ascribed this to the racial clannishness and radicalism of the Jews and Italians and they sought permanence, therefore, by organizing strongly the cutters, who were mostly native born or of the earlier Irish and German immigration, by means of so-called "label shops." They made contracts with manufacturers for the use of a label to be attached to each garment, and since this was of value to the manufacturers of low-priced workingmen's clothes, the employers would do the bidding of the officers of the union, and even force employees to join the organization.

The sale of the label to employers proved a source of considerable income to the union. Since about 85 per cent of the employees in overall factories, which are the mainstay of the labels, are American born, and these together with the cutters were the permanent elements in the union, the leaders who were of American, Irish, and German ancestry were able to maintain control of the union, although they did not have the confidence of the bulk of the immigrants in the industry.

All the foreign born, however, joined the United Garment Workers in a great strike in 1912–13, but they were disappointed with the terms of the settlement which the officials secured in conference with the employers. This led to a determined attack on the leaders of the union, particularly by the Jews, and in this they were aided by the powerful Jewish newspapers. Charges of misdoing were frequently made, as well as demands for the recognition of the foreign nationalities in the control of the organization. When the Convention of the United Garment Workers met in 1914 in Nashville, delegates from strong Jewish unions of New York were not seated, on the ground that their unions had not paid *per capita* taxes to the national organization for the membership that they claimed. Most of the Jewish delegates then left the convention and the Italians and Poles followed them. These organized the Amalgamated Clothing Workers of America, and since that time it has taken in about 80 per cent of the workers in the men's clothing industry of the country, including most of the cutters who came over from the United Garment Workers. At the present time the Amalgamated has several times the membership of the original union, which is affiliated with the

American Federation of Labor and which has very little influence outside of overall shops.

The secretary of the United Garment Workers blames the East Side Jews of New York for the split. The radical Jews are most to blame, he says, but the conservative Jewish papers also aided them in attacking the United, on the ground that it was a fight for recognition of the Jews. While nationalistic feeling was at the bottom of the trouble, radicalism played an important part also. The Italians, Poles, and other nationalities were won over by the Jews largely because of their radical program.

The leaders of the rival movement in effect admit these charges, but they point out that any attempt to unite the workers in an industry without taking into consideration the racial characteristics and social ideals of the various nationalities is bound to result in failure. They charge that it was incompetent union management to ignore the feelings of the immigrants, deny them opportunities for expressing within the union their own reactions to modern industrial life, and try to impose on them policies and methods that would appeal only to Anglo-Saxon skilled workers. Had the United Garment Workers recognized the need for self-expression among the Jews, Poles, and Italians, they say, and had they tried to develop leaders and officials from among these nationalities as the Amalgamated Clothing Workers has done, there would have been no split, and it could have succeeded in uniting all the immigrant races in the industry together with the American as the Amalgamated has succeeded in doing.

There can be no doubt that the success of the Amalgamated thus far has been due to the recognition of the national feeling and the radical sentiment among the various immigrant races in the industry. It publishes weekly papers in seven different languages, and while a majority of the officers are Jews, two Italians are on the National Executive Board, and many Italian, Polish, and Lithuanian, as well as Jewish and American, organizers are employed.

It also has a good many more local unions organized by nationality than most other unions. Nevertheless, when the economic policies of the organization are studied, as they express themselves in agreements and relations with employers, it is apparent that in practice this organization is merely following the general line of development of successful American trade-unionism. It is committed to the preferential union shop as distinguished from the closed shop or the open shop; it works to establish amicable relations with employers by means of negotiation and trade agreements; it prefers arbitration to strikes and favors the establishment of judicial machinery for this purpose; and it has taken a position in favor of improved methods of management and manufacture, as well as for fair standards of production where employees work by the week.

The national feeling and social ideals of its members the union uses to build up the organization, maintain morale, and develop a unified purpose to accomplish the economic objects of the organization. These economic ends grow out of American conditions and in practice are exactly the same as those of other American trade unions; but they are usually couched in radical and revolutionary language.

The Jewish leaders of the Amalgamated are thus trying to assimilate the various immigrant nationalities in the men's clothing industry to American trade-unionism, as the native and Americanized leaders of the miners did in their industry, the task in which the American, Irish, and German leaders of the United Garment Workers failed. It cannot as yet be said that the problem has been solved in the clothing industry. While the Italians and Poles have been given recognition, and leaders have been developed among them who are put in offices of power and responsibility, there is some feeling among these races which here and there threatens to break out into disruptive movements. Among the Poles and Lithuanians particularly there is a good deal of anti-Semitic feeling, and leaders of these nationalities have not been as rapidly developed as among the Italians. The leaders of the Amalgamated realize the problem, and they know that the Italians, Poles, and other nationalities will break away from them, as they broke away from the leaders of the United Garment Workers, unless races, creed, and nationalities are treated equally and all are united for the common task of improving conditions and introducing democratic control over the labor relations in the industry.

CHAPTER XI

UNION MANAGEMENT AND THE IMMIGRANT

IT must be evident, from the experiences of the unions described, that appropriate organizing methods bring foreign-born wage earners into the ranks of labor unions as well as they do native-born workers. The real problem, however, is how to hold and to unite them in permanent organizations after they have been brought in. But this, too, has been accomplished when those in charge of the management of the union study the special problems involved in making immigrants of many nationalities and races work together and in reconciling the conflicting points of view of the skilled mechanics and the unskilled workers in the industry.

COMPANY MANAGEMENT AND UNION MANAGEMENT

Most labor organizations have lagged behind the great industrial corporations in handling the problems imposed on them by the presence of great masses of immigrant unskilled labor in American industries. We have indicated in preceding chapters the attention and study that industrial executives are beginning to give to the management of their employees. By devoting themselves to these problems, employers have been able to develop employees' organizations of their own which threaten to block further growth of trade-unionism among these workers.

Mere denunciation and derision of "company unions" will not stop this movement. If they are really the frauds that trade unionists charge them to be, then the workers who are taken in by them will revolt and turn to organized labor. But the industrial managers are not unaware of this inevitable result of duplicity in dealing with their employees. They have seen cases in which union organizers came along with effective propaganda methods and succeeded in winning away employees from company unions to the regular trade unions. They know also, however, more cases in which company unions have won employees away from the regular labor organizations. In spite of the most bitter opposition from organized labor, works councils and other industrial representation plans are gaining ground, and often at the expense of the trade unions.

As long as employers fought the fundamental principles of unionism, namely collective bargaining and democratic control over labor conditions, the unions had little to fear. But now that they acknowledge these principles and proceed to introduce "industrial democracy" in their plants as a matter of good management policy, the unions face really serious competition, which they can meet only by making their organizations more efficient agencies for industrial self-government than are the employers' organizations.

Some realization of this is dawning upon the trade unions. The American Federation of Labor has made a beginning by establishing an educational and research department. If this is developed to study the technique of organizing and managing the great masses of unskilled workers of foreign birth, the company union movement may be overcome by organized labor. If it confines itself to general propaganda, and does not serve as a laboratory for observation of the details of union administration and development of new methods to be passed on to the constituent national unions, the steady growth of unionism in this country that has been going on since the American Federation of Labor was formed, may be stopped.

UNION MANAGEMENT AND THE IMMIGRANT

Faith in the righteousness of the cause of organized labor alone will not win the immigrants and unskilled wage earners to it. Something more is necessary. There are millions of these workers unorganized and they present the greatest problem of the trade unions. Most important in solving this problem is to study the methods and policies and details of administration and management of the unions that have succeeded in organizing and assimilating these classes of wage earners.

THE METHODS OF THE MINERS

Many other unions besides the miners have won great strikes with the aid of immigrant masses in their industry, but not many have been able to hold them permanently and merge them with the American workers. How did the miners' union accomplish this?

In the first place, it threw its doors open widely to all those who worked in or about the mines, regardless of skill or craft. The constitution of the union provides that no one shall be debarred or hindered from obtaining work on account of race, creed, or nationality. For a time the Illinois unions did have an initiation fee of $50, but this was soon reduced to $10, which has been the fee generally required, and the employers have been free to hire any one who was qualified under the state laws to work in mines, provided he became a member of the union.

Like other unions, the miners have at times used compulsion to force newcomers to join the union if they were unwilling to do it voluntarily. In most of the agreements in the bituminous fields the miners have provisions for the so-called "check-off" system, which requires the employer to deduct from every mine worker's wages the fees to be paid to the union. The effect of this on immigrants has been to make them regard the membership fee as the price they have to pay for their jobs; and at first many of them have entered the union without understanding or any real sympathy for the work of the organization.

But the union has to a large extent realized the responsibility toward the immigrant which comes to it with the great power and the ample funds that this all-inclusive system affords it, and the immigrant was soon taught to sympathize with the aims and purposes of the union. Machinery was established in each mine district to insure each of the miners the benefits of the organization, to educate him in the principles of unionism, to teach him the value of the regulations established by the older members and the importance of conforming to them.[1]

The miners have had such remarkable success in organizing the immigrant worker because of the use of foreign-language organizers and because they encourage immigrant workers to become officials. Immigrants in general are good joiners and strikers, but do not stick or pay dues permanently. The miners tried to counteract this by taking advantage of the joining and striking in demanding the check-off system wherever successful. In this way they got dues from immigrant workers and kept them in the union. They were not content with this, however, but proceeded to educate the immigrant worker through field agents and foreign-language literature. That this educational work is successful is shown by the fact that formerly most immigrant workers paid only trade union dues necessary to cover union expenses and strike fund assessment. This was the minimum dues and obligatory under the check-off system. Very few availed themselves of the voluntary dues for sick and death benefit. At present the situation has been reversed as a result of the process of education, and most of them now have more than the obligatory dues checked off.

[1] Statement of James H. Maurer, President of Pennsylvania State Federation of Labor, in interview, June 22, 1919.

UNION MANAGEMENT AND THE IMMIGRANT

In a typical district organization of the United Mine Workers with 45,000 members we found twenty-five paid officers. Three paid officials and two paid organizers were provided by the district for each subdivision. One of these organizers is generally a foreign-language speaker, and quite often both are. Occasionally the national union also sends in its organizers to help. So many paid officers are needed because the members are scattered in small communities and transportation facilities are usually bad. The large number of immigrants of different nationalities makes this necessary also. Whenever a grievance arises in any community an organizer of the nationality involved is sent to remain there until it is settled. The business management of the local unions is also strictly supervised by the paid district officers.

Immigrants were at first organized in local unions of separate nationalities. This was made necessary both because of the language difficulty and because of the reluctance of both Americans and foreign born to mingle with each other. A great deal of foreign-language literature was used, as well as foreign-speaking organizers, to get immigrants interested in union affairs. The foreign-language locals, however, are regarded as a temporary expedient. Gradually they are disbanded. Immigrants themselves now often object to the separate nationality local, because it keeps them from getting in touch with American workers and from learning English. The organization by nationality also brings together men from different mines where the problems may be different, and conducting the business of the locals is thus made more difficult. The tendency is, therefore, to disband the language locals as soon as possible and organize all the men around each mine. The business is then translated for the various nationalities and the offices are divided among the nationalities. The process of merging all miners is thus accomplished, first, by organizing the immigrants in language locals which are brought into contact with the English-speaking by delegates sent to a council, and later this leads to a closer amalgamation of all nationalities, together with the American, in a local for each mine.

After local unions are organized they are watched closely by the organizers, who teach the members how to conduct meetings and transact business under parliamentary procedure. They instruct the secretaries how to take the minutes and keep books. After that each local is visited by an officer or organizer of the district at least once each month. When officers are to be elected, usually someone from the district office is present to assist and advise. He explains the qualifications needed for the different offices, and advises that each nationality be given representation as far as possible. Hardly ever is there objection to this guidance. On the contrary, the members look forward to the coming of an officer who is in touch with the entire district.

To these local unions every important question affecting labor in the mining industry is referred sooner or later. The delegates to the national conventions which consider these questions are elected by the local unions, and these delegates receive their instructions through the resolutions which are debated and adopted at the meetings of the locals. In addition, policies adopted by the national convention or recommended by the national officers may come up for discussion and a referendum vote in the locals; and the three most important officers of the national organization, the President, the Vice President, and the Secretary Treasurer, have to be nominated and elected directly by referendum vote of the local unions.

UNION MANAGEMENT AND THE IMMIGRANT

What makes all this participation in democratic government particularly effective is its direct connection with the immigrant's need for protection in his employment. He sees the need for taking part and feels directly the effects of it. If he has any grievance, it is taken up for him by a committee of his local union, known as the mine committee, which adjusts the matter with the mining superintendent, and a paid officer of the district will come to assist the committee when necessary. If he is suspended or discharged he may appeal to the committee, which will investigate and, if it finds that he is not guilty of an offense justifying dismissal, it will ask his reinstatement. Should the mine superintendent refuse to reinstate the worker, appeal is made to higher officers of the union and of the operators' association, and if necessary the matter will be finally decided by a joint board of miners and operators or as in Illinois and in the anthracite fields, by an arbitrator or umpire or a board of arbitration. These are the methods not only of handling discharges but of adjusting all other disputes which may arise between the miners and their employees.

METHODS AND POLICIES OF OTHER UNIONS

Most unions adopt the policy of the closed shop as a means of compelling every one in the industry to join and remain in the organization. Under this arrangement the immigrant cannot get work without being a member of the union. He comes in often under pressure this way and with but little sympathy for the organization, because he has to join in order to get work. Later he may learn its principles and become a willing and loyal member. The "check-off" system of the miners has the same effect as the closed shop policy. But, as we have seen, this proved effective only because the miners' union was alive to its responsibilities when it thus used compulsory methods. It used great sums of money and devoted the greater part of its effort to teaching the membership the value of organization, not only by talking to them, but by attention to details of union administration, and efficient handling of the numerous everyday complaints of the members at their work places. This work was not all left to the efforts of local unions, which might lack experience and ability. The national and district organizations step in and see that the services of the union are efficiently rendered to every worker when he needs it. Where the closed shop policy has failed, it has often been because unions have not been alive to their responsibilities in these respects and have not been able or willing to perform these services efficiently.

Insurance benefits are used by many unions for keeping the membership intact after the flush of enthusiasm from a strike or organizing campaign has disappeared. It is an effective device. Death and sickness benefits for both members and their wives are the most common forms used, and in addition there are traveling and out-of-work benefits and tool insurance.[1]

TABLE VII

BENEFITS PAID BY AFFILIATED ORGANIZATIONS OF THE A. F. OF L.
IN 1920

Death benefits to members...............	$5,122,399
Death benefits to members' wives	152,355
Sick benefits.........................	1,329,825
Traveling benefits.....................	94,719
Tool insurance.......................	1,079
Unemployment benefits.................	4,906
Total...........................	$6,705,283

[1] American Federation of Labor, Report of National Executive Board, 1920.

UNION MANAGEMENT AND THE IMMIGRANT

More appealing than insurance, however, because it is more immediate, is the protection that a union may afford the individual member against unjust treatment or arbitrary discharge. To immigrants this protection is particularly important, for they are more frequently liable to discipline and dismissal without any explanation or understanding of the reason. All unions lay a great deal of emphasis on protection against discharge, and if they are effective in actually affording protection, they get a strong hold on immigrant members.

While both insurance and protection on the job assist greatly in holding the membership in unions, it is noticeable among the foreign born particularly that something more than material benefits of this kind, or increased wages and short hours are needed to hold them permanently. Expression for the innate ambitions or aspirations of the workers must also be provided by the unions, or else the interest of the members is lost.

That the foreign-born leaders of immigrant workers have been alive to this is shown by the great amount of formal educational work done by such unions as the International Ladies' Garment Workers and the Amalgamated Clothing Workers. Not only are classes conducted for teaching of English and citizenship, but courses are also given in history, trade unionism, economics, sociology, literature, and social movements. Concerts, entertainments, dances and social affairs, choral unions, and health talks are all parts of the program. In Chicago the Amalgamated Clothing Workers' Union engages the Symphony Orchestra of that city at regular intervals to give concerts for its members and their families, and as many as 5000 at a time attend. In New York the Ladies' Garment Workers have secured the coöperation of the public schools and in a number of these, as well as in one branch public library, lectures and classes are carried on regularly and systematically. Visits to museums conducted by interested leaders are often arranged, and members can obtain passes issued by the educational department enabling them to see good performances in the leading theaters at reduced prices and in groups which discuss the plays afterward.

Insurance, protection, education, and the development of wider interests, are all helpful in maintaining stable organizations; but the success of these, together with the success of the union in improving labor conditions in the industry, and in its relations with employers, depends upon the character and efficiency of their administration. Policies must vary to meet needs and desires of the membership. To some insurance will appeal. Others ridicule union discussions of "cemeteries," as they dub the business of insurance, and they want their imagination and ideals stimulated by other projects. Coöperation and politics always appeal to immigrant working people, and many unions have been rent asunder or destroyed by identifying these activities with the life of the union. But intelligent union management and leadership find ways of permitting expression of social and political ideals of the membership, and yet maintaining the union as primarily an economic organization for dealing with employers.

REQUIREMENTS OF GOOD MANAGEMENT

First and most important in the management of a union are the ability, good judgment, and honesty of its officers. In the packing house strike of 1904 it was a mistake of the officers not to accept arbitration, and it meant practically death to the union for more than thirteen years. The limited vision of the officers of the

UNION MANAGEMENT AND THE IMMIGRANT

United Garment Workers prevented a complete organization of the men's clothing industry. On the other hand, the success of the United Mine Workers must be ascribed in large measure to the managerial ability of John Mitchell and his successors. It is in the conduct of the ordinary affairs of the unions that the leaders are trained; and the incumbent officers of the organizations must assume the responsibility for training new leaders as well as desire to make places for them, particularly for leaders of new nationalities coming into the unions.

In the methods of organizing local unions and in the supervision of their business, this training can be most effectively provided. We have seen how careful the district organizations of the United Mine Workers are to instruct and guide local unions in methods of conducting business, auditing accounts, electing officers, handling grievances, etc. The Amalgamated Clothing Workers pursue a similar policy. In both these unions the locals have little power and responsibility. The district organizations or joint boards handle most of the finances, and they have the power to conduct negotiations with employers and call strikes, subject to the approval of the national unions.

This insures a larger membership from which to draw responsible officials, it makes more talent available for leadership, and by making the stakes larger insures more care in the selection of careful officials. In addition, it prevents newly formed locals from jeopardizing the union by calling impulsive and ill-considered strikes. And it gives the older and more experienced men from the district and national organizations a chance to influence members in the newly organized unions in the direction of stability.

Reckless and unsuccessful striking is a common cause of break-up of unions that can be overcome only by careful supervision and control of local unions. New recruits to unions are particularly likely to indulge in this, thinking that, once they have won a strike, they might accomplish anything by the same method. Often they will make most unreasonable demands and expect to win them by strikes. Only control by district and national officers and the requirement that all strikes and agreements be approved by the national organization can overcome this evil. Local unions must not be left to deal alone with employers, also, because with the best of intentions they often ignorantly do the wrong things.

Unreasonable demands are often made by individual workers, and many imaginary grievances are presented, with the idea that the union will always support the workers. In supervising local unions national organizers and officials can do a great deal to teach local officers to discountenance unreasonable demands, and not to support imaginary grievances.

In so far as a union has the capacity to develop capable leaders, to supervise local organizations to insure honesty in its own dealings and fairness in its relations with employers, it not only maintains the stability and permanence of its organization, but also solves the problem of making good, permanent unionists of its immigrant workers. Essentially, as we have seen, the problem of assimilating the foreign born into trade unions is no different from that of absorbing any other class of wage earners who work under the same conditions. The most trouble is caused by unskilled workers, and unskilled immigrants naturally are as unstable as other unskilled workers. If a union pursues sound management policies in dealing with the ordinary problems of organization and unionism, the same policies are effective in assimilating immigrants.

UNION MANAGEMENT AND THE IMMIGRANT

It is because many trade unions have so largely failed in organizing unskilled and women workers, and have been unable to cope with the problem of maintaining stable organizations among American wage earners of these classes, that they have also failed to organize or hold immigrant men and women in their ranks. After such failures it is easy to blame the "foreigners" if they happen to be the people involved. But we do not blame Americans when the native-born teamsters fail to maintain their organization. Then it is ascribed to their character as unskilled workers. While it is more difficult to maintain organizations among the unskilled, it is not impossible, as the miners and other unions have proved. And if some unions can do it while others cannot, the fault must be primarily with the management of the unsuccessful union.

No better proof is needed that organizing and assimilating immigrant workers is primarily a problem of union management than the experience that unions have had with secession movements or dual unions and with jurisdictional disputes. These occur · again and again in the labor movement, but when the split happens to involve different nationalities it is immediately charged to this difference, rather than to the character of the organization and the management which makes the secession or dual union possible.

The cigar makers afford an interesting example. Skilled cigar workers in many cities where they were organized refused to allow employers to subdivide operations and to introduce labor-saving machinery. They insisted on the entire cigar being made by each worker. The union was able to enforce this policy in small shops by means of the union label. These shops made non-advertised brands and depended upon

227

ADJUSTING IMMIGRANT AND INDUSTRY

the patronage of working men. The label was to them therefore, an asset, and the union was able to dictate terms. The larger manufacturers, however, who sell well-advertised brands and cater to patrons who are indifferent to the union label, would not submit to the cigar makers' organization. They introduced machinery, subdivision of operations, and other labor-saving devices; and they depended on the new immigration for their labor supply. The cigar makers' union was indifferent to these unskilled and semi-skilled workers in the large factories, and these presently organized a union of their own composed mainly of immigrant workers. Then charges were made that the fact that these workers were aliens and radicals led them to organize a separate union. Recently these people have come into the International Cigar Makers' Union, but they are regarded by the officers as a dangerous element, and they are restless under the leadership and policies which do not give sufficient attention to the needs of the less skilled workers in the large factories.

The same sort of secession happens in unions where immigrant members are a negligible factor. The teamsters have had many splits and separate organizations; and the skilled operatives in the United Textile Workers have had many secessions when most of the members were English-speaking.[1]

One difficulty which besets the textile workers lies in contentions between different brances of the trade. If a local becomes dissatisfied with the national management or, as the national officials believe is often the case, if it is unwilling to pay assessments, it is easy for it to secede. And only recently the Mule Spinners' Union was ordered expelled from the American Federation of Labor because it refused to join the United Textile Workers, although the leaders and the membership of both unions are American and of other English-speaking nationalities.

[1] Weyforth, cited above, p. 129.

UNION MANAGEMENT AND THE IMMIGRANT

In the shoe industry, also, a split occurred and a dual organization was formed because of over-conservative policy of the Boot and Shoe Workers' Union, which was more anxious to protect its union label than to extend its protection to employees working in non-label shops. The United Shoe Workers was organized, and it has outstripped the original union in many centers of the shoe industry. Leaders and members in both unions were originally of the same nationalities, although in recent years the United Shoe Workers has greatly extended its membership among the foreign nationalities in the industry.

The causes of these secessions are economic, not nationalistic, though immigrant races complicate the conflicts. With proper policies for avoiding secessions of its members, a union would have little to fear from secession movements or dual organizations of immigrant workers.

This is further emphasized by the jurisdictional disputes among unions. These occur frequently when two unions claim jurisdiction over the same work. Each national union affiliated with the American Federation of Labor has its jurisdiction defined, and conflicts are usually referred to the Federation for settlement. Plumbers have fought with steamfitters, elevator constructors with several other crafts, carpenters with sheet metal workers, coopers with brewery workmen, machinists with glass workers, and so on, where no question of immigrant workers was involved. When, however, a union whose membership is composed mainly of immigrant workers, enters into a dispute with another union of predominantly American membership, it soon takes on the character of a conflict of nationalities.

Thus, the Jewelry Workers' International Union was organized in 1916 as an industrial union and given jurisdiction by the American Federation of Labor over all workers in the industry. This union made rapid progress and soon the machinists and the metal polishers claimed jurisdiction over the tool and die makers and the polishers in the industry. The union of Jewelry Workers is small and its membership is in the main foreign born. It contended that the other unions had done little or nothing to organize their crafts in the jewelry shops, and these skilled men were needed in the Jewelry Workers' Union, for without them as a nucleus, the unskilled could not be organized. It, therefore, refused to give up the skilled mechanics and was suspended from the American Federation of Labor.

Again, the United Cloth Hat and Cap Makers' Union received jurisdiction over the workers on women's hats in 1903 and made considerable headway in organizing them. In 1916 the United Hatters of America claimed jurisdiction over women's hat workers, and the convention of the American Federation of Labor ordered the Cloth Hat and Cap Makers to turn the women's hat makers over to the United Hatters. The latter is an organization dominated by American born and the former is made up mainly of immigrants. The Cap Makers' Union offered to settle the controversy by merging the two unions, but its suggestion was not accepted and it was suspended for refusing to turn part of its membership over to the Hatters which had done little to organize the women's hat workers. At the convention of the American Federation of Labor in Atlantic City in 1919, the Hatters introduced a resolution to have their jurisdiction extended to include cloth hats and caps, while a delegate from the Journeymen Tailors' Union presented a resolution renewing the proposal to unite the two unions. Nothing but the fact that the Cloth Hat and Cap Makers is composed mainly of immigrants can explain the remarkable action of the Committee on the Executive Council's report, which recommended approval of the Hatters' resolution. Only the sound sense and prompt action of President Gompers saved the convention from approving this resolution.[1]

Antagonism and division between immigrants in the ranks of organized labor and the American members are caused by these jurisdiction disputes and secession movements. Unions such as the tailors and the ladies' garment workers, which are predominantly foreign born, support the Jewelry Workers and the Cap Makers at the conventions of the American Federation of Labor, as they did the Amalgamated Clothing Workers in their dispute with the United Garment Workers. The delegates of unions whose membership is mainly of native birth or of the older immigration usually side against them in these disputes. Thus is race division intensified by the purely economic question of jurisdictional disputes, which also occur frequently among many unions where immigrants present no problem.

Here again it is evident that sound policies of union management which make for unity are the best methods also of keeping immigrant and native workers united. Lacking such policies, division and disunion are bound to occur, and whenever foreign-born workers are involved, national prejudices are engendered which are the greatest obstacles to common action. Thus it is most important that the ordinary management of the unions in each industry be based on efficient and sound principles of organization and unionism, that will take in and protect the interests of every worker, that will recognize the needs of every group, unskilled as well

---

[1] *Proceedings, 39th Convention,* pp. 387–388.

as skilled, foreign born as well as native, women as well as men; and thus avoid secessions, jurisdictional disputes, and dual unions, with the possibilities of dividing organizations along racial or nationalistic lines.

The responsibility for seeing that the existing American unions do maintain efficient union management and do not leave large numbers of workers in the industries outside of labor organizations must rest with the American Federation of Labor. It is true that the constitution of the Federation gives autonomy over its own affairs to each affiliated organization. But in the recent organizing campaign in the steel industry, the national organizing committee has shown what could be done to win immigrant workers to the ranks of organized labor; and when individual unions neglect great masses of workers who need to be organized, especially the immigrants, these inevitably turn to other organizations for help. Either the I. W. W., which has no faith whatever in the ordinary methods of labor organization is appealed to, or separate and competing organizations under leaders of their own nationalities are set up, and the entire American labor movement is endangered and threatened with division along racial lines.

Whatever may be the attitude of American labor organizations toward restriction of immigration, the only consistent domestic policy for them is to bring those immigrants who are already here and employed in American industries within the folds of a unified American labor movement. The immigrants need help, guidance, direction, and education in the purposes and practices of unionism. If they get it from the existing labor organizations, they will be won over to these and united in a common mind with the American laboring population. If they do not get it from this source, they will naturally turn to leaders of their own nationalities and depend upon their own resources. Thus will unity be destroyed and the American labor movement will fail to stand for the union of native and foreign born.

CHAPTER XII

TRADE UNIONS AS AMERICANIZING AGENCIES

LABOR organizations meet regularly in local unions, shop meetings, district councils, and national conventions, to discuss the problems of their trade and industry. They send delegates to city central bodies, to state federations of labor, and to annual conventions of their national organizations and of the American Federation of Labor, which concern themselves primarily with matters of common interest to all working people, with methods of unionizing unorganized trades, with financial, and moral support of strikes, with legislation, politics, and with the relations of labor organizations to the state and to the public. They maintain insurance funds against sickness and death, homes for the aged and infirm, employment bureaus and out-of-work benefits for the unemployed, schools, educational classes, and trade union colleges. Recently they have begun to establish banks. Their officers and representatives negotiate agreements with employers fixing terms and conditions of employment, and they set up administrative and judicial machinery for settling disputes.

Obviously the immigrant who participates in organizations, institutions, and activities of this kind learns in a most practical way to coöperate with his American fellow workers for mutual benefit, and through such participation, unity of mind is developed between the native and the foreign born. Through parliamentary practice made necessary by the organizations, through election of representatives, officials, and delegates,

UNIONS AS AMERICANIZING AGENCIES

through voting on agreements with employers and on other policies, through the business dealings of his union, through discussions of men and measures, and through the public activities of his organization and its officers, the immigrant learns American methods, traditions, governmental practices, and problems in the best school the adult can have, the daily experiences surrounding his work.

Professor William Z. Ripley of Harvard pointed out many years ago:[1]

Whatever our judgment as to the legality or expediency of the industrial policy of our American unions, no student of contemporary conditions can deny that they are a mighty factor in effecting the assimilation of our foreign-born population. Schooling is primarily of importance, of course, but many of our immigrants come here as adults. Education can affect only the second generation. The churches, particularly the Catholic hierarchy, may do much. Protestants seem to have little influence in the industrial centers. On the other hand, the newspapers, at least such as the masses see and read, and the ballot under present conditions in American cities, have no uplifting or educative power at all. The great source of intellectual inspiration to a large percentage of our inchoate Americans, in the industrial classes, remains in the trade union. It is a vast power for good or evil, according as its affairs are administered. It cannot fail to teach the English language; that in itself is much. Its benefit system, as among the cigar makers and printers, may inculcate thrift. Its journals, the best of them, give a general knowledge of trade conditions, impossible to the isolated workman. Its democratic constitution and its assemblies and conventions partake of the primitive character of the Anglo-Saxon folkmoot, so much lauded by Freeman, the historian, as a factor in English political education and constitutional development. Not the next gubernatorial or presidential candidate, not the expansion of the currency, nor the reform of the general staff of the army; not free-trade or protection, or anti-imperialism, is the real living thing of interest to the trade-union workman. His thoughts, interests, and hopes are centered in the politics of his organization. It is the forum and arena of his social and industrial world.

---

[1] William Z. Ripley, *Atlantic Monthly*, vol. 93, 1904, p. 307.

ADJUSTING IMMIGRANT AND INDUSTRY

What the mine workers' organization has meant to the immigrant workers and to the districts in which they live cannot be more succinctly stated than in the words of a writer who studied conditions in the mining communities some years ago.[1]

The one bright ray of hope lighting up the uncertain future is shed from the activity in these coal fields of the United Mine Workers of America. With this organization, to a much greater degree than most of us realize, rests the solution of many of the problems presented in the hard-coal producing communities. Its power of uniting the mine workers of all nationalities and creeds and tongues . . . of bringing together the Slav and the English-speaking employees on the common ground of industrial self-interest . . . has only recently been demonstrated. Through this it is breaking down the strong racial ties which until its entrance into the region kept the two groups apart. In brief, this organization is socializing the heterogeneous mass.

But for the effect of the union on the individual immigrant, we may best follow the career of such a worker from the time he first enters an industry in which a union is recognized by the employers as the legitimate representative of the wage earners.

We may imagine an Italian coming into a shop where men's or women's clothing is made, for in these shops he will find many of his own nationality employed, and the membership as well as the leadership of the unions which operate in these industries is predominantly foreign born. The union in the women's clothing industry is affiliated with the American Federation of Labor, the one in the men's clothing industry is not. Both are unions which have succeeded in organizing permanently the so-called new immigrants, and both are chosen to illustrate the powerful Americanizing influences of labor organizations.

As a beginner in the industry the newcomer finds that he is to be paid $12 to $15 per week, or whatever hap-

---

[1] F. J. Warne, *The Slav Invasion and the Mine Workers*, p. 9.

pens to be the wage for beginners, fixed in the agreement between the union and the employers. He may not know this at first, but when the shop chairman, who represents the union in the shop, comes to ask him to become a member of the unions he will be told how the union established the minimum scale for all beginners. He will want to know what this union is, and in most shops he will be given two weeks in which to make up his mind whether he wants to remain in the industry and assume his share of the burden of maintaining the union.

He learns that a shop meeting is to be held after working hours, and he goes with the other employees to a hall a few blocks away to attend the meeting. He finds someone who talks English is in charge of the meeting. He is told that it is a business agent of the union, and there is also an organizer present who will translate into Italian the gist of the chairman's remarks. It appears that a new shop chairman is to be elected. A man gets up and explains something in English. It is translated and our immigrant finds that this shop chairman doesn't like his job. He is tired, he says, of constant request for increases in wages by individual workers who want more than was given in the general increase that all the people in the shop received. The people should know that they cannot get such individual increases. He is a piece worker and he cannot afford to lose time taking up complaints in which the workers have no just claims. He resigns. Then there is a lot of discussion—heated discussion—after which nominations are made and a new shop chairman is elected.

This is interesting. In America, it seems, they elect not only the officials of the government, but also the officers who govern them in the shops. Our Italian friend has decided to join the union. He finds he has to pay dues of thirty-six cents a week—he can understand that—but he objects to paying $10 as an initiation fee. What is that for? The shop chairman explain-to him that this initiation fee was only recently established. When they first formed the union anybody could come in by paying a dollar. But they had to conduct strikes, pay benefits, and there were many other expenses in building up the union and winning recognition from the employers. It was the dues of the members as well as special assessments which paid for all this, and as a result increased wages have been secured for everybody and the working hours have been reduced to forty-four a week. A newcomer gets the benefits of all this and he is required to pay the initiation fee for this reason. The immigrant is still not entirely convinced, but he feels he has to pay it, and is relieved to find that the union will let him pay the fee in small weekly installments.

After a few days the shop chairman brings him a little book, which, he is told, is his union book. On the first page is his name and a statement that he is a member of the Italian Local Union No. 21 of the national organization. Then there is printed the constitution and rules of the union in Italian as well as in English, and in the back are several blank pages, ruled with squares in which a few stamps have been stuck indicating the amount of dues he has paid. Each week when he pays, a new stamp will be put in one of the squares. The shop chairman explains that after he has learned English he can be transferred to another local union where all the people who do the same kind of work that he does belong, whether they are Jews, Poles, or Americans. They all talk English, in that local, however, and he will be more at home in the Italian local until he learns some English. His local has a meeting every other Tuesday, and he had better get his friend in the shop to take him to the meeting the following Tuesday.

He goes to the meeting and he hears the secretary reading many communications. It seems they all come from the Joint Board and they tell what occurred at a recent meeting of this board as well as what the manager of the union and the business agents have been doing. Someone gets up to discuss one of the communications. Our Italian finds out that this man is one of the delegates to the Board. There are seven of them from each of the local unions and all the delegates from all the locals together meet once a week and constitute the Board, the governing body of the union in the city.

The delegate who arose explains that the Joint Board voted to request the employers to change the time of beginning work from 8 in the morning to 7:30. Then the people can stop work at 4:30 instead of 5 in the afternoon, and they will have more time after work to enjoy the summer afternoons, perhaps to work in a garden. The action has to be approved by the local unions before it can be presented to the employers. Some people object. They say the clock has recently been moved ahead an hour and this makes it entirely too early to get up in time for work at 7:30. The chairman calls for a vote. Our immigrant feels impelled to get up and vote for the change in hours. He finds most of the members get up with him. The action is approved. He is pleased. He has had something to say about the working hours he must keep.

Another delegate gets up to speak on the communication which tells that the Joint Board desires to appropriate some more money for educational work of the union. He says that the woman who has charge of this work appeared before the Joint Board and explained that various members had asked for more classes and lectures on different subjects. She needed an additional teacher to start another class in English, and she would like to have some special lectures on the history of trade unionism and also on political economy, but she needs money to get them. After some more discussion the action of the Joint Board in appropriating $116 additional for the education work was also approved.

There is more to this union the immigrant finds than just the work of the shop. He will have to inquire about those classes in English that were mentioned. Presently a speaker is introduced, a national organizer of the union. He speaks in Italian. He tells of the growth of the union and the success it has had in other cities.

Everywhere the workers in this industry are lifting up their heads. They are no longer the sweatshop slaves people used to write about in the papers. They have, by their union, won better conditions for themselves than most American workers have. No longer can it be said that the immigrants in this industry keep down the wages of Americans. It is we who have the higher standards now and we might complain that the Americans hold us back. But we know it is not their fault. Only when they organize and stick together in a strong union can they improve their conditions and maintain high standards. We should be proud to know that they cannot say it is we who are holding them back. And we shall be glad to help them in every way to improve their conditions as we have improved ours.

The immigrant goes away from the meeting with new ideas, new interest in life. He finds at later meetings that people bring up grievances and complaints about wages at the local union. They are told, however, that they must take these complaints up first with the shop chairman in their own shop. It seems that there is an agreement between the union and the employers to this effect. The shop chairman takes the worker's complaint to the boss and talks for the worker.

Then, if the worker is not satisfied, the matter may be taken to the union.

At one meeting a group of workers complained that the employer would not take them back. About a dozen of them had quit in a body because of some action of the foreman. The union business agents, however, would not take their complaint. They said the men had no right to quit work. They should have stayed at their work and then complained to the union. Now the employer does not have to take them and the union officers can do nothing for them. There was much warm discussion. But the chairman explained that the agreement between the union and the manufacturers provided there must be no stoppages. The employer cannot discharge a man unless he has a very good reason; if he does the union can put him back or he will be reinstated by an arbitrator. In the same way, the workers are not allowed to quit work in a body. We must learn not to be hot-headed, but to take up our complaints in the regular way provided by the agreement.

Soon our immigrant finds that he is doing as much work as other men near him in the shop, but they are getting more wages than he does. He doesn't think this is right, but he is afraid the foreman might not like it if he complains. He speaks to his friend about it, who tells him there is no need to be afraid. Go to your shop chairman. He will take it up for you. The shop chairman tells him that the union has made an arrangement with the employers that all the people who do his kind of work shall get $30 a week after they have worked at it six months.

"How long have you been working here?"

"Two months."

"What are you getting?"

"Twenty dollars."

"Have you been raised at all?"

"No. I began at twenty dollars."

"All right, I'll see what I can do for you. In the morning you will go down to the office with me and we'll take up your case."

In the morning he goes down to the office of the labor manager with the shop chairman. The latter talks English. The foreman is called down. He and the office man do not seem at all angry; but it seems that the firm refuses to give him any raise. The next day he is called down to the office again. This time there is an officer of the union besides the shop chairman to talk for him. He is asked by the shop chairman, in Italian, if he is sure that he turns out as much and as good work as the others who are at the same operation. He is sure of it. Still the firm does not agree, and the shop chairman tells him to keep on working—"We'll take it to the 'Impartial Chairman.'"

Several days later at quitting time the shop chairman calls him to go to the Impartial Chairman's office. There he finds things arranged like a court. The chairman sits at a desk. His shop chairman and the union representative sit at one side of a table. At the other side are the men to whom they talked in the office, the labor manager, the foreman, and the man who examines his work. The Impartial Chairman asks the union representatives what the case is about. He and the shop chairman talk in English. Then the foreman and the office man talk. Presently the chairman says something and the immigrant is asked in Italian to tell what he wants and why in his own language. It is translated. After that the examiner is asked to speak, and then there is a good deal of discussion back and forth. The chairman at the desk speaks a long time. Finally everybody gets up, and the shop chairman explains in Italian: "It is all right. You are to

get $1.50 a week raise every month until you reach
$30. He says that it is only fair that you should be
raised right along this way, since the examiner finds
your work as good as any the other men do, and you
are doing as much work as they are."

From this time on the immigrant becomes enthu-
siastic about the union. He wants to become an active
member. He feels the great handicap of the lack of
English, and he joins the union class or he takes lessons
in some other way. He interests himself in the meetings of his union and in the shop meetings of the
people in his factory. He votes on many questions and
he finds that it is important to inform himself on those
questions. He hears that a shop chairman has been
removed in one place because of improper action. He
must be careful to vote for good men as shop chairmen.
He begins to read the paper which the union has been
sending him every week since he joined. It is in Italian
and tells him all about the questions that are discussed
at the meetings. It also tells him about conditions in
his industry in other cities throughout the country.
In this way he learns much about the country. There
is an English edition of the paper he gets every week
and he begins to spell things out in it and gradually
learns to read it. This teaches him much more about
his union, his industry, and his new country.

In the union he finds he has to vote on many questions
submitted by the national organization. Shall the
office of the national treasurer be combined with that
of the national secretary? Shall the membership of
the Executive Board be enlarged from nine to fifteen?
Shall the union work for the abolition of piece work
in the industry and shall it adopt standards of production for all week workers? His paper tells him there
was hot discussion of all these questions at the last
national convention. He reads the reports of the

speeches, and he talks the questions over with fellow members of the union. He goes to the meetings of other local unions and of the Joint Board, to hear further discussions of these questions. He meets many people of many nationalities interested in the same things that interest him. Finally he makes up his mind and votes.

He likes this voting business. It is a new experience to him. He helps to elect officers of his local union, delegates to the Joint Board, business agents, members of the National Executive Board and other national officers, and he takes part in choosing delegates to the national convention. At the meetings he attends and at the conventions about which he reads many resolutions are passed on questions not only affecting his industry, but also on legislation adopted or to be adopted by Congress or state legislatures, on acts of the President of the United States, governors, and courts. He would like to become a delegate or an officer himself and learn more about all these things. The government of the United States seems to be run on the same plan and in the same way as the union is conducted. He could become a citizen and know how to take part in the government just like the Americans.

Thus has the union not only assured him an American standard of living, so he can bring over his family and educate his children American fashion, but it has also furnished him a practical school in citizenship, giving him practice in voting, elections, and lawmaking, teaching parliamentary practices, methods of lawmaking, obedience to the agreements of the union and the employers, which are the laws of his industry, and introducing him to judicial processes and methods through the arbitration procedure which the agreement has established. The union is a miniature republic, training him for American citizenship by teaching him

UNIONS AS AMERICANIZING AGENCIES

American democratic methods of dealing with the problems of his work and wages, the things of most vital interest to him. It is the same kind of a school for Americanism that is provided by the "Junior Republics" for young people, which recognize that American citizenship can best be taught by practice in collective action on problems of interest to juveniles rather than by lectures and exhortation.

A trade union needs to engage in no Americanizing or proselytizing campaigns to make Americans of immigrant workmen. If it is efficient and successful as a union, it unites all the workers in the industry and imperceptibly fuses native and foreign born into a common folk.

CHAPTER XIII

THE GOVERNMENT'S RESPONSIBILITY

"Few years ago when I came to United States," wrote John L—
to his teacher, "I did not understand anything because I were not in
State of Delaware." Perhaps in his enthusiasm, Mr. L— put the
case of Delaware rather strongly, but he expressed a feeling prevalent among the foreign-born people of the state that they have been
given very unusual advantages through the schools. [1]

THIS was the reaction of an immigrant to the work of
the Delaware State Department of Immigrant Education. But the Delaware Americanization Committee,
which started this work and then induced the state to
take it over, realized that schooling is but one of the
problems which the immigrant has to meet, and in
regard to which the people of the state have a responsibility toward the aliens in their midst. The Committee's program includes neighborhood work, community gatherings, and a "Trouble Bureau," to which
any sort of a problem affecting immigrant residents can
be brought for solution. Like the classes in English
these services are undertaken so that the immigrant
may know he "were in the state of Delaware."

Says the report of the Delaware Americanization
Committee:[2]

In attempting to express the spirit of America to the foreign-born
people through these various channels, the Americanization Committee has kept steadily in view an objective which is common to
all the work of the Service Citizens—the progressive development
of activities which should ultimately become a public function. . . .
Most of the responsibilities first undertaken by the Americanization Committee have been progressively transferred to the jurisdic-

[1] *Americanization in Delaware*, Bulletin of the Service Citizens
of Delaware, Sept., 1921, p. 9.
[2] *Ibid.*, p. 51.

THE GOVERNMENT'S RESPONSIBILITY

tion of state and local educational authorities. Beginning with
July 1, 1921, the work carried on by the Committee in class rooms
has been taken over by the Department of Immigrant Education.
All the activities mentioned in Chapter II of this report (teacher
training, publication of Americanization news, community gatherings, etc.) except the financing of community gatherings, have been
provided for in the new budget of the State Department of Immigrant Education, and it is hoped that the public day schools will
take over the "steamer" classes. . . .

With these responsibilities taken off its shoulders, the Americanization Committee will be free to concentrate all its energies on
Home Classes for Mothers and the Trouble Bureau. Each of these
fields offers almost inexhaustible possibilities for service to the
people of Delaware. It is our hope that in the future they, too,
may become a part of the state's official program for its foreign
born—a program that shall not miss any conceivable means of
sharing the best gifts of America with all who seek the protection
of her flag.

SHARING THE GIFTS OF AMERICA

*A program that shall not miss any conceivable means
of sharing the best gifts of America with all who seek the
protection of her flag*—(the words will bear repetition)—
this is the responsibility of the government as it is
conceived and gradually being worked out in the state
of Delaware.

It was in this spirit that most of our states in the
early days of the republic opened wide their resources
as well as the privileges of citizenship to aliens. In
the New York State Laws of 1802 we find the following: [1]

Whereas many good and industrious persons being aliens, have
emigrated to this state with an intention to settle and reside therein
and have expended the greater part of their capital in purchasing
and improving real property; and whereas such emigrations have
tended to promote as well an improvement in the agriculture as the
manufactures of the state; and it is deemed just and right not only
to protect the property which they have acquired, but also to

---

[1] New York State Laws, Chapter 49, p. 78.

encourage others to settle and reside within this state by enabling
them to purchase and hold real property; *Therefore be it enacted by
the people of the state of New York represented in Senate and Assembly,*
that all purchases of land made, or to be made, by an alien or aliens
who have come to this state and become inhabitants thereof shall
be deemed valid to vest the estate to them granted and it shall and
may be lawful to and for such alien or aliens to have and to hold the
same to his, her or their heirs or assigns forever, and to dispose of
the same, any plea of alienism to the contrary thereof notwithstand-
ing. . . .

(A proviso is made limiting the amount of land an alien may
hold to 1000 acres, and it is further provided that any conveyances
that may not have been properly made according to the law may
be corrected within twelve months after the adoption of the act.)

The legislature seems to have thought that protection
to the foreign born, in their efforts at earning a living
and in the fruits of their labor, was most important in
inducing them to remain in the state and become good
citizens.   Agriculture being the main occupation at
that time, the legislature directed its attention to
encouraging the alien to acquire and to own real
property. It did this not by discriminating against the
alien and preventing him from owning land until he
became a citizen, but on the contrary it gave him as
an alien the same rights that citizens enjoyed.

The example of the state of New York was followed
by most of the other states; some limiting the number
of acres to less than 1000, and others placing no limitation whatever on the amount of land an alien might
own.   A few states placed time limits on the alien's
property rights, but most states permitted aliens to
own and dispose of real property, as long as they
remained residents of the United States. This policy
of our states with respect to land ownership is further
illustrated by a law enacted in Delaware in 1881,
which exempted from state and court taxes for a period
of ten years certain marsh lands occupied by colonies
of immigrants.

THE GOVERNMENT'S RESPONSIBILITY

RESTRICTING THE IMMIGRANT'S OPPORTUNITIES

In striking contrast with this earlier policy of sharing
the land of America with the immigrant is the present
policy of many states in limiting his opportunities
both for land ownership and for employment.[1] In
Michigan an alien cannot get a barber's license. The
labor law of New York requires that stationary engineers, moving picture machine operators, master pilots,
and marine engineers shall be licensed, and non-
citizens are disqualified by the license laws. Florida,
Oregon, Texas, and Washington prohibit aliens from
catching and selling fish and oysters, while in Arizona,
California, and Idaho license fees for fishing and hunting are from two and a half to ten times as high for the
alien as for the citizen. Virginia prohibits aliens from
planting oysters in certain river beds; and game laws,
either placing prohibitions entirely on aliens or charging them higher license fees than citizens, are common
in many states. In Louisiana an alien printer may
receive no public printing to do. Virginia requires
licenses for junk dealing and no non-citizen may receive
such a license. In Georgia a person must have declared
his intention of becoming a citizen before he can secure
a peddler's license; and in Delaware a discriminating
fee of a hundred dollars is charged to aliens for traveling
peddler's licenses in addition to the fee charged to
citizens. In pre-prohibition days liquor licenses were
issued to citizens only in many states, such as Ohio,
New Jersey, Pennsylvania, Vermont, Texas, Florida,
and Washington.[2]

---

[1] See *Immigrant's Day in Court.* Kate H. Claghorn. Americanization Studies, p. 298.

[2] See *Immigrants in America Review*, Sept. 1915, p. 73.

ADJUSTING IMMIGRANT AND INDUSTRY

This is not an exhaustive list of restrictive laws. It is merely illustrative. And in addition to the state laws there are innumerable municipal ordinances excluding aliens from licensed businesses and occupations. In Philadelphia only citizens may get licenses as "hawkers, peddlers, etc., of fish, vegetables, fruits, berries, general produce, coal, wood, or any wares of merchandise." New York City denies licenses to "cartmen, hackmen, expressmen, drivers, junk dealers, dealers in second-hand articles, hawkers, peddlers, vendors, coal-scalpers, common show men, dirt carters, or stand-keepers within stoop lines" who are aliens. Toledo denies licenses to aliens who would be taxi drivers, and Buffalo will not permit non-citizens to operate pawn shops. Licenses for street trades are denied to foreigners in Bayonne, N. J., Niagara Falls, N. Y., and other cities; and several Massachusetts cities prohibit aliens from dealing in junk or second-hand articles. Where liquor licenses were controlled by municipalities, as in Connecticut, California, Oregon, and Wisconsin, many cities also prohibited these to aliens.

The City Council of Chicago, in December, 1917, adopted an ordinance providing that no person shall be granted a license to engage in any occupation for which a license is required, unless such a person is a citizen of the United States or has legally declared his intention of becoming a citizen. This ordinance came to the attention of the Swiss consul in Chicago and he entered a vigorous protest to Secretary of State Lansing. The Secretary wrote to the Governor of Illinois, pointing out that such legislation might involve the United States in serious difficulties with other nations who, under treaties with this country, grant rights and privileges to Americans in their jurisdictions on the condition that the same treatment shall be accorded their people in America. Treaties of the United States being among the supreme laws of the land which are binding on the states, the Secretary requested that the Chicago ordinance be repealed. It was only when the Mayor of Chicago called attention to these facts that the Council repealed the ordinance.[1] The discriminations against the alien usually remain effective, and where the state or city acts in a proprietary capacity, as in employment on public works or regulation of hunting, fishing, oyster planting, etc., the discriminations against the immigrant are probably well within its powers.

But the policy of restricting the alien's opportunities for employment is not confined to licensed callings. States like California, Idaho, Louisiana, Pennsylvania, and Wyoming exclude alien common laborers from employment on public works. Many other states, including New York, Massachusetts, Indiana, Louisiana, Utah, and Washington, give preference to American citizens on all public works and permit aliens to be employed only when citizens are not available. The same policy of restricting opportunities of employment on public works is followed by most of our municipal governments. City charters, local ordinances, or civil service regulations discriminate against aliens who may want to earn a living at street contruction, sewer digging, subway building, or any other public work. Cities like Baltimore, Providence, Philadelphia, and Pittsburgh forbid entirely the employment of aliens on public works. Others permit them to do the com-

---

[1] The treaty between the United States and Switzerland provides that citizens of either country shall have the right to "acquire, possess, and alienate property, to manage affairs, to exercise their professions, their industry, and their commerce," in either country, and that "no pecuniary or other more burdensome conditions shall be imposed upon the enjoyment of the above-mentioned rights than shall be imposed on the citizens where they reside nor any conditions whatever to which the latter shall not be subject."

mon labor, but usually only after citizens cannot be secured.

In 1915 Arizona attempted to extend her restrictive anti-alien labor law to private industries, by an enactment which required that employers who have more than five employees must see to it that at least eighty per cent of these are citizens of the United States. This law was declared unconstitutional by the United States Supreme Court on the ground that it conflicted with the Fourteenth Amendment to the Constitution, which prohibits the states from enacting laws denying the equal protection of the laws to any persons within its jurisdiction.[1] Morally the laws and ordinances discriminating against immigrants on public works also violate the principle laid down in the 14th amendment, but legally they have been upheld by the courts, on the ground that cities and states, when they stipulate the kind of workers who may be employed on public works, are acting in the capacity of proprietor, and as such they may employ or not employ whomever they see fit.

But the Fourteenth Amendment could hardly protect nonresident families of immigrant wage earners who suffer industrial accidents in this country and whose families are excluded from the benefits of workmen's compensation laws. In fourteen states the compensation laws contain no provision for nonresident alien dependents of immigrants killed or injured in industry. Fourteen others recognize such dependents, but limit the benefits they may receive under the compensation laws either to amounts smaller than resident families, or to restricted classes of beneficiaries or both. Two states, New Jersey and New Hampshire, exclude all nonresident alien dependents of any immigrant

---

[1] Traux *vs*. Raich, 239 U. S. 33.

workman injured in their industries. Only seven states include beneficiaries of alien and citizen alike, and provide full compensation.

EFFECTS OF DISCRIMINATION

The reason for the laws prohibiting or restricting employment of aliens on public works is stated as follows in the Constitution of the State of Illinois: "to protect the labor of native and naturalized citizens." [1] This is, no doubt, the motive behind most of the state and municipal legislation which discriminates against unnaturalized immigrants. But another motive is to hasten the naturalization of immigrants; and many private employers, in furtherance of what they consider patriotic endeavor, are following the example of the state and municipal legislatures and denying employment to aliens. [2]

To the Trouble Bureau of the Delaware Americanization Committee came an Italian who was "sent in by the Associated Charities to get a copy of his naturalization certificate," without which it was almost impossible for him to obtain employment. Investigation revealed that the Court had no record of his naturalization. Then it came out that he had not gotten his papers in court at all, but from a "boss" who had charged him $5 for his declaration and $10 for his final paper. "I guess maybe that boss, he fool me," he said simply. "No speak English—no understand." He had been under the impression all these years that this is the way the great American nation bestows the priceless gift of its suffrage upon newcomers. A man must live in Rome for thirty years before he can become a Roman citizen.

Yet this man's conception of American citizenship is not so different, after all, from that of the employer who would compel all aliens to take out papers or be cut off from the employment without which they cannot find food for themselves or their families. Since jobs began to be scarce, the office of the Trouble Bureau has

[1] Chapter 6, sec. 10.
[2] Report of the Delaware Americanization Committee, 1921, p. 41.

been besieged by men and women who want to become citizens,
and incidentally not because they have learned to love this
country better than any other in the world, but because would-be
patriotic employers insist on the nation's granting a vote to all whom
they employ.

Just as the Delaware Americanization Committee
does not find that employers tend to make better
Americans of immigrants by denying them employment, so the New York State Bureau of Industries
and Immigration did not find that the laws which
discriminate against aliens tend to make better citizens
of them. On the contrary: [1]

One of the results of such legislation has been to educate the
immigrant in law-breaking and to debase his ideals of citizenship.
When laborers are in demand, "first papers" are sometimes given
to them so they may "comply" with the law; when their votes are
needed, politicians use them. In one of the states where, as soon as
an alien has filed his declaration of intention to become a citizen,
he is given full electoral privileges, the number filing their declara-
tions in a presidential election year was 660 from July to October;
from October to July there were only 71. On one public contract,
when the alien labor law was being tested in the courts, first papers
were supplied to each laborer who renounced his allegiance to his
own country and pledged his faith to a new one for the sole consideration of $1.75 a day.

These experiences make it evident that we cannot
deny opportunities for employment to the alien immigrant, in order "to protect the labor of native and
naturalized citizens," and at the same time expect
these aliens to become loyal and patriotic Americans.
We have seen the undesirable effects of a trade-
union policy which excludes immigrants from its membership, how it develops antagonism between the native
and the foreign born, and prevents the development of
a common mind. We have seen how the employer

[1] New York Bureau of Industries and Immigration—First Annual
Report, 1911.

who discriminates against foreign labor in hiring methods and other labor management policies tends to produce the same effects. For a state or municipal government to restrict opportunities for employment or otherwise to discriminate in its legislation against its alien residents is not essentially different from either of these. Congress may see fit to prohibit or restrict immigration in order to protect American standards; but those immigrants who have been admitted by the federal government cannot be denied the privileges of America without danger to the nation. The framers of the Fourteenth Amendment to the Constitution saw this clearly when they provided that no state shall "deprive *any person* of life, liberty or property without due process of law; nor deny *any person* within its jurisdiction the equal protection of the laws." It was intended to guarantee the privileges of America to all persons resident here, not to citizens alone.

A nation whose hope it is to weld together its immigrant and native-born population into a single citizenship can pursue no other policy and expect to see its hope realized. Not by exclusion from American industrial opportunities and privileges will the immigrant be adjusted to American economic life. Such a policy, whatever its purpose, can result only in making it more difficult for him to establish himself on a basis of self-support and well-being. If we desired to have a subordinate class of alien laborers who are not to be of us, but who would merely work for us, then this would be a proper policy to pursue. As long as our aim is to fuse the immigrant with the native born into a common citizenship, he will have to share in the privileges and opportunities of America, and he will need guidance and assistance during his first years of residence in the country, his most trying period of adjustment.

255

ADJUSTING IMMIGRANT AND INDUSTRY

The State of Connecticut seems to have realized this when in 1895 it enacted a law providing that: [1]

> The commissioner of the bureau of labor statistics is hereby authorized to appoint some competent person or persons, familiar with the language of Italian, Polish, or other alien laborers, as special agents of the bureau, whose duty it shall be to inform said laborers, either personally or through printed matter in their language, as to their right of contract under the laws of the State and to prevent, as far as possible, any illegal advantage being taken of said laborers by reason of their ignorance, credulity, or want of knowledge of the English language.

With such assistance from the state the employment contracts of the recent immigrant could be given the same protection as the real estate contracts of the older immigrants received. The law, however, appears to be a dead letter on the statute books. Under date of November 26, 1918, the Commissioner of Labor of Connecticut wrote to us: "The law you referred to was passed in 1895, and I have no means of knowing now what the reason for its enactment was. I find upon inquiry that no question was ever raised under it during the term of my predecessor nor has there been any appointment during my term of office."

While Connecticut was the first state to recognize in legislation the special protection which the immigrant wage worker needs to remove the handicaps under which he labors and to place him on an equality with his American fellow workers, it failed to create the agencies for putting the law into actual practice. The state of New York, however, created in 1910 a Bureau of Industries and Immigration as a division of its Department of Labor, for the purpose of dealing

---

[1] Public Acts, 1895, Chapter ccxcv, 9. 638.

THE GOVERNMENT'S RESPONSIBILITY

in a comprehensive way with the problems of protection, supervision, and assimilation of the immigrants arriving and residing in the state. The creation of this bureau resulted from the investigations and recommendations of an Immigration Commission authorized by the legislature of 1908, and it was the first attempt by an American state to organize deliberately the forces and agencies of Americanization under a public authority, and to create the administrative agencies necessary to further the work of assimilation.[1]

Believing that an alien's first impression, his first experiences on arrival, and his first contract with American institutions, are the most lasting; that if his property rights and liberty are not respected on arrival he can not be expected to respect those of people resident here; and that if he has not been given a square deal he will later visit his early experiences upon his newly arrived brothers; the state has undertaken, so far as its facilities permit, to make these early experiences forces for real civilization. . . .

The report of the legislative commission brought to light a great volume of frauds and exploitations practiced upon these foreign-born people. It emphasized the need for greater correlation of activities on the part of public and private agencies for their protection and preparation for citizenship. On the commission's recommendation the bureau of industries and immigration was established with functions broad enough to enable it to become the agency for inspecting, investigating, and promoting coöperative effort to meet these increasingly difficult problems.

New Jersey, shortly after New York, appointed an Immigration Commission to investigate the same problems in that state, but the legislature did not see fit to enact the laws it recommended. California, however, created, in 1914, a permanent Commission of Immigration and Housing which has during the seven years of its existence done some of the most effective work with immigrants that has come to our attention.

---

[1] First Annual Report, New York Bureau of Industries and Immigration, 1911, p. 15.

ADJUSTING IMMIGRANT AND INDUSTRY

This Commission states its duties and outlines its responsibilities in the following words:[1]

All the problems which touch the immigrant take on a distinct aspect peculiar to no problem of the native born . . . The foreign born suffers great hardships because, from the moment of his arrival, he is placed at a disadvantage, and that, in order that he may be placed on an equal footing with his native-born neighbor, definite constructive aid must be given him in overcoming his handicaps. Furthermore . . . as the immigrant suffers from his shortcomings so does the community in which he lives suffer with him.

Ordinarily the immigrant is so situated that he becomes an easy prey to exploiters, that he finds it almost impossible to get on his feet economically; misfortune drags him into the overcrowded quarters of our slums, those breeding places of disease, immorality, crime, and ignorance; education in English and civics is almost impossible to attain. Such a man is not on the road to becoming a useful citizen. Indeed, unguided and unprotected, he is liable to become a menace. The correction of these evils is no more than a matter of our own self-protection. . . .

But the immigrant is not merely a potential menace from whom we must protect ourselves. With the proper encouragement, he may become a positive source of benefit to our civilization. Each man brings to our shores certain inherited racial and national talents as well as certain personal faculties which we may encourage and develop to our own advantage. . . . The protection of the foreign born from exploitation, the building up of proper standards, and the opening up of economic and educational opportunities are what are involved in the conception of a domestic immigration policy.

About the same time that the California Commission was created, the city of Cleveland established an Immigration Bureau in its Department of Public Welfare with functions similar to the bureau in the state of New York. In 1917 Massachusetts also established a Bureau of Immigration following recommendations of a legislative commission, and the law creating the bureau states its purpose as follows:

---

[1] California Commission of Immigration and Housing, Annual Report, 1916, pp. 131–2.

THE GOVERNMENT'S RESPONSIBILITY

It shall be the duty of the bureau to employ such methods, subject to existing laws, as, in its judgment, will tend to bring into sympathetic and mutually helpful relations the commonwealth and its residents of foreign origin, to protect immigrants from exploitation and abuse, to stimulate their acquisition and mastery of the English language, to develop their understanding of American government, institutions, and ideals, and generally to promote their assimilation and naturalization. For the above purposes, the bureau shall have authority to coöperate with other offices, boards, bureaus, commissions, and departments of the commonwealth, and with all public agencies, federal, state, or municipal. It shall have authority to investigate the exploitation or abuse of immigrants, and in making any investigation it may require the attendance of witnesses and the production of books and documents relating to the matter under investigation.

We have already mentioned the Delaware Americanization Committee, which is gradually turning over its work to the state. The "Service Citizens of Delaware," the organization which finances this work in coöperation with the state, thus states its purpose in its last annual report:

When the people of Delaware began three years ago to plan how they might bring the foreign-born residents of the state closer to the best life of the American community they called the plans they made "an Americanization program." The purpose of the movement they thus described has always been very simple and direct. We referred to it in a previous report as "the planting in the hearts of all who live under our flag an understanding love for America."

For many immigrants the love they bore the America of their dreams has faded in cruel disillusionment before a grim reality which they have learned to call by her name, but which is no less unlike the America we know than was their first idealistic vision. Those of us who have found America a country beautiful and dear must somehow share our experience with our friends from overseas if we expect them to believe in it, too. There are two ways of doing this. The first is by the spoken word. The second is by the living deed. Delaware is using both to reach her foreign born to-day.

ADJUSTING IMMIGRANT AND INDUSTRY

In discussing factory English classes in a preceding chapter we mentioned the tendency of state and local school authorities to take over the responsibility for instruction in these classes. The prevailing system at the present time is for the employer to furnish the classroom with heat, light, and other equipment while the schools furnish instruction, supervision, and educational material. In Massachusetts, New York, Pennsylvania, Delaware, Connecticut, Illinois, California, and other states divisions of immigrant education have been established, for the purpose of giving special attention to the schooling of adult immigrants, and classes conducted by school authorities in the daytime at the place of employment have proved to be the most effective means to the end desired. In states where no special laws have been enacted providing for adult immigrant education, local school authorities have been just as eagerly entering into arrangements for "coöperative classes" in the factories.

These coöperative classes have emerged as the most successful method of teaching English to immigrant wage earners, after many experiments with public evening schools and factory classes conducted by employers, both of which failed to bring the results which were expected of them.

The old idea of community responsibility for the education of adult immigrants was limited to the

---

[1] For much of the material in this section we are indebted to an unpublished report by John T. Mahoney and Charles M. Herlihy entitled "Industry and the Non-English Speaking Employee." Mr. Herlihy is now supervisor of Americanization in the Massachusetts Department of Education, and Mr. Mahoney formerly occupied the same position.

THE GOVERNMENT'S RESPONSIBILITY

establishment of evening schools. The facilities for evening instruction were provided in most of the larger cities, but the idea seemed to be that the instruction was for the benefit of the immigrant only, and if he chose not to take advantage of it or was unable to do so, after a long day's work, so much the worse for him. The result was that only the unusually ambitious took advantage of the evening schools and the main body of non-English-speaking immigrants was left untouched.

During the war, when the presence of great numbers of illiterate and non-English-speaking immigrants in industrial plants began to be recognized as a danger to industry as well as to the community, factory classes sprang up like mushrooms. All sorts of pressure was brought to force attendance at these classes and almost any foreman or clerk who was willing to undertake the work was considered competent to teach the classes. The result of this, as we have seen,[1] was that the classes died out as fast as new ones were being started.

As a result of this experience with evening schools, a few states enacted compulsory attendance laws for illiterate minors.[2] But the model act designed to provide English instruction for adult immigrant wage earners is that of Massachusetts, adopted in 1919. This law authorizes the holding of classes in industrial establishments and other convenient places, and provides for state aid to local educational authorities who undertake the work to the extent of fifty per cent of the expense.[3]

---

[1] Chapter VI.

[2] See Thompson, *Schooling of the Immigrant*, Chapter X, for details of these laws.

[3] "The Massachusetts Law. General Laws, Chapter 69, Sections 9 and 10. Section 9. The department (of education) with the coöperation of any town applying therefor, may provide for such instruction in the use of English for adults unable to speak,

ADJUSTING IMMIGRANT AND INDUSTRY

A national conference of educational directors in industrial plants was held in Nantasket in June, 1919, and this conference came to the same conclusion that public educational authorities had reached. They recommended:

"1. That instruction in English for non-English-speaking people should be carried on in coöperation with the public educational forces, provided those forces are prepared and will assume the responsibility. We pledge our aid in our respective communities to bring about this coöperation.

"2. That the industrial representatives here gathered disapprove making naturalization a condition of employment."

Pursuant to the Massachusetts law the State Department of Education and the Associated Industries of Massachusetts held a conference under joint auspices, and at that conference the following report on state policies and procedure with respect to adult immigrant education was adopted:[1]

POLICIES

(1) The significant statement has been made in this conference that 800,000 immigrants landed on our shores during the year ending June 30, 1920, in contrast with 141,000 the previous year. The

read, or write the same, and in the fundamental principles of government and other subjects adapted to fit for American citizenship, as shall jointly be approved by the local school committee and the department. Schools and classes established therefor may be held in public school buildings, in industrial establishments, or in such other places as may be approved in like manner. Teachers and supervisors employed therein by a town shall be chosen and their compensation fixed by the school committee, subject to the approval of the department.

"Section 10. At the expiration of each school year, and on approval by the department, the commonwealth shall pay to every town providing such instruction in conjunction with the department, one half the amount expended therefor by such town for said year."

[1] Massachusetts Department of Education, Division of University Extension, Americanization Letter No. 5.

THE GOVERNMENT'S RESPONSIBILITY

immigrant tide is again on the rise. America welcomes these new-comers from overseas. America has learned, however, the danger of allowing in our midst thousands who are with us but not of us, mainly because of the language barrier. Hence the imperative need of education in English and the principles of American citizenship to the end that our American institutions may endure.

(2) Thousands of our non-English-speaking immigrants are to be found in the industries. Because of this, the coöperation of the industries with the educational authorities will go far to help us solve the difficult problem of assimilation. The spirit of co-operation between the industries and the schools displayed at this conference is a happy augury of achievement for the coming year. We believe that the delegates here gathered should do everything within their power to spread this coöperation over a wider and wider area.

(3) The education of the immigrant is a public function, and wherever possible should be carried on by public educational authori-ties, in accordance with the plans formulated by the State Depart-ment of Education following out the provisions of Chapter 295, Acts of 1919. Industry should avail itself of the educational facili-ties offered by the public schools, and should coöperate in every feasible way to perfect these facilities.

(4) Public educational authorities must appreciate that adequate plans for educating the immigrant call for the expenditure of many times more money than is now being provided. The choice, however, is between illiteracy which breeds anarchy, and education which indoctrinates good citizenship. There is nothing between. This convention goes on record as endorsing a generous expenditure of public funds for this public work, and urges that public educational authorities everywhere become more keenly alive to their duty in this field of educational endeavor.

(5) The Americanization movement has been subject to some criticism because the term Americanization has been given so many false connotations. We believe in an Americanization which has for its end the making of good American citizens by developing in the mind of everyone who inhabits American soil an appreciation of the principles and practices of good American citizenship. We conceive of Americanization as a process of giving, not of taking away. We believe that English is only the first step in this process, but it is a very necessary step, and the task to which the school should primarily address itself. We deplore wholesale denuncia-tions of immigrant groups as constituting a menace to our American institutions. We hold to the opinion that Americanization should not be compulsory. And we boldly express our confidence that if

we in the true spirit of America will do our duty towards the immigrant, he will not be found wanting in his attitude towards that America which native born and immigrant are together daily building.

Procedures

To carry out the foregoing policies, this Committee, after carefully analyzing the findings of the industrial and the school groups and considering the suggestions given in discussion, recommends the following set-up for the two agencies, respectively:

(1) The Schools:

    (a) Accept provisions of Chapter 295, Acts of 1919.

    (b) Appropriate enough money to get the work well done.

    (c) Provide for classes in industries whenever organized.

    (d) Provide a director of immigrant education.

    (e) Train and supervise teachers.

    (f) Provide suitable text material, including motion pictures.

    (g) Organize courses of study.

(2) The Industries:

    (a) Centralize responsibility in a plant director or committee or other effective agency.

    (b) Conduct preliminary study to learn the extent and nature of the problem.

    (c) Recruit classes.

    (d) Provide satisfactory school accommodations.

    (e) Establish an efficient follow-up.

    (f) Provide incentives.

    (g) Collaborate in training teachers and in providing special text material.

As a corollary to the above, we endorse the report of the Findings Committee of the industrial group to the effect that "no dictum should be expressed as to the time when classes in industry should be held. Each industry should decide this question on the basis of its own hours of labor and other working conditions." Furthermore, we hold with them that any community plan for the education of the immigrant will be successful only when it has received full endorsement and support from both management and workers in industry, and from teachers and all other responsible parties in the school. And, finally, we most heartily concur in their findings that any coöperative program such as is suggested above will be effective only when based on mutual confidence and respect on the part of the two agencies, each for the other."

THE GOVERNMENT'S RESPONSIBILITY

That this new policy of government responsibility for English classes in industrial establishments promises to overcome the failures of the earlier efforts with evening schools and classes conducted entirely by employers is evident from the following records of the factory classes conducted by public school authorities in Massachusetts since the law referred to was enacted:

Year	Number of Classes
1919–20	131
1920–21	327
1921–22	366

Most significant in this record is the increase in the number of classes during the years of industrial depression and restriction of immigration. In many states where public responsibility for such instruction had not been assumed, as in Massachusetts, factory classes dwindled and disappeared as industries were struck by the depression.

COMPLAINT OR TROUBLE BUREAUS

In his attempts to adjust himself to American industrial conditions the immigrant often gets into trouble because of his ignorance, his inability to speak English, and the presence of people in every community who are ready to take advantage of the helpless. The government that desires to assure the immigrant the protection of our laws and to assist him in the process of adjustment must find out what his troubles are.

So in California the Commission of Immigration and Housing reports:[1]

From the start the Bureau of Complaints became the point of contact between the state and the people whom the Commission was to serve. From the start it became evident that it was to be

---

[1] Annual Report. 1919, pp. 13–14.

the chief protective branch of the Commission and from the start its work divided itself into three parts. . . .

Not to theorize concerning the problems and difficulties met with by newly arrived immigrants, but to find out from the immigrants themselves what those facts are, this was the first work of the complaint bureau. . . . In the capacity of clinic, the bureau takes up the work of research. . . . Here the causes of the immigrant's difficulties are sought out.

Then the individual complaints are adjusted. Land frauds, insurance frauds, wage claims, industrial accidents, bad housing conditions, unsanitary camps, and unnumbered other difficulties are referred to their proper departments and settled in the best way possible.

The work of legislation forms the third part of the work and is the logical end of research. And the Commission takes just pride in the laws which have been enacted for the protection of the stranger.

Similarly in Delaware: [1]

Our attempt to demonstrate to the foreign people of Delaware that America is in very truth the land of "liberty and justice for all" would be empty indeed if we ignored the tragic injustices and misunderstandings that do occur and have done so much to destroy the foreigner's faith in the country of his adoption.

If we are unwilling to face these facts and to take definite steps to change them, all our fine phrases about patriotism will be worse than wasted. That is why we could not feel that we were keeping faith with the foreign people of Delaware or with the fair name of America if we did not have some such institution as the "Trouble Bureau" to which any sort of a problem affecting immigrant residents can be brought for solution.

The nature of the troubles and the kind of assistance immigrant wage earners need may be gathered from the experience of the Massachusetts Bureau of Immigration: [2]

The Bureau has received numerous applications for assistance regarding collection of wages. The Bureau in no sense aims to act as a collection agency, but difficulties due to the migration of the immigrant from place to place, his inability to speak English or write

---

[1] *Americanization in Delaware*, 1920–21, p.37.

[2] First Annual Report, 1919, p. 18.

for himself concerning money due him, the uncertain delivery of mail, and the confusion which sometimes arises from the use of check numbers were often eliminated by friendly correspondence with the employer, which cleared up many of the misunderstandings—frequently those of the employee—in the matter of wage contracts. Such cases as could not be settled by friendly intermediation were referred to the State Board of Labor and Industries, if the evidence warranted such reference, or to the Legal Aid Society.

Once the work of a government agency becomes known, immigrants come to it not only with their complaints, but also with requests for information and advice.[1]

Men come to ask concerning laws on land, on wages, on naturalization, on housing, on bad camps. Men come for help with money orders, with letters, with loans, with investments. The Commission's agents must know how a divorce is obtained, where free blankets and free seed samples are to be had, must be able to advise on labor unions and pastimes, on charities and dentists—on everything which touches human life.

The Bureau[2] has aimed to become a clearing house of information useful to the immigrant, whose ignorance of the language renders him particularly liable to misunderstanding, fraud, and abuse. He is often ignorant of the civic, social, and philanthropic resources of the community.... In many cases our service has been to personally bring the applicant coming for advice and assistance into direct contact with the proper agency. Often additional aid in interpretation has been given because of ignorance by the applicant of the English language. In many cases, a preliminary investigation by the Bureau assisted in the solution of the problem by the agency to which it was assigned. From the beginning of the Bureau, September, 1917, up to December 1, 1918, 3905 applications for service have been made at the Bureau on which it has been necessary to have correspondence. For the same period of time, 2018 applications for service have been made which needed no correspondence.

---

[1] Annual Report, California Commission of Immigration and Housing, January, 1919, p. 15.

[2] First Annual Report, Massachusetts Bureau of Immigration, March, 1919, p. 13.

ADJUSTING IMMIGRANT AND INDUSTRY

The complaints registered with immigration bureaus and the nature of the advice and information sought, have been the best guides for these public agencies as to the methods to be pursued in accomplishing their tasks. Among the complaints and requests for assistance, industrial maladjustments stand out most prominently. Of the 10,800 complaints received by the New York Bureau in 1918 over 2500 were claims for wages, more than 1300 related to employment agencies, 511 concerned conditions in labor camps.[1] Of the 5000 cases handled by the Massachusetts Bureau during the first year of its existence, 102 related to employment, 179 to compensation for injuries, 100 to claims for wages.[2] And the California Commission reports almost 2000 wage claims, 483 industrial accidents and compensation claims, 812 cases of breach of contract, 400 cases of employment agency frauds and misrepresented employment, 927 complaints of unsanitary labor camps and 460 land frauds of a total of 7200 complaints between January 1, 1916 and July 1, 1918.[3]

The need of better industrial adjustments which these complaints show cannot be met by the action of a public bureau for immigrants alone. Licensing, inspection, and supervision of private employment bureaus are usually in the hands of another authority. The State Department of Labor commonly conducts the public employment bureaus, and where wage payment laws have been enacted these, too, are enforced by labor departments. Industrial accidents are handled

---

[1] Annual Report of the Industrial Commission of New York, 1919, p. 214.

[2] First Annual Report Massachusetts Bureau of Immigration, p. 42.

[3] Annual Report of California Commission of Immigration and Housing, 1919, pp. 68–69.

by workmen's compensation commissions, and conditions in factories and labor camps are supervised by various authorities. The bureaus for immigrants, however, undertake the duty of making these public agencies function for the immigrant, bring him in contact with them, impress upon them the special needs of the immigrant, and assist them in giving the special services that he needs.

PUBLICITY MEASURES

It is not enough to have a bureau where complaints may be made and advice secured. Many will come, but many more will never hear of the bureau, and active efforts are needed to reach the immigrant. A public authority desiring to help the stranger in its jurisdiction cannot afford to wait for him to learn through his own efforts of the existence of a bureau for immigrants. It must advertise.

To tell the immigrant that the government is ready to lend a helping hand various expedients are used. The Massachusetts Bureau of Immigration placards railway stations, public buildings, factories, churches, etc., with notices in English and in numerous foreign languages making its existence known, giving the location of its offices, the office hours, and the character of the services rendered to immigrants. This bureau also uses local correspondents to acquaint the foreign born with its work in cities and towns where it has no branch office, but where any considerable number of them live.

The Cleveland City Bureau published small handbooks in various languages, describing its operations as well as the services that other agencies in the city were ready to render to immigrants. These were widely distributed in the districts where the foreign born live, and given to the arriving immigrants at the depots.

In New York the Bureau of Industries and Immigration established a press information bureau and kept almost a thousand foreign-language newspapers supplied with information relating to the activities of the bureau. A file was created showing the editors, location, and nationality of each paper, and the policy and nature of the material it uses. Through this medium any group of aliens could be immediately reached. Realizing that prosecutions and remedies in individal cases will not necessarily prevent further frauds, a group of fifty newspapers, representing all nationalities and languages, was selected by the New York Bureau early in its existence, and whenever widespread frauds were detected and proved, exploiters apprehended, or fraudulent institutions closed, notice was sent to these papers, asking them to acquaint their countrymen with the facts.

A placard widely distributed by the California Commission of Immigration and Housing was this organization's first step in making its existence known to the foreign born of California. This was printed in twelve different languages and offered assistance to immigrants. These posters were placed conspicuously in all immigrant centers throughout the state.

This Commission is firm in the belief that Americanization must begin before the immigrant can learn English, that his need of knowing America and her institutions is greatest before he can hope to understand the language. Aside from the regular interpreters, therefore, it sends foreign-language speakers among the immigrants of the state to make clear to them in their own tongue those things which perplex and baffle them in their new environment. They

THE GOVERNMENT'S RESPONSIBILITY

explain the laws which so often the foreign born transgress through ignorance; they learn the grievances of immigrant laborers in labor camps and act as mediators between them and their employers; they make clear to the newcomers their duties to their new country as well as their rights and privileges.

SUPERVISION OF WORK PLACES

Labor camps on construction works, in the woods, on railroads and in connection with mining, road building, reclamation projects, and harvesting fruits, hops, and other agricultural products are typical work places of the newly arrived immigrant. In New York the Bureau of Industries and Immigration has power only to inspect these and to make recommendations, but the California Commission in 1915 was also given authority to enforce the Labor Camp Sanitation Law. The Commission prepared plans and specifications with drawings and descriptions for building and maintaining sanitary labor camps, and its agents assist superintendents in making camps habitable and up to standard at a minimum of expense.

As a result of five years' work in this direction, labor and living conditions in California's camps have been revolutionized and, whereas in previous years strikes and riots were common forms of rebellion against unsanitary camp conditions, no serious labor trouble of this kind has arisen recently. In the lumber camps the Commission visited when it began its work only one bath was found. At present practically every lumber camp in the state has bathing facilities. The standards of sanitation for fruit, berry, and miscellaneous camps have been entirely changed, and in connection with these the Commission has evolved plans of community camps, a number of small holders erecting a camp at a central point and operating it jointly, thus making it possible to maintain decent camps which no small holder could individually afford. Railroad companies are building model car camps for their section and extra gangs and bridge crews, and mine operators have made many improvements in their camp conditions.

What these improvements may mean to the country as well as to the immigrant is suggested in a letter from a ranch superintendent to the Commission. He wrote:

> During the past summer there was a labor shortage in the Imperial Valley. While many other farmers in the valley were unable to handle their crops promptly on account of shortage of men, we scarcely felt the shortage at all. . . . We attribute this largely to our housing accommodations. . . . We farmers must realize that the farm laborers, as in fact almost all laborers, have really never had a fair chance and are entitled to better things. . . . Imperial Valley farmers should show good profits, provided they can get their crops harvested. . . . Part of these profits rightfully should and must go into the installation of sanitary labor camps and living accommodations.

It makes little difference whether the enforcing of American standards of working and living conditions for the immigrant is entrusted by law directly to the immigrant protective authority, as in California, or is left to other authorities as in New York and Massachusetts. The bureau for immigrants must, however, have power to investigate, inspect, supervise, and recommend the special measures necessary to insure American standards for the immigrant which it learns to know from its daily contact with him.

EDUCATION AND NATURALIZATION

The work of fostering citizenship may be illustrated by the Division of Naturalization in the Massachusetts Bureau of Immigration. The division gives assistance in filling out both first and second papers, it explains and eliminates technical difficulties, and it organizes instruction for better preparation for citizenship. Lists of those eligible for second papers are kept on file, and letters are sent to declarants informing them of the assistance and instruction available to prospective citizens and by whom given in all the communities of the state. There are many educational agencies willing and anxious to give this instruction to immigrants. The division helps to organize classes, and it conducts conferences and classes for practical training of teachers of citizenship. The difficulties and complaints brought by the immigrant to the Bureau are discussed by the teachers and they learn to teach not the right and duties contained in formal legal documents, but the living responsibilities and privileges that the foreign born may encounter in their daily experiences.

INADEQUATE APPROPRIATIONS

These descriptions are sufficient to indicate the nature of the responsibilities which some states and municipal governments have assumed toward the immigrant worker and the manner in which they attempt to meet these responsibilities.

It should be mentioned also that the California Commission and the New York Bureau of Industries and Immigration are given authority to inspect and supervise employment agencies dealing with immigrants, labor camps where immigrants are employed, docks, ferries, and other landing places of immigrants, relations between immigrants, and steamship or railroad ticket agents, banking and savings institutions and sheltering of immigrants in hotels and lodging houses. The New York Bureau licenses lodging houses and the California Commission is given broad authority over the housing conditions of the immigrant population of the state.

Unfortunately, however, only the California Commission has received anything like adequate financial support to enable the work to be carried on. The New York Bureau began with an appropriation of less than $10,000 and much of its work had to be done by volunteers and with financial aid from private sources. By 1914 the appropriation was increased to $26,000, but in 1917 it was cut to $19,500. A report on the administration of this bureau by the New York Bureau of Municipal Research made in 1917 showed that [1]

> In two years the number of employees has been reduced from twenty-nine to sixteen, and the salaries of those retained have also been reduced. . . . The work described does not measure up to the possibilities for constructive undertaking in the field covered by the law creating this bureau. It shows lack of vision and efficient administration. The broad functions laid down for the bureau at the time it was established are of no less importance now than then. The bureau can be of inestimable service to the state. To abolish it would be a step backward. What is needed, rather, is a complete reorganization and the preparation of a thoroughgoing program for its work in the future.

A visit to the Cleveland Bureau not long ago showed a similar decline in activities. It seems to be assumed that because fewer immigrants have been arriving during the last few years, therefore, there is less need for the activities of the bureau. California seems to realize that the primary work of its immigration commission is protection and help in assimilating the aliens that are already with us, but in most states, while great interest is evidenced in educational and naturalization work, little attention is given to the establishment and maintenance of public protective and guiding agencies which are needed to lay the basis for a proper

---

[1] *American Labor Legislation Review*, June, 1917, pp. 451–462.

adjustment of immigrants. The Massachusetts Bureau of Immigration began with an appropriation of $10,000 in 1919. Since then it has been made a division of the Massachusetts Department of Education, and in 1922 its appropriation was $37,500.

A UNIFIED POLICY

Public policy with respect to the foreign born has become confused since the days when immigrants were solicited to come to our land and inducements given them to stay and become part of us, equal members of a new American nation.

Then our duty was clear. The stranger's necessities in earning a living had to be safeguarded. He had to be assured equal opportunities to adjust himself to the economic life of the country. Laws were enacted by our states to safeguard the immigrant's right to acquire, own, and dispose of property; to look after the comfort and welfare of aliens in transit across the states; to assist those who became residents in finding work and proper boarding places; and to care for the orphans of deceased immigrants. In New York masters of vessels were required to report to the mayor the name, age, occupation, place of birth, and other information about each incoming immigrant passenger, and every alien who was landed was required to report himself to the mayor, so that the city might know its newcomers and proper care could be given to them.[1]

When, however, the federal government adopted the policy of immigration restriction, the exclusion from the country of those who were considered undesirable was carried over into the states in laws and policies of

[1] First Annual Report of the New York Bureau of Industries and Immigration, 1911, p. 11. See also Report of the U. S. Immigration Commission, vol. 39, State Immigration and Alien Laws, p. 489.

exclusion from economic opportunities and rights that citizens enjoy.

This meant not only conflict of policy between the nation, which permits the immigrant to enter and the states which limit his opportunities for employment; but also confusion in the mind of the immigrant as to whether it is desired that he should become an American and as to what he may or may not do in America. If we do not want immigrants among us, working side by side with American workmen, living as neighbors and equals of Americans, then let us keep them out. But they cannot be admitted to the country and at the same time opportunities for earning a livelihood denied them and handicaps placed in their way to prevent raising of their standards—if we are to remain a united nation. If those aliens who are admitted by the federal government are not to be reduced to the position of a subject class, if we want all that live among us to develop a common American mind, then the old policy of the states toward alien residents must be re-established.

To accomplish this, the repeal of discriminatory laws is necessary first. But this negative action alone will not suffice. Positive measures and constructive governmental agencies are also needed to insure protection and guidance to the strangers in our midst, and to make certain that they are put on an equality with their American neighbors in their struggles for a footing and existence in America. The States of Massachusetts, New York, Delaware, and California, and the City of Cleveland have pointed the way for the nation to follow, and they have developed the methods which need but to be extended and expanded.

For, in the words of the Delaware bureau: [1]

---

[1] Bulletin, September, 1921, p. 50.

THE GOVERNMENT'S RESPONSIBILITY

These services, important as they are to the individuals to whom they are rendered, have an even greater significance to the community. Not one in ten of those whom the bureau reaches gives the credit for benefits received to the Delaware Americanization Committee. It all goes to "America." The first experience in the new land is often bitter and discouraging; but this is the faith that has been put into the hearts of the immigrant people of Delaware: "No matter what happens, America cares, America helps, America never willfully neglects her adopted children."

CHAPTER XIV

IMMIGRANT SELF–HELP

PRACTICALLY every immigrant race and nationality has formed some kind of organization to assist newcomers of its own kind to self-support in this country. In addition, groups of immigrants of various nationalities have developed other agencies for meeting special problems in connection with finding work, with trade-union control of jobs, and with employers' policies, as well as with efforts to keep down the cost of living.

IMMIGRANT AID SOCIETIES

The earliest and most familiar of these organizations are the immigrant aid societies, which concern themselves mainly with new arrivals. Their purposes may be gathered from a statement of the president of one of the oldest and most successful of them, the Hebrew Sheltering and Immigrant Aid Society: [1]

Away back in the eighties, at the outset of the early immigration, when the pioneer Jewish immigrants who came here had neither kith nor kin to receive them, the Jewish Community acted as their relative pro tem, and looked after their welfare until they became independently self-supporting. In so doing they were maintaining the sacred covenant of the first Jewish immigrants to guard and cherish their own poor and to administer to their own sick. . . . Our Society has assumed the rôle of Agent for the Community and welcomes the new arrival as a guest for a short time, affording the means for him to reach his relatives. . . . We must know what becomes of him, and make sure that he finds what he is seeking—a home and a living. We owe a debt also to our country, in that we

---

[1] Address of President, Annual Meeting, January 21, 1912.

must be sure that each newcomer from our own race is an acquisition to, and not an incubus upon, the country, that he is self-supporting, and that he duly falls into the ranks as an American.

To make sure that he finds a home and a living, that he is self-supporting and that he duly falls into the ranks as an American—these are the results to be achieved from successful adjustment of immigrant and industry. Concretely the "objects" of the Hebrew Sheltering and Immigrant Aid Society, as stated in its constitution, are:

> To facilitate the landing of Jewish immigrants at Ellis Island; to provide for them temporary shelter, food, clothing, and such other aid as may be deemed necessary; to guide them to their destination; to prevent them from becoming public charges and help them to obtain employment; to discourage their settling in congested cities; to maintain bureaus of information and publish literature on the industrial, agricultural, and commercial status of the country; to disseminate knowledge of the United States Immigration Laws in the centers of emigration in Europe with a view of preventing undesirable persons from emigrating to the United States; to foster American ideals among the newcomers and to instill patriotism and love for their adopted country through the medium of lectures and literary publications.

The Society begins its work abroad. An information bureau sends circulars and warnings to foreign co-operating societies, to prevent people from leaving their homes who cannot hope to be admitted to the United States. The number who are deported is still large and the Society is giving careful consideration to methods of preventing people liable to deportation from leaving their homes. Plans are afoot to elect men of the highest standing in Europe as members of the Advisory Board of the Society and also to station at the leading seaports of Europe representatives of the society, trained in this country, whose business it would be to warn immigrants likely to be refused admittance to the United States from embarking.

279

ADJUSTING IMMIGRANT AND INDUSTRY

At Ellis Island the Society has stationed a representative who meets and greets people of his own nationality who have not been called for by relatives or friends. He turns them over to guides, who take them to the home of the Society. Here they are carefully questioned as to the name, address, and relationship of the people to whom they are destined, and a staff of guides is employed to deliver them safely to the addresses which they have. If an immigrant's address proves to be wrong, the guide brings him back to the home, where he is given lodging and board until his friends can be located. An advertisement is then inserted in the Jewish daily papers, giving the name and a full description of the immigrant who has arrived, and asking readers to inform the Society of the present whereabouts of the people whose address he had. Almost invariably this method leads to prompt discovery of friends or relatives of the immigrant.

The immigrant who is destined to mere acquaintances and not to relatives remains at the home until a representative of the Society ascertains what they are able and willing to do for him. If it is found best to keep the immigrant at the home and assist him to establish himself, it is done without hesitation, and work is sought for him through the Society's Employment Bureau.

The employment agent in charge of this bureau solicits work for immigrants from employers who are in a position to use such labor. Many of the immigrants wish to observe the Jewish Sabbath and all the Jewish holy days, and employers are sought who will permit this. Then there are those who have no trades whatever and for whom must be found opportunities for learning a trade, while those having occupations must be placed in positions where they can learn American methods of work. In many cases the immigrant has to be guided to his place of employment until he becomes familiar with the streets and car lines. The guides of the Society are used for this purpose.

How the immigrant is assisted in dealing with work problems that confront him at the very beginning of his career in America, is thus described by the employment agent of the Society:

In case of difficulties arising in respect to wages, etc., the Employment Bureau has settled these matters without having recourse to court proceedings. . . . Through the agency of the Bureau, immigrants detained at Ellis Island have been admitted when it was shown that there were *bona fide* offers of employment. . . . When offers of employment came from cities outside of New York, the standing of the employer and local conditions, whether there is a strike, etc., were carefully investigated, and not until it was made certain that the immigrant would be well placed was he allowed to proceed to the destination. . . . The Employment Bureau has made arrangements with many labor unions, whereby concessions for immigrants applying for admission to these labor organizations have been obtained.

The Hebrew Sheltering and Immigrant Aid Society maintains branch offices in Baltimore, Boston, Philadelphia, San Francisco, and Seattle, and it is supported by voluntary contributions from its members and from other Jewish organizations.

Almost every other race and nationality has a similar organization doing similar work at the ports of entry. The Polish National Alliance maintains a home in New York City for Polish, Lithuanian, and Ruthenian immigrants who do not promptly locate relatives or friends. It maintains a representative at Ellis Island; furnishes information and employment; investigates cases of abuse against immigrants, and aids them in their complaints or grievances against unlawful treatment. The Irish Emigrant Society and the German Society of New York jointly maintain an Immigrant Labor Bureau which seeks work for immigrants

throughout the country and places them in positions
free of charge. Swedish, Spanish, Russian, Norwegian, Italian, Greek, and Belgian societies do the
same work of meeting people of their nationalities at
Ellis Island, sheltering them and placing them in
employment, as well as affording that guidance and
protection which the newcomer so sorely needs. In
addition, there are religious and missionary societies
engaged in similar work.

The work of the Society for Italian Immigrants is
probably more extensive than that of any other of these
organizations. It has given temporary lodging to more
than 22,000 Italians in a single year, and has found
employment and aided in various other ways as many
as 45,000 a year. This society also meets immigrants
at Ellis Island and guides them to their destination or
to a place of shelter. It conducts a lodging house for
Italian immigrants temporarily in New York, maintains an employment bureau, and affords protection
of all kinds that immigrants need. In addition, it
establishes and conducts schools for Italians in labor
camps and maintains agents on steamship docks, to
assist Italians leaving the United States to return to
their native lands. It is supported by voluntary contributions and also by a subsidy from the Italian
Government. Says the New York State Bureau of
Industries and Immigration:[1]

It is obvious that the sudden influx of thousands of reservists
into the city and their concentration here awaiting embarkation
during the winter months would have created a hardship had not
the situation been so admirably handled by this society. The fact
that this Bureau has not received a single complaint in consequence
of these extraordinary conditions attending the arrival and depar-
ture of 81,000 Italian emigrants, and that the Society for Italian
Immigrants has cared for, housed, and assisted 45,495 aliens, the

---

[1] Fifth Annual Report, 1915, p. 28.

bulk of whom arrived in this city during the past seven months, is the most remarkable achievement ever attained by an institution of this character. This society is highly organized and its agencies coördinate throughout the United States and Italy. . . . The immense number of 2313 immigrants were lodged by the society during the year 1915, totaling 44,024 days maintenance. A total of 25,058 Italians were met at railroad stations and accompanied to steamship docks direct and 20,437 were met at railroad stations and accompanied to the society, making a total of 45,495 Italians assisted during this year by this society. . . . The statistical report of the society for 1915 is a truly remarkable document and its activities for the year 1915 are highly commended by this Department as a social and economic benefit not only to Italian immigrants but to the state as well.

IMMIGRANT DISTRIBUTION AGENCIES

The Society for Italian Immigrants and most of the other immigrant aid societies attempt through their employment bureaus to direct their people away from the congested centers of immigrant populations, as far as this can possibly be done with non-English-speaking immigrants. Jewish philanthropists and social workers, however, have developed a specialized agency, known as the Industrial Removal office, to distribute Jewish immigrants over the land and help them settle in the more sparsely settled centers where the process of adjustment would naturally be less difficult. It was clear that if the Jewish immigrant population was to reap the full benefit of the opportunities offered in the new land, many of them would have to settle in the less congested cities, where competition was less severe and housing conditions more favorable.

A beginning was made when the Baron de Hirsch Fund supplied transportation to those immigrants who had expectations of employment outside the large cities, or who had relatives or friends in small towns willing to receive them and care for them. In 1900 the Industrial Removal Office was organized through the

coöperation of the National Conference of Jewish
Charities and with the aid of Jewish communal agencies
throughout the country. Since that time this organization, maintained by the Jewish people for the distribution of Jewish immigrants, has been more or less
of a model of what proper distribution work ought to be.

The work of the Industrial Removal Office is thus
described in the *Jewish Communal Register* of New
York City.[1]

To bring home the importance of the proper distribution of
Jewish immigrants, educational work was at first carried on among
the newly arrived immigrants and in the interior communities
through every available agency of publicity. Within a few years
after the movement was first inaugurated, the work of the office
and the number of applicants had assumed such large proportions
that it became possible to discontinue practically every form of
propaganda, as the reports of the successful settlement of a great
majority of persons sent by the organization to the interior, brought
to the central office a larger number of desirable applicants than it
could properly make provision for.

The general method of procedure was to receive applications for
removal at the central office in New York, to make a careful physical
examination of the applicant, to secure if possible evidence of good
moral character and fair competence in some trade, to select from
carefully compiled data on industrial opportunities throughout the
United States a community where the applicant and his family, if
he had any, could make a reasonable living, to make arrangements
for his reception, and then to keep in touch with him through the
local agencies and the traveling agents of the central office. While
in some cities the entire work is in the hands of a paid agent of the
central office, who works under the supervision of a small committee,
composed of representative members of the community, in other
localities it is the function of the Independent Order B'nai B'rith.
In the smaller communities the Rabbi is the acting representative
of the central organization.

From 1900 to 1917 almost 74,000 people were sent
from New York City to about 1500 cities and towns

[1] Published by the Kehillah (Jewish Community), 1918, pp. 1246–
1247.

situated in every state in the Union. Of these 37,700 were adult wage earners and the rest members of their families. Over 1500 families were moved, together with the heads of the families, while 5900 families were moved to join their heads. Married men whose families remained in New York numbered 3700 and 11,600 married men were moved whose families were in Europe. Unmarried men and women, all wage earners removed from New York, were 17,176. In addition branch offices, established in Boston and Philadelphia, distributed from those cities about 5000 individuals, making a total number of removals in seventeen years close to 79,000.

The Industrial Removal Office is not an employment bureau. It does not send immigrants directly to employers who apply for help. The people are sent to communities where it is thought they can adjust themselves most easily. Local committees in these places receive the immigrants, care for them, and find employment for them.

IMMIGRANT LABOR FEDERATIONS

In adjusting himself to the trade-union movement of the country, the immigrant has found it necessary to develop his own organizations just as he has had to do in locating himself in the country and finding work. The prototypes of these labor organizations were the United German Trades, central labor federations made up of delegates from German-speaking local unions of various crafts, which were organized in the 'seventies and 'eighties in New York, Chicago, Milwaukee, and St. Louis. These bodies carried on a propaganda for trade-unionism among German workmen by means of the labor papers which they supported and published and by lectures and speaking campaigns. After they were thus organized, they could be brought in touch with American trade-unionists and joined to the latter's organizations.

An offshoot of these German organizations is still to be found among the Bohemian wage earners of New York City, a federated central body consisting of delegates from about a dozen Bohemian local unions. This body carries on organization campaigns among Bohemian workers, raises strike funds, distributes relief during strikes, and conducts negotiations with employers for local unions affiliated with it.

In 1888 a similar central body of Jewish immigrant workers was formed in New York City, known as the United Hebrew Trades. It grew slowly at first, but now has affiliated with it over a hundred local unions with a combined membership of more than 250,000 workers. Its purpose is to spread unionism among Jewish-speaking working people, organize them into local unions, and affiliate them with the American trade-union movement. It is recognized by the American Federation of Labor as a valuable aid in bringing immigrant workers into the American labor movement, and has the support of that body. It provides leadership and funds during strikes of Jewish unions, conducts negotiations with employers for the weaker unions, and carries on a constant campaign for trade-unionism among Jewish wage earners. Similar bodies have been formed also in Chicago and Philadelphia.

Samuel Gompers, who was a member of the New York State Factory Investigating Commission, in questioning the secretary of the United Hebrew Trades at a hearing of the commission brought out clearly the relationship between these immigrant labor federations and the American Labor Movement: [1]

---

[1] Preliminary Report of the Factory Investigating Commission, 1912, p. 1628.

IMMIGRANT SELF–HELP

By Commissioner Gompers:

Q. What is your trade, Mr. Weinstein?

A. I was at several trades. The last one was the boiler business. Originally I was a cigar stripper. I went all the way through. Most of the time I have been devoted to labor organizations.

Q. You worked with me at one time?

A. I worked with you in the same shop, Mr. Gompers. I was floor boy in Stachelberg's shop twenty-nine years ago. I used to pick your cuttings while you made Spanish cigars.

Q. For the information of the Commission and for the value it may have, will you relate the primary purpose of the United Hebrew Trades in its organization?

A. We found out that the Jewish-speaking people coming over into this country, in order not to compete with the workers over here who were previously in this country, ought not to work for cheaper wages. At the same time, that they should have better conditions, better wages, and shorter hours, we found that they would have to be unionized.

Q. That is it.

A. To keep up the standard of wages.

Q. That is it, to prevent the exploitation of their helplessness, either to their own injury. . . .

A. That is the main thing.

Q. Or to the injury of America?

A. The main thing is to give the same protection and we have our hands full with it . . . getting short hours now. I remember twenty-five years ago—not as far as that, but twenty-two years ago, when the sweating system in the tailoring trade prevailed, tailors would go to work at three o'clock in the morning and work until ten o'clock at night. Now the longest they work in the tailoring industry at present is ten hours, not all of them. They average about nine hours for work, every one of them.

Q. Without going into the details of these matters, is not one of the purposes of the formation and the work of the United Hebrew Trades to form a sort of probationary class of Hebrew workmen who come here as immigrants, so that they may take their position among the workmen of the United States, who have preceded them?

A. Exactly, but those who are first-class mechanics, they can join at once.

Q. It is a probationary step?

A. Exactly.

Q. Toward a fuller membership of the workers of America?

A. Exactly so.

287

ADJUSTING IMMIGRANT AND INDUSTRY

In November, 1919, an Italian federation of this kind was organized, known as the Italian Chamber of Labor. At the convention where the organization was formed there were delegates from the following trades: barbers, carpenters, excavators, hod carriers, ladies' garment workers and men's clothing workers, painters and decorators, piano makers, and printers. These delegates came from local unions whose membership was either entirely Italian or in large part Italian, and it is claimed that 30,000 Italian wage earners were represented.

The purpose of the Chamber of Labor is trade-union organization. It will help the trades in which Italians are employed and which are not organized or weakly organized to form strong organizations of labor. In addition, the Chamber proposes to regulate the flow of Italian immigration to this country by exchanging information with the Confederation of Labor in Italy and discouraging wage earners from coming to this country when the American labor market is overcrowded. It issues monthly bulletins in Italian and in English. At present the Italian Chamber of Labor operates only in New York City, but it plans to establish branches in other cities as well.

AN IMMIGRANT BUREAU OF INDUSTRY

In 1914 there was established by the Jews of New York City a Bureau of Industry to study and deal with the special industrial problems existing in those industries where both employers and employees are mostly Jewish immigrants. This bureau was active for three or four years, but since then it has practically ceased functioning. However, its purposes and plan of operation offer an excellent program of immigrant self-help in industry, which sooner or later is likely to be revived.[1]

---

[1] *Jewish Communal Register* (1917–18), pp. 1158–1159.

IMMIGRANT SELF-HELP

The Jew in industrial life in this city presents a distinct and separate problem.

The problem is due largely to the fact that the overwhelming majority of Jewish workers and employers in the city belong to the first generation of immigrants, who were trained for industry under conditions entirely different from those obtaining in New York City at the present time. . . .

Industry, as far as the Jewish population of New York City is concerned . . . presents the following specific problems: Race prejudice; Sabbath observance; employment of minor boys; working girls; oversupply of labor in certain trades and undersupply in others . . . unsatisfactory relations between employers and employees; handicapped workers; untrained adult workers.

A comprehensive plan to alleviate the distress and to overcome the difficulties resulting from this maladjustment presents a problem of economic and human conservation which only social engineering by the entire Jewish community can adequately meet. . . .

The Bureau of Industry, through its Division of Surveys, gathers, analyzes, and interprets the vital facts bearing on the various specified Jewish industrial problems of the city.

Through the Division of Mediation and Arbitration, it helps in the development of rational organized effort among groups of employers and employees. . . . The Bureau mediates in the settlement of strikes and lockouts; it arbitrates specific disputes between employers and employees submitted to its representatives; it negotiates collective agreements between unions and employers' associations. . . .

The Division of Employment is for the present conducting an employment bureau for such workers whose needs at the present time are not and cannot be met by another agency.

Through its Division of Vocational Guidance and Training . . . the Bureau of Industry hopes to coördinate and develop facilities to improve, through training and guidance, the condition of workers, many of whom have not had, and have not now, full opportunities to acquire skill in their respective trades and callings.

IMMIGRANT COÖPERATIVE SOCIETIES

Another group of organizations have been developed by the immigrant wage earners to meet their needs as consumers. These are the coöperative societies.[1]

---

[1] James Ford, *Co-operation in New England*, 1913, p. 4.

ADJUSTING IMMIGRANT AND INDUSTRY

Many conditions of the immigrant's life in America make co-operation on racial lines desirable. Newly arrived immigrants are unfamiliar with American goods and prices, have difficulty in understanding and making themselves understood in trade, and when unorganized are often the victims of fraud. Coöperation is frequently resorted to in self-protection, a linguist from among their number being chosen store manager. An added reason—that delicacies from the home country can be imported cheaply in large quantities.

In the large cities these needs are commonly met by groceries and other stores, conducted in the ordinary way by business men of the nationality of the people inhabiting the neighborhood. Outside the large cities, however, particularly in mining and steel towns, the problem of buying the things that he needs and wants is a serious one for the immigrant. This was first met by large immigrant mercantile houses conducted by clan leaders to cater to the wants of the newcomers. The following description of a Bulgarian mercantile house in a steel town of the Middle West may be cited as typical: [1]

A number of separate enterprises united under one central management somewhat like an American holding company with subsidiary corporations. The business centers in the banks, which act as a central point of management, is a clearing house. Mercantile houses are not incorporated and are usually under an informal partnership. A typical house of this description will own a number of brick buildings, usually grouped together, the ground floors used for business purposes, and the upper floors used for living purposes. A typical mercantile house includes the following lines of business: grocery, meat, dry goods and clothing shop, saloon, coffee house, bakery, bank steamship agency, pool room, theater, real estate and rental, newspaper, dairy, restaurant, baths.

The stores are as good if not better than the average American store. Bakeries turn out Bulgarian bread. Direct patronage of saloons comes from Austrians, Servians, Magyars and Croatians. . . . These institutions tend to retard Americanization.

---

[1] U. S. Immigration Commission, *Iron and Steel Manufacturing*, Vol. II, pp. 107–113.

IMMIGRANT SELF–HELP

The remarkable fact to be noted is that the expansion of business has been made through the profits realized. We must infer that profits could not have been earned by ordinary business methods. They must have made exceptional gains from labor agencies or similar sources.

These larger mercantile houses control and give the stamp to the business life of the immigrant sections.

Public opinion is largely influenced by the alien press and the press in turn is controlled by representative mercantile houses.

The typical mercantile house will have a patronage of from four to five hundred persons, who look to the manager for advice in all the affairs of life.

Partly to get away from the influence of these foreign mercantile houses and from company stores, or as the miners call them the "Pluck Me" stores, the United Mine Workers began about eight or nine years ago to stimulate the organization of coöperative stores in the mining communities. This movement has attained its greatest success among the foreign-born miners of Illinois, where at the present writing there are about one hundred coöperative societies.[1]

Successful coöperative enterprises, according to all authorities, require mutual understanding among the coöperators and an interest in small savings. It has been observed by British coöperators that Americans, as a rule, are not interested in small savings on their purchases, and this is one of the reasons that coöperation has made so little headway among them. On the other hand, when mixed races unite in a coöperative enterprise mutual understanding is likely to be lacking; and, therefore, the success among coöperatives has attended mainly those enterprises which are carried on by persons of a single racial or national group.

---

[1] Details of immigrant coöperative societies are omitted here, as they have been fully described in the volume of this series entitled *America via the Neighborhood*, by John Daniels.

ADJUSTING IMMIGRANT AND INDUSTRY

Does this tend to separate such groups from the American community and thus make adjustment more difficult? The answer may be found in the values obtained through coöperation as described by a close student of the subject: [1]

There are many values obtained through coöperation not readily obtainable from other sources. (1) It provides important practical education in business methods for adult wage earners. (2) It provides training for citizenship. Questions of broad policy are inevitably discussed in meetings of coöperative associations. This discussion develops knowledge, ability to understand, and to handle men, which renders the coöperator valuable in public service. (3) It discovers what Professor Marshall calls "our greatest waste product," namely the latent abilities of workingmen, and utilizes those latent abilities not only in the fields of business and citizenship but throughout the entire range of social conduct. (4) It habituates men to altruistic modes of thought and of conduct. The motto "each for all and all for each" finds daily expression in coöperative activities. The more a man buys from the coöperative shop the more he stabilizes the business and increases his profits and his neighbor's dividends. (5) It not only increases the income of individual members, but creates a collective capital which can be used on occasion to free the working classes from any form of exploitation.

It is in the isolated immigrant colonies that coöperatives among the foreign born have been most successful. The immigrant's activity in these coöperative societies tends to bring him into contact with American economic life and to teach him to know it in a way that few other agencies can provide.

In the state of New York the law concerning coöperatives provides that the Division of Foods and Markets shall aid in the organization and operation of coöperative associations, and agents of the department are in constant touch with these immigrant

---

[1] "Distributive Coöperation," address by James Ford at National Conference of Social Work, Pittsburgh, 1917.

societies, giving them the encouragement of the state government. The Director of the Department writes:

As to the things we are doing to assist consumers' coöperation, we are first of all at the service of any group of people in the state who want to start a consumer's or a producer's coöperative enterprise. We advise them as to the methods of organizing their undertaking and how to incorporate it under the laws of the state. Any group of people interested in coöperation that will communicate with our Department will receive our assistance. If it is possible a representative of the Bureau of Coöperative Associations will meet with the group and help them work out the details of their plans. We will see that the articles of incorporation are sound from a legal and business point of view and file them with the Secretary of State. The same assistance is given in the preparation of by-laws governing the details of operation of the business. It is our purpose to bring to the new association the experience of others, to steer them away from the rocks on which others have capsized. It is our desire that they come back to us whenever they have problems of organization or problems of business operation in which the Department can help them. But we do not attempt or desire to exercise any control over those organizations, once they have become established on a sound basis and started to work.

In New York City the consumers' societies may find out from our office the wholesale market prices on any of the principal food commodities. If they are in doubt as to whether they are getting a good price on a commodity, or have doubt as to the quality, and have no facilities for finding out themselves, we will find out for them. We will tell them whether or not they are getting fair treatment from the tradespeople with whom they are dealing. We hope in the near future to be able to establish a course of training for coöperative store managers, to teach them, not the principles of coöperation, because the Coöperative League of America can do that better than we can, but to teach them the practical details of buying and store management. The purpose would be to cover the things they have to know in order to make their store efficient and render the same quality of service to their customers as their customers can get elsewhere.

It is also our intention to serve as a clearing house of information regarding the condition of existing coöperative societies and to analyze their experience for the benefit of each other and new societies.

There are now twenty-eight states having fairly comprehensive statutes covering the incorporation of coöperative businesses. Such direct contact as this between all these states and the immigrant coöperatives would not only bring the members of these societies more quickly into adjustment with American economic life, but it would also bring to the American people a contribution in thrift, efficiency, and social outlook in the ordinary business of supplying daily needs that would be of the utmost value to the nation.

THE IMMIGRANTS' OWN AGENCIES AND THE AMERICAN COMMUNITY

What is true of the immigrant coöperative societies in bringing people of foreign nationalities into adjustment with American economic life is also true of the immigrant aid societies and immigrant labor federations. But there is also a certain amount of danger in these organizations. It is not America which is doing all these things. It is the immigrant's own nationality, perhaps even the government of the country from which he came, that is affording him these services.

As in the case of the immigrant aid societies, the immigrant labor federations serve a very useful purpose during the transition period between the immigrant's arrival in this country and the time when he has acquired enough knowledge of English to join an American union. We have seen, however, how some American trade unions have held themselves aloof from the immigrant, been indifferent to his interests, neglected to organize him, and even have deliberately excluded him from their ranks. This made the existence of racial and nationalistic organizing bodies all the more necessary, and engendered some antagonism between these bodies and the American trade

unions. Quite frequently local foreign-speaking unions
were kept from affiliation with existing national unions,
and sometimes dual unions were formed. Under such
circumstances the loyalty of the immigrant trade
unionist is apt to go to the organization of his own
nationality which brought him into a union, and secured
increases in wages and improved working conditions
for him, rather than to the general labor movement of
the country. Again, the immigrant labor federations
naturally interest themselves in problems of their native
lands, in which the American trade unions have little
concern. This tends to give them a consciousness of
their own, distinct from that of the general labor
movement in America; they are inclined to perpetuate
themselves as nationalistic organizations, instead of
merging with the general labor movement of the country as soon as their membership becomes English-
speaking.

Although the United German Trades of New York
City was one of the constituent organizations which
helped to form the American Federation of Labor,
serious difficulties arose between it and the Federation
at a later time. Similar difficulties have arisen between
the Federation and the United Hebrew Trades, and
almost invariably when the Federation has expelled
trade unions for violation of its rules, as in the case
of the Jewelry Workers, Cloth Hat and Cap Makers,
or when it has refused to recognize a union which com-
petes for jurisdiction with one of the unions affiliated
with it, as in the case of the Amalgamated Clothing
Workers, the United Hebrew Trades has supported
the expelled or unrecognized union.

As long as the American Federation of Labor has
no immigrant organization department of its own to
do the work of these federations, these difficulties are
bound to arise, for the individual foreign-born wage

earner will adhere to the organization which was most helpful to him in improving his status in America. Each new nationality as it becomes conscious of its position in American industry, is likely to seek self-expression. The Italian Chamber of Labor represents the latest foreign-born group of wage earners to seek such self-expression and it has already asserted its opposition to a number of policies of the American Federation of Labor.

When the national trade unions affiliated with the American Federation of Labor learn to follow the policies of such organizations as the United Mine Workers, the need for separate immigrant labor federations will disappear, and the immigrant wage earner will be more likely to feel that it is the American unions, the American labor movement, and America itself which has helped him to join hands and unite him with his American fellow workers.

CHAPTER XV

SPECIAL PROBLEMS OF THE WOMAN IMMIGRANT WORKER

WHEN the immigrant worker is a woman, her adjustment to conditions of American industrial life requires the assistance from the employer, the trade union, the government, and the people of her own nationality which has been described in the previous chapters without regard to sex. Her adjustment involves something more, however. She combines the problem of the immigrant in industry with that of the woman in industry. The difficulties which she would naturally encounter as an immigrant, in finding work in America, in becoming accustomed to new occupations and new industrial methods, and in acquiring a new language, new associations, and new customs are greatly multiplied by the fact that she is a woman. We propose in the present chapter to describe some of the problems that are peculiar to the immigrant woman in industry, and the methods of solving them which have been helpful in bringing her into closer adjustment with American life.

EXTENT OF EMPLOYMENT OF IMMIGRANT WOMEN

To just what extent immigrant women are at work outside their homes it is difficult to estimate. Preliminary figures of the Fourteenth Census show that there were 8,549,000 women gainfully employed in 1920. This represents an increase of nine per cent over the figures for 1910. The war was responsible for bringing great numbers of women into industrial employment, and it was confidently expected that the Census of 1920 would show a much greater increase in the number of women employed than has actually been reported. Of the 8,075,000 gainfully employed women in 1910, fifteen per cent were foreign born. The percentage for 1920 is not yet available, but it will probably be somewhat less than fifteen per cent, as the percentage of foreign-born population as a whole fell slightly between 1910 and 1920. The comparatively small increase in the total number of women employed between the two censuses, however, may be due to the change in census date from April 15, 1910 to January 1, 1920, and it is possible that if the last census had been taken on April 15, a great many more women might have been found in employment. April is normally a month of full employment, while January is usually a slack month.

Of the 1,222,000 foreign-born women gainfully employed in 1910 about one third were in manufacturing and mechanical industries and 46 per cent in domestic and personal service. In each of these groups they constituted 22 per cent of the total women employed.

A square of which the corner posts are Maine, Minnesota, Missouri, and Maryland comprehends most of the foreign-born women industrially employed in the country. The only outposts in which the United States Census of 1910 shows a concentration of 1000 or more so employed, are California and Florida. A clear contrast is found in the case of domestic service; for in this work foreign-born women stretch their thousands from Atlantic to Pacific, skipping only a South Atlantic section, and a state-wide belt in the mountain region bordering upon the states of the western coast. Foreign-born women, serving as wholesale and retail dealers, midwives, and nurses, are concentrated in Middle Atlantic and Lake states, and in California.

PROBLEMS OF THE WOMAN WORKER

In the manufacturing and mechanical industries, covering what is ordinarily referred to as industrial employment, we find the foreign-born women distributed among the industries, as follows:

TABLE VIII

TOTAL NUMBER OF WOMEN, AND NUMBER AND PER CENT OF FOREIGN-BORN WOMEN, GAINFULLY EMPLOYED IN MANUFACTURING AND MECHANICAL INDUSTRIES IN THE UNITED STATES.[1]

INDUSTRIES	TOTAL NUMBER	FOREIGN-BORN		Per cent of foreign women
		Number	Per cent of total women	
All industries........................	1,712,157	386,140	22.8	100
Building and hand trades.............	48,000	5,883	12.2	1.5
Chemical and allied industries..........	9,322	1,032	11.1	0.3
Cigar and tobacco factories...........	79,486	21,886	27.5	5.7
Clay, glass, and stone industries........	15,872	1,683	10.6	0.4
Clothing industries...................	301,685	112,330	37.2	29.1
Dressmaking and seamstress work (not in factory)........................	443,919	69,040	15.3	17.6
Food and kindred industries..........	54,440	10,382	19.1	2.7
Iron and steel industries..............	18,847	2,890	15.3	0.7
Leather industries....................	77,411	11,807	15.3	3.1
Liquor and beverage industries........	3,005	395	13.1	0.1
Lumber and furniture industries........	16,626	1,892	11.4	0.5
Metal industries, except iron and steel...	32,820	6,166	18.8	1.6
Milliners and millinery dealers.........	122,447	13,640	11.1	3.5
Paper and pulp industries.............	37,180	6,444	17.3	1.7
Printing and bookbinding.............	76,676	5,087	6.6	1.3
Textile industries....................	379,977	116,633	30.7	30.2

Almost half of all foreign-born women in industry are in branches of the sewing trades, and the greater number of these are in clothing factories, where they constitute over 37 per cent of the total women employed. About 17½ per cent of all foreign-born working women are employed at sewing or dressmaking not in factories, and of all the women thus engaged 15 per cent are immigrant. In the textile industry, especially

---

[1] Compiled from United States Census, 1910, vol. 4, table vi.

cotton, wool, and silk manufacturing, 30 per cent of the women employed are foreign born, and these are also 30 per cent of the total foreign-born women in industrial employments.

The industrial distribution of foreign born women is largely a concomitant of that of men. Even though the immigrant man and his wife both work, the trade or "job" opportunity of the man is likely to control the home location; and wage-earning daughters, among the foreign born generally, will be found where their parents are. Women and girls who come to this country apart from families of their own—with the special exception of some who intend to find work in textile centers or in domestic service—are likely to make propinquity to family groups of their country people a consideration prior to occupational selection. If industries are found in the neighborhood of such groups, they will probably enter them; if there are no industries, they will find other employment as best they can. Thus it is that we find in mining regions of Pennsylvania, Michigan, and other states, as well as in localities in which the principal or only industries are iron and steel manufacturing, large aggregations of foreign-born women, but an insignificant industrial showing.

OCCUPATIONS IN EUROPE AND AMERICA

A study of 610 foreign-born women in the slaughtering and meat packing industry showed that 520 had worked "in the fields" abroad; only four had ever been in a factory before coming to this country.[1] This is typical of all the nationalities from southern and eastern Europe, with the possible exception of Italian and

---

[1] Louise Montgomery, *The American Girl in the Stockyards District*, University of Chicago Press, 1913.

Russian-Jewish women. These, together with the immigrant women from north European countries, show apparently high percentages of industrial employment in their native lands; but it must be remembered that the general name by which an occupation

TABLE IX

PER CENT OF FOREIGN-BORN WOMEN EMPLOYEES IN EACH SPECIFIED OCCUPATION BEFORE COMING TO THE UNITED STATES, BY RACE, FOR SELECTED RACES.[1]

	NUMBER REPORTING COMPLETE DATA	PER CENT OF FOREIGN-BORN WOMEN EMPLOYED IN			
		Industrial Work	Farming or Farm Laborers	Domestic Service	All Other Occupations
Bohemian and Moravian..........	107	37.4	36.4	16.8	9.4
Canadian, French..	995	38.2	42.2	8.9	10.7
English..........	1,804	95.9	.1	1.8	2.2
German...........	437	70.9	16.7	6.0	5.5
Greek............	107	27.1	61.7	8.4	2.8
Hebrew, Russian...	360	85.5	.6	.8	13.1
Irish..............	603	72.7	12.3	11.3	3.7
Italian, North......	542	69.6	20.8	3.7	5.9
Italian, South......	738	72.0	14.6	7.6	5.8
Lithuanian.......	554	14.6	78.5	6.0	.9
Polish............	4,057	8.1	86.9	3.6	1.4
Portuguese........	408	36.0	20.1	36.5	7.4
Russian...........	369	19.8	75.3	2.4	2.5
Scotch...........	282	96.1	.4	1.4	2.1
Slovak...........	105	23.8	64.8	11.4	.0

is designated abroad and here gives no clue to identity or even similarity of process. Industrial experience abroad by no means needs to connote either life in an

[1] Compiled from Report of U. S. Immigration Commission, Abstract, vol. i, table 19, p. 362.

industrial center, or any of the plant organization which is so forceful a factor in the newly arrived immigrant's impression of industry here. Those who were textile workers in continental Europe encountered machines different from ours, and a tempo of work much slower. The clothing shops met by the Jewish girl abroad rarely initiated her to the power machine, and the organization of processes was entirely unlike that which she finds in this country. It is commonly known that Italian women, overseas, have proficiency in fine hand-sewing; but this sewing is likely to have been done at home.

The experience that immigrant working women are likely to have in their native lands may be illustrated by the stories of two women who applied for work at a public employment office:

The first, a Bohemian, now in Chicago, comes of a family which owned only the cottage it lived in and very little land. At twelve the little girl was provided with a "pillow" which contained her bedding, and was taken by her father to a peasant who lived some distance away. Here she was to work for a year receiving in return a training, her living, and eighteen dollars not for herself but for her father.

Early in the morning she went out into the fields; she fed and milked the cows; she washed the dishes and helped the cook; she went out into the fields again, looked after the children, watched the geese, brought the sheep home; fed cattle and washed dishes again— getting to bed at ten or eleven o'clock to be called early in the morning again for a new day's work. Sunday mornings she went to mass, but Sundays except for this were just like other days. The year over, she went home for a little vacation; and then, for twenty-four dollars a year, when she was not yet fourteen, she became the cook for a wealthy family living in a city.

A childhood story similar in experience is that of an Italian woman. She was sent to school in or near Naples when she was four; at six, after she had finished the second grade, but before she had learned to read or write her parents decided to let her "live out" with a fine family several miles away who wanted help in the household. The mistress of the house promised her mother that

she would have the child taught reading and writing, but there
never seemed to be time for this, and though the promise was re-
newed still more solemnly at the beginning of the second year, she
cannot remember any real teaching. She prepared the vegetables,
helped in the garden, carried water, and received ten cents a week,
which was paid to her mother. For four years she lived with this
family, going home on holidays. Her sisters worked on farms and
went home nights, so that their mother taught them needlework
after dark, but she never had a chance to learn any skill with a needle,
for she rarely saw her mother. When she was ten it was decided
that she would live out regularly at housework, receiving two dollars
a month. It did not mean a great change, except that she had
heavier pails of water to carry and did a larger share of the washing.

ADJUSTMENT ADVANTAGES IN EMPLOYMENT

The women, in the case of the foreign born, may find
their employment the best means they have for learning the ways and spirit of this country; and for many
it may be, for a time, the only means. It is common to
find among the non-English-speaking women, who do
not "go to a job," complete ignorance of the city's
streets and street car lines. If the children's school is
not within a few blocks' radius from the home, that,
too, is covered with mystery; and of the work places
to which the mother's boys and girls go, not even the
name may be known. She tries to live the old country
life as well as she can, with the handicap of new conditions of tenement living and piecemeal buying.

But her neighbor, who came to America when she
did, takes a half-hour's walk or ride to work, every day,
crossing perhaps the main thoroughfare of the city.
She can say a few words of English, and if she cannot
"read the cars," at least she can tell one car from
another; and the destination of some, at least, is not
a blank to her. She knows how to pay her fare and use
a transfer. She passes people of many kinds on the
street, she notes their way of dressing, and forms an
idea of what she thinks they are like. She sees many

things in shop windows—clothing, furniture for one's
house, and food. When she reaches her shop she joins
a group of workers, among whom are some of her own
nationality, whom, naturally, she chooses for her com-
panions. But those of other nationalities are not overlooked. She watches their workmanship and habits,
and reacts from them or toward them, as the case may
be. Unconsciously, perhaps, she will appropriate or
imitate whatever appeals to her as of value in the life
that goes on around her. Americans in the shop will
especially interest her. She will gradually build up a
little English vocabulary, which, small as it may be,
will give her a decided advantage over her shut-in
neighbor at home in the process of adjustment.

There is a Bohemian girl on the upper East Side of
New York City who finds excellent working conditions
in the little dressmaking shop where she is employed;
and she is proud of her good salary. She looks at
America, as through a windowglass, and thinks it is a
wonderful country! But she finds she does not share
in American life, because of her handicap in English
speaking; she cannot, seemingly, make American
friends or other American contacts because she "talks
like a greenhorn"—and she is very lonely. Her eleven
years here have been spent, in work, in a Bohemian
shop; and, in living, with a Bohemian family. And
although she goes to night school for English, and understands the language readily and speaks it grammatically
the "foreignness" does not wear off. She enjoys
reading and music, has an intelligent understanding of
a wide range of interests; and she could be a companion
that any girl, American or otherwise, might be proud
to have. But, through lack of the language and consequent timidity, she finds her only diversion in the
Bohemian theater, on Sunday afternoons, and she is not
what she wants to be—an American in America, find-

ing joy in America, in the fullest sense of the word. If this girl had worked in an American factory these eleven years, it is possible life would wear for her a brighter color now, because of the daily opportunities she might have had for improving her English in the shop, and the acquaintances made there who might have enlarged her experience outside.

To the elements of American life which make for an improvement of the status of the foreign-born woman—in the eyes of her family and herself—industry can and does contribute in several important ways. The question of status concerns itself largely with the immigration of peasant women from southern and eastern Europe, especially Italian, Greek, and Slavic. Repetition of statements from such women shows that among the prizes of American freedom are more considerate treatment from the men of their family than was received in the old country; more freedom than they formerly had in going and coming—although Italians assimilate this slowly; and, in the case of girls who come unmarried, more freedom of choice in the matter of taking a husband. If an industry employing both foreign-born men and women pays some attention to the human relations of its women workers, and if it has forewomen as well as foremen, and both women and men serving as representatives on its shop committees, the effect of this cannot help reaching back into the home attitude of the foreign-born men who are witness to it. They thus learn in a poignant way America's standard for women. They may not, immediately, adopt this standard, but it means something that they have seen its demonstration.

The opportunity, through industry, to have money of her own is of great significance to the foreign-born woman and it gives her acknowledged importance if she is the housekeeper. But younger, unmarried girls in foreign households in America may not know much about this independence, so prevalent is the custom, with them, to turn over the pay envelope—unopened it may be—to the family budget.[1]

Economic independence for the woman in a sense conveyed by the modern use of these words is as yet unknown and incomprehensible. It follows that what the girl earns is easily appropriated by the parents, and, broadly speaking, obediently surrendered by the girl. Among the 300 girls between sixteen and twenty-four years of age, there are 290 who have no independent control of their own wages.

The parents here referred to are, predominantly, Poles, Bohemians, Irish, and Slovaks. A New York employer of several hundred girls of foreign birth or parentage found in this situation a resultant lack of personal interest in the pay, which acted as a deterrent to ambition in earning; and he was considering the possibility of assembling the foreign fathers and mothers at an evening entertainment and of attempting to persuade them that their daughters would earn more money if they were allowed even a small share of it, for their own disposal.

The shop lunchroom, too, is an important educator. Here the women may learn much more than they would otherwise know of the varieties of inexpensive food available in America, and of ways of preparing and serving it. If there is table service, they have additional opportunity for observing customs that are American. It does not need to be inferred from this that American cooking and table customs are necessarily better than the foreign ones; but we know that being "different" through ignorance of American ways works hardship on the immigrant girl. Moreover, the food available in the stores is likely to be the Ameri-

[1] Louise Montgomery, *The American Girl in the Stockyards District*, p. 57.

can kind, except in the case of those who live in self-dependent national groups.

Association in employment with service workers and nurses, or with native and foreign fellow workers of higher living standards than their own may have a favorable effect on the personal habits and appearances of some foreign-born women who consciously care to improve their condition. An employer in a metal industry proudly cites the case of Italian immigrant girls who, as soon as they are adjusted to the work in his factory, appear in silk stockings and high-heeled shoes. If any are dubious of the advantage of this Americanism, at least they must grant that it serves to illustrate the power of imitation. Companies which maintain summer homes or camps, and are successful in getting the foreign-born women to visit them, have an opportunity to show these women the whole daily cycle of American living.

IMMIGRANT MARRIED WOMEN IN INDUSTRY

A Western company which employs 1000 women, 55 per cent of whom are foreign born, has taken a definite stand against the employment of married women who have working husbands. This action was taken after the company had made a voluntary inquiry into the home situation of its family women employees and proved to its own satisfaction that the living standards and the children are the worse because of the outside work of these family women. The prevalence of married women among foreign-born workers has been apparent throughout this study, some of it due, without doubt, to circumstances attending the war. But, whether or not the influx of married women brought into industry by the war has become a permanent factor, we have evidence in the Report of the

Immigration Commission that their employment even in normal times is, in certain trades, extensive. Table 10 shows the percentages of married foreign-born women to be highest in cigar and textile manufacturing, of the industries for which information is given.

TABLE X

CONJUGAL CONDITION OF FOREIGN-BORN WOMEN SIXTEEN YEARS OF AGE AND OVER, GAINFULLY EMPLOYED IN SELECTED INDUSTRIES [1]

INDUSTRY	TOTAL NUMBER	SINGLE	PER CENT MARRIED	WIDOWED
Cigar and tobacco manufacturing....................	4,122	55.6	37.4	7.0
Clothing manufacturing......	5,004	71.9	22.6	5.5
Cotton goods manufacturing..	19,329	56.6	37.3	6.1
Shoe manufacturing.........	956	64.1	27.9	8.0
Silk manufacturing..........	1,853	66.9	27.5	5.6
Woolen and worsted goods....	9,238	60.0	34.3	5.4
Slaughtering and meat packing	1,788	69.8	24.9	5.3
Total..................	42,290	60.2	33.8	5.9

The war-time shortage of labor drove many employers, previously unaccustomed to relying much on married women workers, to take them on in numbers; and even to solicit their help. There is little doubt that the high war wages tempted some women to desert their families for the shop unnecessarily; and others were forced to do it by high prices and by the reduction of the usual income from the male members of the family and the boarders who had gone to war. The great cause which in normal times sends a continual stream of immigrant women, mothers of families, into industry

[1] Compiled from Report of Immigration Commission, vol. 20, Table 41, p. 818.

must be financial necessity. No other reason could
make them submit continuously to the lack of leisure
and neglect of home which daily employment entails.

An inquiry among 580 married foreign-born women,
employed in several plants located near together in
the region of their homes, drew from the women these
statements of their reasons for working:

TABLE XI

NUMBER, PER CENT, AND REASONS FOR WORKING, OF MARRIED
FOREIGN-BORN WOMEN

REASONS FOR WORKING	NUMBER	PER CENT
Insufficient income (Husband working).........	249	42.9
Insufficient income (Husband ill, dead, or absent)	176	30.4
To pay debts..............................	50	8.7
To educate children..........................	12	2.0
To buy property............................	69	11.9
To save money.............................	24	4.1
Total.................................	580	100.0

A Lithuanian woman asserts that many of her
countrywomen come to this country alone, unmarried,
expecting to find life easier, and after coming they
refrain from marrying because they see that the married
women have it harder. The single woman has only
work; the married woman has work and all the responsibility of a household added. The Franco-Belgians,
who have an insistent desire to maintain a good and
ascending living standard, find a way to meet the economic stress by limitation of children.

The attitude of husbands seems to be a factor in
pushing many family women into mill and factory
work. Especially has this been found true of Greeks
and some of the Slavic people. They seem to look upon

wives as an extra pair of hands to help boost the family income. A French girl with a young baby said she was not going back to the mill—her husband, an Italian, would not make her go. "Would most husbands?" she was asked. "Oh, sure," was the answer. This family lived in a small mill town. Among Italians in cities, "there is to some extent a certain social sentiment with regard to women leaving home to work after marriage and mingling with men in the shops. Some of the Italian men who would not permit their wives to go back to the shop after marriage, have not the same delicate feeling regarding home-work, and are satisfied to have the family income supplemented in this manner." [1] Syrian men, too, as a rule, seem to favor their wives remaining at home, or doing only occasional, supplementary work outside.

The appearance of a day nursery in the neighborhood of a plant or of the homes of its workers suggests three things: the kind and social-minded endeavor of the employer or other agency to make the best of a bad situation by giving comfort and protection to children who would otherwise be neglected; the inevitable plight of family women whose husbands are lost to them or incapacitated for work; and the fundamental wrong in an industrial condition that seems to compel the combined, daily labor, away from home, of both adult members of a normal family, of father, mother, and children—so that there is no care for the children and no person to make a home. This third consideration has been brought out arrestingly in studying the situation of the foreign-born woman worker.

A labor leader in a mill town who ascribed the employment of married women to low wages paid to heads of families said to an investigator for this study:

---

[1] *Women and Child Wage-Earners in the United States,* vol. ii, p. 300.

PROBLEMS OF THE WOMAN WORKER

These wages make it in almost all cases necessary for the mothers to be earners. You can scarcely find a Portuguese family in which the mother does not work. The French-Canadians somehow manage to avoid this situation. This is possible, to some extent, because the French men do not get so low in work as the Portuguese do; and the French, because they believe so strongly in the need for the women to stay at home and take care of the younger children, put their older children to work just as soon as the law allows them to be taken from school. This is a city of neglected children. They are practically unlooked after when the days get good enough for them to play out of doors. When in the house, they may be carelessly treated by women who are supposed to look after them, and they are very ill-fed.

This city is one of those wherein the government has thought best to make inquiry into the causes of the high rate of infant mortality.

Of another mill town, a Polish community worker who has since done special work for her people in the employ of the United States government, said:

It is the custom for foreign-born married women to work just as unmarried women do. It is an unusual thing to find a woman in the foreign section who does not go to the mills. Children are taken care of in groups by old women, or other women incapacitated for work, or not taken care of at all. It is even true that the women seem to lose caste among their neighbors if they do not work; but the underlying reason for their working is that heads of families are so insufficiently paid that every person in the family of working age must do his share to make an existence budget.

There is an arrangement, by no means unusual among the foreign born, whereby a husband and wife alternate with day and night work, so that one or the other will always be at home on the children's account. The woman often chooses the night work, so that she may have the daytime with the children; and of course the one who does this is bound to get few hours of sleep. So well is this plan understood that employment agents in plants and persons in charge of public or other

311

employment bureaus have given their coöperation to promote it.

The neglect of housekeeping, incident to the mother's work at the factory or mill, has helped to earn for foreign-born women newcomers the generalization that their standard of living is low. Even women who have the intelligence to plan and organize their housework and possess a high standard in the matter of being clean and of making their families comfortable, may find it difficult to realize all this in the fringes of time before and after the daily work outside. Is it to be wondered at that women less favored in training and mental development fall down when the odds are apparently all against them? A French woman told us:

High living cost and relatively inadequate wages—these keep up a continual struggle. Wives must work in the mill or factory with their husbands and in addition they must come home at night, cook the dinner, fix the house, get the lunch ready to take to the mill next day, go to bed perhaps not before eleven o'clock, and be up early in the morning, because of the children. So it goes on forever.

An Italian woman tells of getting up each day at five o'clock in order to have time to take the children to the woman who is to care for them. When work is over, after five-thirty o'clock in the afternoon, she gets the children, and takes them home. When supper has been prepared, and finished, it is after nine o'clock. It takes such a long time because she "has to light the stove." On Sunday she does not go to the mill, but then she must do the washing. Another Italian woman tells of a similar program. She takes her three children to her mother, who "holds them for her." After she comes home at night, she gets supper and puts the children to bed. This done, she has no more time.

Helene, a French girl, is a young mill worker. When the family finances get in a bad way, as they have done after illness or when the brother was in service, Helene's mother goes back to the mill. But this is very unsatisfactory. There is no one at home then to keep the house clean, and Helene's evenings have to be spent washing dishes and "cleaning up"; and her Sundays in helping her mother to do the washing and ironing. "What are we in this world for," she said, "if we have to work all the time and can never go out and have any fun?"

PROBLEMS OF THE WOMAN WORKER

In various parts of the country experiments have been made with part-time work, as a solution for the problems of married women workers. These experiments have been made by persons in charge of public or philanthropic employment bureaus, or by other social agencies, and have grown out of a desire to compromise wage earning and home making. Whether this compromise can meet the situation, is a matter of individual circumstance and capacity. But although employers have given sincere coöperation in the working out of such employment, through shifts, alternates, or reorganization of process, and small groups have been carried for a period on a part-time basis, the success of this as a plan for great numbers has not yet been demonstrated.

A summer evening's walk through the mill section of a New England town revealed streets overhung with great shade trees, rows of little white cottages with a continuous sweep of green lawns, and flowers here and there. In the growing dusk people were resting and chatting pleasantly, sitting on doorsteps or in hammocks or swings in the yards. So far as one could see, the surroundings were faultlessly neat, with no sign of litter or waste either in front or back of the houses; and it could be imagined easily that the housekeeping, inside, was consistent. The paint on the houses was very white; and on nearly all of them window boxes bloomed. One caught the impression of relaxation, contentment, and comfort. Next day, at the mill it was learned that these people are French Canadians, Poles, and Italians, very few of whom were born in this country. The secret of the apparent cleanliness and comfort of their living may have been exposed when the superintendent showed a register of mill families, which records the occupation or school grade of all the members, and takes care to indicate for each

313

family which person is housekeeper. It is the policy of the mill, he said, to know that there is a housekeeper in every home, and that wherever possible this person is the mother.

LEARNING THE LANGUAGE

Time and place, seemingly important to both men and women workers in any plan of English instruction, are perhaps of utmost importance to women. If men's leisure is precious after the hours of labor, the women's is more so; for all women, single or married, are likely to have certain household responsibilities, which make the margin for recreation, personal needs, or relaxation still more narrow. Even those foreign-born girls who board with friends or relatives may find themselves included in the family when it comes to doing the "work"—and all women have necessary sewing and "fixing" to do. Among several nationalities, notably Italian and Syrian, there is a traditional disapproval in regard to permitting women to go out at night for any reason, unescorted by their men, and so long as this persists it makes daytime lessons for such women the only practicable arrangement.

Two factors of place invite consideration; these are convenience and familiarity. Convenience is really only another expression of time. The desire for a familiar place, if based on reticence and group feeling, is more insistent for women than for men; the fewness of women's contacts outside of the home makes for greater shyness. Moreover, as in the matter of being out at night, the foreign tradition is likely to oppose going to "strange places" on the part of the women. It seems to have been demonstrated by many cities and many agencies, that the enrollment and regularity of attendance of women at English classes are largely dependent upon the points here noted; and thus the work place or the parish house, the hall or school of the home neighborhood, has been experimentally tried, and each has reaped its set of pros and cons. We can only point out, for the industrial worker, that from a standpoint of time saving, classes in the shop, during working hours or just before or after working hours, obviously rank first; and such classes satisfy the two conditions of place.

In providing for the teaching of English or definitely encouraging workers to learn it elsewhere, employers generally have lagged in interest so far as the women have been concerned. Provision for teaching English was greatly stimulated by the war. Thus it was to be expected that this inquiry, made in 1919, would uncover many incipient or experimental English teaching arrangements. The women in most plants have been left out of these; in some instances, where classes for men had been launched, the company was considering the women's side of the matter, with the hope that something might later be started.

The reason for overlooking women in English-teach-programs is in part accounted for by the fact that practical demands, like the pressure of citizenship and the necessity to carry on business transactions, bear less obviously upon the women. The connection between shop safety and knowledge of English is felt less for women than men. It does not so often happen that the women are doing work which endangers life if accident precautions are not understood; and such injuries as they are personally subjected to are likely to be of a minor sort. Moreover, it is true that the employer has to contend with the women's reluctance to learn; and this reluctance is, with most nationalities, greater among the women than among the men. The women are less optimistic than men about their ability to learn. It is easy for a woman past her youth to think she is too old; and instances are known of Greek, Syrian, Lithuanian, and Polish husbands who discouraged their working wives from learning on the ground that a woman does not need to know things.

An illustration of conquering the reluctant attitude of the women by change of method is provided by a steel plant. The Polish women employees knew so little English that their work on war orders was handicapped. The company tried by the usual methods to give them instruction, but the women's interest was not reached and classes did not "go." Then, the company took its problem to a local Girls' Trade School, believing, with reason as it proved, that the trained teachers at the school could find a solution. The answer was a clever and promising experiment which the director of the school devised, and has described as follows: [1]

With the entry of foreign-born women into industry, came the great need of their understanding enough English so that they could comprehend what a foreman meant when he gave them the simple directions for carrying on the work which was assigned to them.

In certain parts of some industries a high degree of intelligence was not essential and work could well be done by the "scrub-woman" type, a group who had not found it necessary to know much English up to the present crisis. Now some vocational English of a simple nature would make the worker much more useful in the part of the job she was hired to perform.

This type of worker is not stable on the job, being easily disturbed by higher wages somewhere else, or by an unusual demand made in connection with the work. How was it possible to teach her English without opposition on her part? Going to school had not been an attractive matter in the past, and might arouse antagonism which the employer could little afford to risk when it was very difficult to find all the help needed in the rush of war work.

During the summer of 1918, conservation of food was being pushed in many quarters and was popular with all women. During a visit to one factory, wishing to train these women above described,

---

[1] Helen R. Hildreth, Worcester Girls' Trade School, Worcester, Massachusetts.

it was observed that many of the operations in the industry were analogous to those of canning fruits and vegetables. The women sorted the good from the imperfect shells, placed the good ones in baskets and dipped them into a liquid solution and out again. Vegetables were sorted, the good placed in baskets for blanching and dipping, and then canned.

Consultation with the foremen brought out that certain phrases would be advantageous for the women to understand and be able to use. These were very simple and could be repeated many times during a canning demonstration when the attention could be easily held; "education" was not apparent and interest was uppermost. The phrases were as follows: "Good keep, bad throw away"; "Dip basket into water"; "Take basket out of water," etc. Other words used in the demonstration were not rehearsed by the pupils, but were explained by one or more women who happened in class and understood a little English. The drill was only on the few words which were of vocational value to the work. The operation of canning would get over, without special emphasis on the words used in describing its process, except those referred to.

The women came directly from the shop with dirty hands and clothes, so some idea of cleanliness could be enforced by having them wash their hands before sorting the vegetables and repeating, "Clean hands with food"; "Dirt makes sick"; etc. This association with health is very fundamental.

The idea of time could be developed, for the vegetables had to be blanched for from five to ten minutes and cooked or sterilized for one or two or more hours. These time durations could be shown on the face of the clock and their name lengths learned.

The pupils were held for half an hour only, without any loss of pay and with little loss of time to the employer.

Since the chief aim of these lessons was to form a habit of coming to class, no attempt was made at this time to teach any great amount of English; that was to be followed up later when the women had become used to submitting to instruction. Four of these canning lessons were given as an experiment and then the teacher was on vacation until September.

In the fall regular instruction in English based on familiar actions of everyday life was begun, but was soon discontinued because there were, by that time, too few women employed to make the class worth while.

This method of getting the interest of the women seems sound, but it could not be thoroughly tested since the same women did not come each time, due to press of work as well as to the change of personnel of the employees. War conditions seemed to breed constant labor turnover, and the women drifted out of one factory and into another in a bewildering succession. This vocational training should hold them if one could get their attention once focused on it.

The other alternative for English teaching is the night school; but if employers do not admit a maximum of eight hours for the working day, there is slight use of dependence upon voluntary night education for foreign-born women employees.

The best way to arrive at understanding of the foreign-born women's situation with respect to night classes, especially of the married working women of whom there are so many, is to try to think of one's self in her place—and thus to imagine the early rising, the quick necessary touches to things of the house before starting to work, the hours of application in factory or mill, the home-going and probably the preparing of the evening meal; and this over, washing the dishes. If she has had a nine or ten hour day, it is seven o'clock now at least; and she is facing the questions: Shall she go to night school? Shall she sit on the doorstep instead and chat with the neighbors, if it is a mild spring evening? Or shall she let the warm kitchen lure her, if a winter wind is blowing?

If she is married, can she with easy peace of mind, forget the heap of washing that ought to be done, the children who may need attention, the ragged rents that should be mended somehow, the food that should be prepared in advance of another work day? Against all this can she array the advantage of knowing ultimately the English which falls so strangely on her ears, and makes her so sleepy when she hears it read in class? If she could go one night in the week and be done with it! But one should give up two or three evenings, if it is really to count. Of course there are women who have all these duties, and the same apparent question of time, who can nevertheless transcend them, and go to night school with persevering regularity until they at last are "English speaking." But we have no evidence that most of the women have the understanding to treat their problems this way when the working day is long; and it is for the "most" that present plans must be laid.

BOARDING HOMES FOR IMMIGRANT WORKING GIRLS

Charles Dickens, on his trip to New England mills, was witness to this country's earliest development for housing wage-earning women. He wrote in *American Notes:*

> They reside in various boarding houses near at hand. . . . I am now going to state three facts, which will startle a large class of readers on this side of the Atlantic very much. Firstly, there is a joint-stock piano in a great many of the boarding houses. Secondly, nearly all these ladies subscribe to circulating libraries. Thirdly, they have got up among themselves a periodical called "The Offering."

From the days of a housing problem for little groups of American girls and women, who came from homes in neighboring towns, industry has passed to the much more complicated problem of enormously greater numbers of workers, of widely ranging nationalities, and for most of them an ocean between them and their homes. Or perhaps their present housing plan is all there is, and—so far as they know—all there is to be, of home.

It seems impossible to know, from any comprehensive statistics, the number of such "non-family groups of women," who, in normal times, have been coming here from foreign lands. Figures by age and nationality, for single, widowed, or separated women are available; but they do not show how many of these came with or to join families, or how many of the single girls came expecting to be married immediately on reaching this country. Between the years 1910 and 1915 the total number of unmarried women immigrants, under thirty years of age, was 525,600.[1] More than 100,000 of these were Poles; more than 80,000 were Hebrews; nearly 75,000 were Italians. The remainder represent about twenty different nationalities. During these years the Immigrants' Protective League of Chicago received from ports of entry the names of 26,909 women and girls, all of whom came from Europe to Chicago.[2]

In all of the city of Chicago there is just one organized home designed especially to give permanent accommodation to foreign-born girls. This is a Polish home, in a Polish and Lithuanian district; and the capacity is forty-six. A woman physician interested in the children of this community, eight or nine years ago, became aware also of the crowded, unsuitable living situation of unmarried, foreign-born girls. At her instigation the Catholic Woman's League of Chicago raised funds necessary for starting the home. It is now under the direct guidance of the priest of a nearby Polish church, although it is open to residents of any religion. Among its wage earners' boarding houses of general character, Chicago has a few which intend to serve foreign-born workers as well as natives; but at the time of inquiry none of these had in residence as many as a dozen girls of foreign birth.

In Cleveland, a small home for Jewish girls is the only one that has been established specifically for the foreign born. This home, during the period of normal immigration, received some girls directly from Europe. It was then located in a good residential part

---

[1] Report of Commissioner General of Immigration, 1915, p. 56.
[2] Grace Abbott, *The Immigrant and the Community*, p. 61.

of the city, in a neighborhood largely Jewish, of the American generation. It has since moved to another section which is not essentially Jewish, and some non-Jewish girls are among the residents. The home is attractive, comfortable, and pleasant in all its arrangements. The girls are looked after and given freedom in ways that are likely to bring individual capacities or talents to discovery, and needed educational help is found for those who seem to show that they will use it well. The immigrant girl who comes to this home has an unusual opportunity for adjustment under most favorable circumstances; but the very care, expense, and individualness of the method almost preclude a large undertaking along these lines. This home is aided by philanthropic contributions and is directed by trustees. Four homes, of general character in Cleveland, are open to the foreign-born girl. One of these, however, seems always to have its capacity of residents as well as a waiting list filled with American-born girls. In the other homes the number of the foreign born actually in residence is negligible.

New York City's list of homes for wage-earning women seems, on the surface, to give some hope that the foreign-born unmarried woman is being taken care of. But inquiry has shown that homes planned especially for her are chiefly the temporary type—the needed refuge which a great port of entry and debarkation like New York must provide for the emergencies connected with landing, meeting relatives, deportation, or voluntary return; or they are transient homes designed to care for governesses, maids, servants, and other homes or institutions for workers in the intervals between positions. The table, appended to this chapter, shows that the only permanent, non-private facilities in Manhattan for organized living specifically intended for foreign-born women industrial workers are two, a home for Jewish girls, and the boarding home of the International Institute of the Y. W. C. A. The combined capacities of these homes is fifty-one. The table shows also a few permanent Jewish organizations which admit the foreign-born industrial workers, but the number of these in residence was found to be very small.

There are, in addition to these possibilities, twenty-seven organized homes in Manhattan which are willing to serve foreign-born girls, among others, and they do have some representation of girls of this class. Eight of the homes, whose combined capacity is 550, have "many" or a "majority" of foreign born; the nineteen remaining homes, whose capacity totals 1223, have "only a few," or "a small minority." Thus, by the most liberal estimation, only a few hundred of New York's thousands of foreign-born industrial women workers, away from their families, are being accommodated with organized aids in their living arrangements.

All homes open to the foreign born in Manhattan are from the standpoint of support and control of four classes; those carried by the church or church societies, those carried by philanthropic agencies of foreign or native origin, projects which combine commercial and social interests, and schemes of coöperative boarding. The reasons given for maintaining these homes and organizations include religious influence, protection, necessity of providing low living cost, and the desire of girls to escape the dreariness of a furnished room in a great city.

A number of these homes give employment-finding service, which is in most cases more or less unorganized. One home has a graphophone for teaching English; another has extensive provision of teachers and equipment for teaching trades, in preparation for wage earning. The home designed especially for young foreign-born Jewish girls is run as a "republic," and this method is believed to aid in home harmony and in developing initiative. The International Institute Home, which serves a wide range of nationalities and only the foreign-born, tries to arrange the manner of living so that girls who have been in this country several years can be helpful to newer comers, especially in the matter of learning English. It is the policy in assigning rooms to put girls who cannot speak English with those who can; though in the seating at table this policy is not strictly observed. The director's only thought about the dining room is that all shall feel at home and have a good time, so that here there is likely to be a considerable amount of foreign language speaking.

There is undoubtedly some "clubbing together" for living among immigrant working women, after they have become adjusted enough to the country to make it possible; yet various private and governmental studies of housing have found this an occasional arrangement only. Nearly all of these thousands of girls crowd into the homes of relatives or other fellow-country people which are probably, before the coming of the new arrivals, as full as they should be. The cheapness of this method of living is what makes it endurable; but discomfort and lack of privacy are obvious concomitants. In speaking of the living situation of some of the foreign-born women workers in Chicago, a government report states: [1]

All were Slovaks or Galicians, and all worked in the stockyards. They lived with foreign-born families who had crowded into their households a number of lodgers. All were living in a most wretched way. . . . In two families, there were eight persons in three rooms.

---

[1] *Report on Condition of Woman and Child Wage-earners in the United States*, 1910, vol. 5, p. 64.

ADJUSTING IMMIGRANT AND INDUSTRY

This condition is repeated in other cities, and can be fairly understood as, at present, this country's accepted standard of provision for new-coming foreign-born women workers who come alone from overseas. Further illustration is provided by the Massachusetts Immigration Commission, which records among others the following pictures.[1]

In a mill town which has one of the largest Greek colonies in Massachusetts, in the downstairs tenement of a two-story house, is a group of eight people living in this way. There are four girls ranging from sixteen to twenty-four years of age, and four men. They have two rooms and a kitchen. The apartment is clean and orderly.

A Lithuanian girl has lived four years in a family of three who have four rooms and eight lodgers—five men and three women. The girl works as a stitcher in a tailor shop. She started to go to night school when she first came, but the landlady objected, as she wanted her to help out with the housework in the evening.

A sixteen-year-old Jewish girl came with her father, but is not living in the same house with him. She is lodging in a house where there are four in the family, three men lodgers and herself, all in five rooms.

A Lithuanian girl who was eighteen years of age at the time of arrival has been in this country four years. She lived in three different places since coming to this country. In the first place there were five rooms, four in the family and two men and two women lodgers. At present, she is living in a tenement of five rooms with a family of three who have three men and one woman lodger.

A Polish girl of eighteen who has been in America four months, having borrowed her passage money from her brother in this country, is lodging with a family of four who live in four rooms with five lodgers, three men and two women. This girl is working seven days a week washing cars in the railroad yards in Boston.

A recent study of Italian women in industry in New York found young girls boarding or lodging in Italian homes where they had not an inch of space which they could call their own. Even the bed which was theirs to share at night was folded into a chiffonier by day.

---

[1] *Report of Massachusetts Immigration Commission*, 1914, pp. 60–61.

PROBLEMS OF THE WOMAN WORKER

Among other pictures drawn by this study are the following. The last picture is given to illustrate the contrasting experience of the woman who did have a bit of space which was unencroachably hers.[1]

Two sisters were each paying fifty cents a week for sleeping space in a four-room flat, the home of nine other adults.

A woman was boarding with a brother's family on Elizabeth Street, where eleven persons were huddled into two rooms.

Caterina, twenty-six years old, who sewed on men's coats and earned $6 a week, shared the household expenses with a brother and his wife. As she helped considerably with the housework, her share of the rent was only $2 a month, although she enjoyed the luxury of being the sole occupant of a bedroom.

Another woman, who had earned $8.50 in the preceding week as a finisher on cloaks and suits, but who had been idle about five months during the year, rented an unfurnished room with the privilege of gas and the use of the kitchen stove for $1.50 a week. A folding bed, two trunks, three chairs, and a table made of a soap box, were the principal articles of furniture, but the room was decorated with several shelves of gay dishes. The images of eighteen different saints adorned the head of the bed, bright pictures of the rulers of Italy, advertising calendars and panels, an alarm clock, and a guitar hung on the wall. The care of her room was a daily joy and her only recreation. She prepared her own meals, which cost between $2 and $3 a week. She was an economical housekeeper, buying what she could in large quantities.

Five factors have to be considered in any comprehensive workable plan for the organized housing immigrant industrial women workers. These are, location in a neighbrhood of their fellow-country people; opportunity to economize living expenses in their own way; household arrangements controlled by a fellow-country woman of their own class; the sanction of the church—in the case of the great majority who come from Catholic countries; and a non-philanthropic financial base.

---

[1] L. C. Odencranz, *Italian Women in Industry*, pp. 222, 223, 226.

ADJUSTING IMMIGRANT AND INDUSTRY

In Passaic, New Jersey, there is a well-established demonstration of a boarding home system which is workable for unlimited numbers; and it appears to take care of the five factors which this study calls requisites. This is a coöperative idea which may contain special adaptation to girls of Slavic tradition and temperament. The Passaic plan is taken as the most suggestive because it has not only proved its practicability through more than fifteen years, but it is specifically adapted to industrial workers; it can serve incoming immigrants by providing a temporary or permanent home, as well as a model which they can follow later if they desire in starting independent homes of their own. It is true that the Passaic coöperative homes are the projects of girls who are members of the Tercyarki, a religious order, which has its origin in Europe; and girls who live in the homes must become members of it. The code of conduct to which the girls bind themselves may take care of the government of the home in an important way; but the financial scheme and general plan of organization should be found readily adaptable for the great army of thrifty, simple, well-meaning Slavic girls, and probably some of those of other nationalities in the great industrial centers of this country.

The Passaic coöperative boarding houses, of which there are seven, are neat, comfortable cottages, housing, in most cases, about thirty girls each, and recognizing a rule whereby a sleeping room is shared by not more than two persons. The residents are Galicians; and all the homes are in neighborhoods of the same nationality. Four houses are in the better residence section known as the Eastern End; the remaining three are in "Dundee," a district wholly industrial. There is a high standard of cleanliness for all these homes; clean, simple white curtains are at the windows, and the tiny yards are neatly planted with vegetables or flowers.

The history of the Passaic homes goes back more than fifteen years, when a young non-English-speaking Galician woman left a Buffalo convent and came to Passaic to work in one of the mills. With native thrift, she had saved, at the end of a few years' work, nearly two thousand dollars. It was at that time that the woolen mills of Passaic were offering work and pay which attracted unmarried or non-family Galician girls, and they were coming to the town, to the mill work, straight from Europe. It is estimated by a local organization which serves the foreign-born population that there are now in Passaic about 1200 Galician women whose families are in Europe; and that some of these women are married. The single Galician women in Passaic far outnumber the single men of the same nationality. Thus, since the immigration of girls began, the town has had a special housing problem, created by their coming. This was the situation which the young Galician woman recognized; and stimulated by her own experience in trying to live in Passaic comfortably and decently, she determined to use the money she had saved, in order that something better might be realized for others.

She unfolded to the priest of the parish her plan for the first coöperative home, and for establishing the Tercyarki for single girls in Passaic. The priest approved, and from that time has given moral but not other support to all the coöperative boarding ventures. This woman, with another who also had saved some money, bought a house, which they soon had filled with mill girls. She charged them $3 a month apiece for rent; and, regarding this as a chance to devote her life to a good cause, she acted as housekeeper and laundress for three years without being paid. She marketed carefully for food, dividing the cost equally among the residents. At the end of three years the rental paid by these girls had reimbursed her investment. She was then married, and gave the responsibility of the home to another; but she has continued to aid with advice when new hones are started.

Subsequent houses have been self-maintaining. Three or four mill girls who have been in the country long enough to have money saved pool their savings and thus jointly have sufficient to make a good first payment on the house they decide to buy. The house is at once occupied by as many as it can hold without overcrowding; all rooms except the kitchen being given up, as a rule, for sleeping. The rental of $3 or $4 a month, paid by each girl, is applied to payments on the house, and to a salary for one of the owners who acts as housekeeper. She is usually a young woman, like all the rest who live there. The other owners and the girl tenants work during the day in the mills. They have "coffee" at home in the morning, and dinner at the end of the day; and in one of the homes, the rate for these two meals, in the high-cost-of-living times of 1919, was about $3 a week. The housekeeper divides the cost equally among all, every week. Each girl does her own laundry work, for which the facilities are provided in the rent. The girls who have a room together usually furnish it jointly; but some rooms are already furnished when the girls come.

During the period of immigration before the war new-coming girls were welcomed by those who had had a partial initiation here, and when there was evidence of demand, a new home was started by girls who had been living in one of the homes, and had learned the method by which they are carried on. It is stated by the parish priest, and others who are familiar with the situation, that all the girls who have been in the country a few years have savings with which they can combine to buy new homes; and should the gate again be opened to immigration it is prophesied that many more of these homes will be started by such girls. In its whole development, this Passaic coöperative plan relies largely upon the foreign-born girl already here, to help meet the problem of the foreign-born girl who has newly arrived.

ORGANIZED BOARDING FACILITIES FOR FOREIGN-BORN WOMEN WAGE

NATIONALITY	NAME	ADDRESS	CAPACITY
Finnish.......	Finnish Women's Co-operative House	241 Lenox Avenue	40
French.......	French Branch, Y.W.C.A.	124 West 16th Street	12
	French Evangelical Home	341 West 30th Street	21
	Hugenot Home	237 West 24th Street	40
	Jeanne D'Arc Home	253 West 24th Street	130
German......	Maedschenhein	217 East 62d Street	26
	German Governess' Home Assn.	235 East 60th Street	21
Hungarian....	St. Mary's Home, Our Lady of Hungary	231 East 72d Street	26
Italian.......	St. Raphael's Society for Italian Immigrants	8 Charlton Street	
Jewish.......	Clara Di Hirsch Home	225 East 63d Street	150
	Hannah Lavenburg Home	319 East 17th Street	30
	Unity House	135 Lexington Avenue	40
	Workers' Co-operative House	1786 Lexington Avenue	153
	Young Women's Hebrew Assn.	3 West 110th Street	
Scandinavian	Danish Mission Home	154 East 64th Street	
	Norwegian Evang. Lutheran Home	45 Whitehall Street	30
	Norwegian Home for Girls	167 East 60th Street	20
	Swedish Epsorth House	588 Lexington Avenue	30
	Swedish Lutheran Immigrant Home	5 Water Street	65
Slavic........	Polish National Allicande Immigrant Home	180 Second Avenue	60
	Slavonic Immigrant Society	436 West 23d Street	30
Spanish......	Casa Maria	251 West 14th Street	30
International	International Institute Boarding Home	116 East 29th Street	21

OTHER NATIONALITIES SERVED	RESIDENCE PERIOD	OCCUPATION
None...............	Transient	Coöperative, chiefly domestic servants
None...............	Permanent and transient	Governesses and maids, chiefly
None...............	Transient	
None...............	Transient	
American and Italian.	Transient	Governesses and maids, chiefly
None...............	Permanent and transient	Domestic workers, chiefly
None...............	Transient	Governesses
None...............	Chiefly transient	
None, usually........	Temporary	Chiefly married women going to join family
A few; most are American born..........	Permanent	Trade workers, chiefly
A few; all foreign born	3–6 years permitted	Factory and domestic workers
A few; not primarily for foreign born....	Permanent	Coöperative. For members of Local 24. Dress and Waist Makers' Union
Intended for workers of any nationality...	Permanent	Coöperative. For men and women, chiefly in garment trades. Private enterprise
Primarily for Jews, most are American born..............	Permanent	
None, usually........	Transient, chiefly	Domestic servants, chiefly
None...............	Temporary	(For arriving immigrants) Domestic servants, chiefly
None, usually........	Transient	Domestic servants, chiefly
None, usually........	Transient and permanent	Men and women, arriving and returning
None, usually........	Temporary	Few women arriving alone
None...............	Temporary	(Men and women)
	Transient and permanent	(Men and women, chiefly men) Women are domestic servants
Cuban, French, and some Americans....	Permanent	Teachers, office workers, and fine hand-sewers
All.................	Permanent	Office workers and factory workers

CHAPTER XVI

ADJUSTING IMMIGRANT AND INDUSTRY—A NATIONAL POLICY

ASSUMING that we do not want our immigrant wage earners to be either "birds of passage" or an inferior caste for doing the hard and disagreeable work of the country; assuming that we do want them to thrive and prosper here and to be merged and fused into a united American citizenship, what are we doing and what can we do, as a nation, toward this end?

Whatever may be our ideal of American citizenship, the basis for common thought and action between the native and foreign born lies in the adjustment of the immigrant to the conditions of American economic life. For most immigrants the necessity of earning a living and the problems arising in the course of their employment constitute the major interests of their lives. It is in these interests, therefore, and in the methods of solving the problems of their working lives, that the basis for fusing the native with the foreign born must be sought.

Whether the nation consciously directs the process or not, an adjustment of some kind between the immigrant wage earner and American industry is constantly taking place. If, on account of inability to speak English and ignorance of American industrial opportunities, the immigrant is unable to find a job and to hold it, he gets a padrone, an interpreter, an employment agent, or a straw boss of his own nationality, to help him overcome these difficulties. Industry, too,

adjusts its methods, processes, and management policies to the practices of such intermediaries, as well
as to lack of skill and ignorance of its immigrant labor
forces. These methods of adjustment, however, while
ofttimes helpful, develop abuses of their own, which
tend to separate the foreign-born from the native population rather than to unite the two.

It is in the first years of the immigrant's life in America that he is particularly subject to these abuses and
maladjustments, and it is the newly arrived immigrant
that presents the greatest difficulties to American
industry. After a period of years, when he has learned
the language and the methods of the American industries in which he is employed, when he has familiarized
himself with the social agencies of American life that
function in behalf of the wage earner, the immigrant,
in most cases, has substantially improved his economic
position, and is able to command the same treatment
and consideration that native-born wage earners get.
But the newly arrived immigrant is apt to upset the
wage scales, working conditions, and management policies, often to the detriment of both the immigrant and
the industry; and the experiences of the early years
of his life in America frequently remain in his consciousness as a nightmare, which often crops out to interfere
with the maintenance of proper relations between
employer and employee, as well as between native-
born and foreign-born population.

An attempt has been made in the preceding chapters
to describe the immigrant's industrial experiences in
America and to indicate their effect on his mind and
on his attitude towards things American. The maladjustments which alienate, and the adjustments which
tend to draw the immigrant closer to American industry and its people, have been described in connection with the problems he has with finding a job and

learning to work, with management methods and trade-union policies. And in connection with each of these problems, it has been our purpose to indicate the helpful measures and the agencies, public and private, which have tended to prevent maladjustments, remove difficulties, and further as complete and favorable adjustments as is possible between American industry and its immigrant employees.

COMBINING EXPERIENCE IN A UNITED STATES IMMIGRATION COMMISSION

But the methods that have been found helpful in assisting the process of adjustment have in the main been disconnected instances. Employers here and there, a few trade unions, a number of states, some immigrant societies, and private or philanthropic labor agencies have developed technique, policies, or administrative organizations, which show what can be done in uniting the immigrant with the native born, and how to do it. These instances are, on the whole, increasing from year to year. More and more is being done, but there is as yet no concerted national movement, and the work of uniting all this disconnected experience into a national policy or program still remains to be done.

This should not be a difficult task, for all the elements of such a program are already at hand in the various experiments described in the preceding chapters. All that is necessary is for some national authority to take the leadership in spreading information about the things that are being done and the results achieved, and in assisting those employers, trade unions, and government agencies which have remained backward to adopt the methods of the most progressive.

Such a national authority would naturally be the United States Immigration Service; but the policy of restriction of immigration, to which our Congress is committed, is bound to throw more and more quasi-judicial functions on this Service in addition to its regular administrative duties and in addition to the guidance functions which a national adjustment policy would make necessary. It has been the traditional policy of the federal government in dealing with problems involving conflicting economic interests—such as between shippers and carriers, bankers and borrowers, employers and employees—to create quasi-judicial bodies like the Interstate Commerce Commission, or the Federal Reserve Board and the Railroad Labor Board, to hold the proper balance between the conflicting groups. The restriction of immigration has already developed conflict between those groups of our population which desire abundant supplies of labor and those which desire to restrict labor supplies as a means of raising wages and other standards of American life. To adjust these interests properly, it will be necessary that the immigration authority be organized in the form of a Board or a Commission with quasi-judicial functions.

It is outside the purpose of the present volume to discuss problems that have to do with the admission of the immigrants into the country. But there is bound to be a relation between a domestic policy for immigrants, with which we are here concerned, and the policy of admission or restriction. We cannot refrain, therefore, from pointing out that the sound lessons of American experience have been to leave to a fact-finding and quasi-judicial board or commission such disputable facts as to whether the country is in need of more labor or more immigrants of any kind, while Congress enacts the general law stipulating when and under what conditions immigrants are to be permitted to enter or be denied admission.

ADJUSTING IMMIGRANT AND INDUSTRY

Just as the Interstate Commerce Commission is given authority to investigate and determine what are reasonable rates and adequate service, while Congress enacts the general law that rates must be reasonable and service adequate; so the Congress might similarly enact that normally healthy and moral immigrants may be admitted into the country when there is need for them, but may be excluded when the industries of the country could not absorb them. And the United States Immigration Commission could be empowered to ascertain and determine what the needs of the country are for immigrant labor, and to issue orders from time to time fixing the number and kind of immigrants who are to be admitted in accordance with the ascertained needs of the country.

IMMIGRATION POLICY—DOMESTIC AND FOREIGN

A national policy of adjusting immigrant and industry would thus require a United States Immigration Board or Commission with two main functions:

1. Admission—the foreign immigration policy;
2. Americanization—the domestic policy for immigrants.

We pass over the first as being beyond the scope of this work. But the domestic policy must also have its roots abroad. We have seen how some immigrant aid societies have their agents in foreign countries, to discourage those who cannot be admitted to this country and to assist those who are on their way. Here is suggestive experience for a United States Immigration Commission to follow. If the government is to assume more responsibility toward the immigrants in this country and assist in their adjustment to the conditions of American life, it ought to know in advance what immigrants are coming over in number and kind. At the same time it is only fair to the prospective immigrant that he should know before he begins his long journey whether he will be admitted into the United States and whether there are opportunities for him to make a living.

At present he gets this information in letters from fellow countrymen in this country, who may be little better informed than he is; from steamship companies which are interested in securing passengers; and occasionally from immigrant aid societies organized for the welfare of the immigrant. It is proposed, therefore, that the United States Immigration Commission shall have stations abroad for examining those who apply for admission to the United States, and that these agencies should indicate on the immigrant's papers before he starts that he will be admitted under the laws of the United States.

Such a procedure would be equally advantageous to the immigrants and to the United States, and the organization of stations in foreign countries would be one of the first steps necessary in any comprehensive plan of adjusting immigrants and industry in the United States. For, besides examining immigrants for purposes of admission, the agents of the immigration authority stationed abroad might have the duty of disseminating accurate information regarding industrial opportunities, to discourage from coming those classes of labor for which there are abundant supplies in the United States, and to aid in the proper selection of those for whom there may be a special need.

Secretary of Labor, J. J. Davis, has proposed the examination of immigrants abroad. But under the present law there can always be an appeal from an immigration agent to the Secretary of Labor, and the Commissioner General of Immigration has explained that most immigrants will take a chance on coming over and having their cases heard by the Secretary while friends interest Congressmen and Senators in their behalf. Under such circumstances examination abroad is useless. But if an Immigration Commission could pass final judgments abroad, and had facilities for securing accurate information to support its judgments, then the maintenance of immigration stations to visé the applications of immigrants who desire to settle in the United States would be both desirable and practical.

DISTRIBUTION AND PLACEMENT

In the purely domestic policy of adjusting immigrant and industry, the distribution and placement of immigrants among our industries would be one of its first functions. We have seen how finding a job is the first need of the immigrant, how private labor agencies as well as public employment bureaus, trade unions, employers' associations, and philanthropic organizations have all attempted to meet the need. All of them may be said thus far to have failed to meet the need, but each of them has contributed something that has been helpful, has had some measure of success. On the whole, however, our conclusion must be that only public enterprise on a national scale, a national employment service coöperating with the states and municipalities can ever meet the need with any measure of completeness; and this will have to be supplemented to some extent by carefully regulated private and philanthropic bureaus for specialized services which the national system is unable to provide.

With such a national system of employment bureaus, the proposed United States Immigration Service would have to be closely connected, not only for the purpose of proper placement of immigrants, but also because in any policy of admission or restriction of immigration, a most important consideration must be whether those who are admitted are able to find employment in this country.

A United States Employment Service coöperating with states and cities which operate public employment bureaus is already in existence. It is wofully crippled because of lack of funds and lack of civil service requirements for its directors and managers. But the measures necessary to enable it to render effective service are known and established. They have been described in Chapter III. All that is needed now is the will on the part of the representatives of the Nation in Congress to *do it*, and the financial means to make an efficient administration possible.

The functions of the United States Immigration Commission with respect to the distribution and placement of immigrant labor may be briefly outlined as follows:

1. It would license and regulate the activities of those private labor agencies which supply immigrant laborers. Most of these agencies "ship" immigrants, as they call it, across state lines, and the states which have attempted to license and regulate the work of such agencies have on this account found it almost impossible to protect the immigrants against the abuses which the state laws were designed to remove.

2. The Commission would assist the public employment bureaus in organizing separate departments for the handling of non-English-speaking workers, lending its agents to act as interpreters in such departments or perhaps operating such departments of the public bureaus outright, in order that immigrant labor might be placed in industry, to the best advantage of both the immigrants and the industries of the country.

3. The collection of information about opportunities for employment of immigrant labor would be primarily

in the hands of the Employment Service, for it is seldom that an employer uses foreign-born labor exclusively. His requests for labor would be registered at the employment offices, and through these the Immigration Commission would be able to secure accurate measures of the real need for labor and the available supply.

4. The special services which immigrants need in their search for work, some of which we have described in Chapter III, would be the concern of the Immigration Commission, and as it ascertained these needs and developed the measures for meeting them, it would see to the installation of these in the departments for non-English-speaking workers in the employment offices.

5. For the purpose of determining whether additional immigrant labor is needed, whether this is done by Congress or by the Immigration Commission, the information secured through the employment offices would be the most reliable. The ordinary statements made by employers of shortages of labor and by trade unions of oversupply of labor are partisan attempts to increase or decrease supply. Requests for help which employers register at employment bureaus, however, are "orders" for which they may be held responsible. And if the bureaus are united in a national service, an attempt can be made first to supply the demand from labor available anywhere in the United States, both native and foreign born. Then, if this available labor cannot supply the entire demand, the residue can be certified by the Immigration Commission as a *bona fide* need of the country.

In Canada this is the actual procedure. Labor may be imported into that country with the approval of the immigration authorities. But when requests are registered with the immigration department, these are first referred to the Canadian Employment Service and

whatever labor is available in Canada is sent to meet
the demand. Only such workers as cannot be supplied
from within the country are then permitted to come
in. Importation of labor in this manner is prohibited
by our laws; but for the purpose of determining accu-
rately the need of immigrant labor in the United States
an Immigration Commission may well follow the same
procedure.

ADJUSTING THE IMMIGRANTS' INDUSTRIAL RELATIONS

Next to the distribution and placement of immigrants
in a domestic immigration policy would come the adjustment of the industrial relations between immigrant
employee and American management. Corresponding
to this the proposed United States Immigration Commission would need a Division of Industrial Relations
to study and help in the solution of three problems
which confront our immigrants and our industries alike:

1. Training of immigrant labor;
2. Labor management of immigrant employees;
3. Trade-union policies with respect to immigrant
   employees.

Training for work in America is primarily the work
of the employer who uses immigrant labor. The experience of the war industries in training women and other
unskilled workers to new and unfamiliar tasks has
pointed a way toward the solution of the problem.
"Vestibule schools" conducted by employers, through
which every new employee must pass on his way into
the shops, guarantee that the immigrant's special problem of adjustment to new tasks and a strange industrial
environment will receive special attention. His capacities can thus be ascertained and his instruction can
be directed to make him fit to hold the place into which
he is put.

But just as the spreading of "vestibule schools" and other methods of training had to be stimulated and directed for war purposes by the Section on Industrial Training of the Council of National Defense, by a War Department Committee on Education and Special Training, and by the U. S. Training Service in the Department of Labor, so a United States Immigration Commission will have important duties in connection with the development of "vestibule schools" and special methods of training immigrants in American industries.

The methods themselves have been described rather fully in Chapter VI, but they are far from universally in use among plants employing immigrants. It took a good deal of education, propaganda, and advisory services on the part of the agencies mentioned to induce employers to install systems of training for war purposes, and it will take a good deal more to induce them to develop training methods in pursuance of a national policy of adjusting immigrants and industry. The Immigration Commission will, therefore, have to follow the methods of the war agencies designed to promote training of industrial workers. It will need to publish and distribute bulletins describing the methods and results of such training of immigrants in industrial plants. Its agents will have to address Chambers of Commerce and other employers' organizations, as well as trade unions, in the interest of training of immigrant workers; and the Commission must be ready to supply information and lend assistance in installing "vestibule schools" and immigrant training departments in industrial plants on request from employers.

A national policy designed to aid in the adjustment of immigrant and industry requires also that the labor management methods and policies of those employers who have been most successful in uniting their employees in common thought and action should be spread as rapidly as possible to all the industries which employ immigrant labor. The United States Immigration Commission in administering the domestic immigration policy for the country would have to make this a most important part of its work.

It would have a considerable body of successful experience in this kind of work to follow. During the war the proper management of labor was recognized by the nation as an important factor in developing a united purpose among all our people, and several agencies were created to assist in spreading the best labor management policies among the war industries. An employment Management Section of the Council of National Defense and a Division of Labor Administration in the Department of Labor collected and distributed information relating to methods of hiring, selecting, transferring, promoting and otherwise managing labor in industrial plants. They also aided employers in organizing employment departments to carry out the most successful policies designed to maintain peaceful and friendly relations between employers and employees and to develop a coöperative spirit.

Similarly, a United States Immigration Commission would have to collect and distribute information regarding the most successful experience in managing immigrant labor, and to advise and assist employers in the installation of such methods and policies in their plants.

The development of the science of personnel management and its widespread application in American industries have been due largely to the activities of war agencies established for the purpose; and theoretically the new labor management policies developed by this science were to be applied to all employees without discrimination. In actual practice, however, many employment managers drew a dividing line between English-speaking and non-English-speaking employees, and the latter have often been left out of consideration when the new policies designed to promote a more just and democratic relationship between employer and employee were inaugurated.

This neglect was quite natural, for the employment manager usually understood neither the languages nor the ways of the foreign-born workers they employed. But it is just these non-English-speaking employees that need most the understanding and the humane labor policies developed by the science of personnel management. The Immigration Commission would, therefore, have for its duty the raising of the standards of labor management of immigrant workers, just as general labor standards were raised by governmental agencies in the war industries. Where laws are violated in the employment and treatment of immigrant labor, it would see that these laws are properly enforced, and where no violation of law is involved, its bulletins and other information would advise employers as to the best methods of understanding and handling wage earners of various nationalities.

We have seen that trade unions, like the industries in which they operate, need to adjust their methods and policies to the characteristics and capacities of the immigrant nationalities which abound in so many of our industries. A number of unions have been markedly successful both in organizing and holding immigrants of many nationalities in the common comradeship of a permanent organization; and the basis of their success has been the special methods they have adopted for appealing to and educating the foreign-born workers.

The breaking down of division and antagonism between American organized labor and the masses of immigrant workers in our midst, and the building up of a spirit of common citizenship is another task for an Immigration Commission entrusted with carrying out a domestic policy for immigrants. This would be promoted by the study of the methods and policies of labor organizations which have been most successful in uniting native and foreign-born in their membership, and the publication and distribution of such information among labor organizations in the same manner that development of proper management policies for immigrant labor is spread among employers.

RELATIONS OF IMMIGRANT TO AMERICAN GOVERNMENT

Our governments, state, local and national, play their part in all the problems of industrial adjustment. They have at times assisted both the immigrants and the industries in the processes of adjustment, by legislative and administrative action, and sometimes they have made adjustment more difficult, by legislation restricting opportunities for employment or discriminating against aliens in the protection of the laws. A few states have taken positive action toward developing a domestic immigration policy for the aliens in their midst, and, though usually working under handicaps of inadequate appropriations, these have shown both the need of such a policy of studying at first-hand the problems of the immigrant through complaint and trouble bureaus, and the effective results that may be secured by such a policy in helping the immigrant to adjust himself to life in America and in enlisting him as a loyal member of a united citizenship.

The immigrant in America has also developed many agencies of self-help in all the fields of industrial adjustment which we have mentioned, and organizations of the foreign born help people of their own nationality to find work, to settle problems with their employers, to organize trade unions, to coöperate in maintaining stores and restaurants, as well as to learn English and prepare for the duties and responsibilities of American citizenship. These organizations have developed the practical methods in many cases, which have later been adopted by American employers, trade unions, and public authorities. But when the immigrant has to depend in large part or for a long time on such organizations to help him meet his problems of adjustment, there is danger that his loyalty to the organization of his own nationality, and through it to his native land, may be perpetuated, and so hold him back from participation in American organizations and American affairs.

To assist and to control the immigrant's own agencies for adjustment, as well as to work in coöperation with the agencies created by state and local governments, the proposed national Immigration Commission would need another division which might be called the Division of Governmental Relations. In states like California, Massachusetts, New York, and Delaware, where public bureaus are maintained for the purpose of learning the immigrant's problems and helping him to solve them, this division would merely have to encourage the work by coöperation, especially in helping with problems that involve national laws or that go beyond state lines and require action by federal authorities. Where no such state agencies exist, however, the division might perform this service itself as best it can until the states are led to undertake it by the example of the federal government and other states.

Organization of the immigrant's own agencies for help in adjusting himself to the conditions of American industrial life would not be discouraged by a United States Immigration Commission. On the contrary such self-help would be encouraged. But the commission, as well as the state agencies, would want to advise and assist in their work; to make it plain to the immigrant that America is ready to help, and is helping through the people of his own nationality, and to make sure that he will get the most sympathetic and intelligent kind of help during the time when he is unable to speak English and unable to take care of himself through the ordinary American agencies.

CONCLUSION

In addition to the work thus outlined concerning the direct relations of the immigrant and industry, the proposed Immigration Commission ought to have most important functions with respect to immigrant education and naturalization. We omit detailed consideration of these, because the problems of schooling of the immigrant and naturalization have been treated fully in two other volumes of this series, and we are concerned here primarily with industrial adjustments.

With respect to education, however, it is not the immigrant alone that needs to be taught. The American people, too, need education with respect to the problems which immigration presents to the nation; and they need to know more intimately the characteristics and the quality of the alien peoples who are manning our industries and whose children will make up a very large part of the American people of the future.

To meet these needs, as well as to aid in the teaching of the immigrant, a United States Immigration Commission will have important duties to perform in connection with the study of immigrant races in America, their distribution, industrial as well as geographical, the kind of work they are doing, skilled or unskilled, the progress they are making in the economic structure, etc. Something along this line has in recent years been begun by the states. The Illinois Department of Registration and Education, for example, has published bulletins one of which is entitled: "The Immigrant and the Coal Mining Communities of Illinois." And the Massachusetts Bureau of Immigration began the publication of a series of short bulletins under the general title of "Immigrant Races in Massachusetts," each bulletin treating of a separate people, e.g. "The Greeks," "The Syrians."

These studies and the publication of the results could be much improved if they were directed by a United States Immigration Commission which was in close contact with all the immigrants. The data on which conclusions are based would be more extensive and correspondingly more reliable. The facts of the Census Bureau, the immigration stations, employment offices, employers' records, trade-union experiences, and "trouble bureaus" conducted by local, public, or private agencies, all could be more easily studied, and the results distributed throughout the nation.

A national policy designed to adjust immigrant and industry requires no elaborate legislation or governmental administrative machinery. What we have attempted in these chapters—to study the experiences of immigrants and industries, and the methods of adjustment that have proved most successful and beneficial—this needs to be continually done. And a national public authority like a United States Immigration Commission, if charged with this authority, would be in a position to hold up the example of the most advanced states and the most progressive employers and trade unions to the rest of the country, and thus enlist the coöperation of the whole nation in helping to merge the foreign born with the native industrial population.

INDEX

349

INDEX

INDEX

INDEX